# Dandy Kim

## The Extraordinary Life of
## Michael Caborn-Waterfield

by

## Nigel Hamilton-Walker

# CONTENTS

# PROLOGUE

## January 1st 1930 – May 4th 2016

**SEX... Actresses... Aircraft... Aristocrats...
Arms... Automobiles... Casinos... Champagne...
Crime... Gambling... Gangsters... Guns... Hedonism...
Heiresses... Hookers... Helicopters... Intrigue...
Lies... Models... Money... Nightclubs... Orgies...
Parties... Police... Pornography... Prison...
Racehorses... Restaurants... Robbery... Royalty...
Scandal... Secrets... Smuggling... Socialites...
Starlets... Villains... Yachts...**

These are just a few key words I would choose when thinking about my dear old friend and soul mate who sadly passed away last year. I feel very honoured and privileged to have known him so well.

For the second half of the twentieth century his debonair devilish schemes and capers captured headlines worldwide and yet he always remained composed, suave and silent.

Although his name was Michael Caborn-Waterfield, I always knew him simply as Kim' (Not 'Dandy Kim') for over fifty years. I will refer to him as Michael in the first chapter of this book because the Catholic nuns at St Patrick's in Miami didn't actually 'christen' him 'Kim' until 1937.

His list of friends was an eclectic Debrett's mixture of the World's most influential, rich, powerful and notorious icons. His list of lovers is a bedroom guide to some of the most fascinating and beautiful women of all time.

There were many heated discussions about him from Hollywood to the White House, from Interpol to No 10 Downing Street and Scotland Yard.

Kim had a happy knack of being in the right place at the wrong time. The tales of his escapades and the intriguing characters he encountered, often in the most compromising situations, are wonderfully entertaining. A cavalier cavalcade of adventure from wartime Bermuda to the post war high society of London to Manhattan, Havana to Tangiers and Florida to the Cote d'Azur. Some of his stories are truly mind-blowing and unbelievable.

I have never written a book before, but having read some of the recent unpleasant obituaries published by certain tabloids, I felt it was necessary to recite some of this unique gentleman's amazing adventures as accurately as I could and create a lasting testimony to him which might help put the record straight and take the 'lid off' certain rumours and speculations. I feel qualified to do this considering the number of long lunches and endless evenings that I have spent reminiscing with this very unique and unusual character, as well as reading and looking after many of his documents and notes personally.

I often suggested to Kim that he should write his autobiography, but his reply to my suggestion was always the same...

*"Nigel, if I blow the lid off that damned lot, I could open up a bloody can of worms that will come back and haunt me for what's left of my life. You have been privy to my most sensitive of papers, so best you write it after I have departed from this World."*

Well, I have done my best!

My background and career have always centered around 'classic' cars, a subject about which Kim was very knowledgeable, having owned and driven some of the World's most exotic automobiles.

I first met Kim in 1965 when I was eight years old. My late father, Geoffrey Hamilton-Walker had an exclusive car showroom in London's Sloane Street just opposite the Carlton Tower Hotel. He had just sold Terence Young (the director of the famous James Bond movies 'From Russia with Love' and 'Thunderball') a magnificent dark blue Rolls Royce Silver Cloud III convertible with a plush white hood and leather upholstery. Kim was due meet with Young the following evening at Les Ambassadeurs Club, in Hamilton Place where the new Rolls Royce had just been parked outside by the uniformed doorman. Kim saw the car, which was by chance painted and trimmed in his registered horse racing colours, he tried to buy it there and then from Young. The well-known film director told Kim where he had purchased the car, and suggested he visit the Sloane Street showroom. My father duly met him and sold him a similar Rolls Royce. I was present when he took delivery of this beautiful automobile and remember thinking what an elegant gentleman he was, attired in an immaculate Prince of Wales check suit, a lemon woven tie and very expensive alligator boots. His debonair appearance reminded me of the Duke of Windsor, whom Kim believed was a fashion icon.

The Duke and Duchess of Windsors lives intertwine with Kim's throughout the first half of this book.

The second time we met was in the mid-1970's at 'Le Casserole' restaurant on Chelsea's King's Road. He had just returned from Australia and the Philippines promoting 'Miss Topless Universe'.

His reputation preceded him, I was already aware of his involvement concerning the infamous robbery of Jack L. Warner's palatial villa on the French Riviera, but I was not aware of the subsequently sworn 'non-disclosure agreement' promising a forty-year silence that was signed in 1960, securing his early release from a filthy French jail, or the incredible sensitivity of the documents linked to the

Royal Family that he uncovered during the theft. I also knew that he was the founder of the Ann Summers sex shop empire.

He had recently been making the front pages again. This time he was contesting the late property tycoon Clive Raphael's will, on behalf of his ex-wife, model and actress Penny Brahms in the High Court. Raphael's private plane had mysteriously blown-up mid-air near Paris, killing him and his passengers instantly. Penny Brahms had been Raphael's very young wife prior to marrying Kim, and Raphael had bequeathed his then widow five pennies and five nude photographs of herself.

Kim wanted to buy a Bentley S3 Continental Coupe from me and part exchange another much rougher one, which had been used by Peter Wyngarde in the TV series 'Jason King'. After much haggling with Kim and a certain Count Liechtenstein (the restaurant owner and one of Kim's business partners) a deal was struck. I am sure that the homosexual Count was not from the famous European dynasty!

Kim was due to collect the car the following day from my showroom in Elvaston Mews, Chelsea but telephoned me and said:

**"My poor darling girlfriend is suffering from growing pains, could you please deliver the Bentley Continental to my home in Eaton Terrace instead?"**

I shall never forget it. Our friendship began.

Years later, Kim would often come to stay with my family in London, Bournemouth and Kent, all I had to do for my house guest was keep the fridge topped up with Stella Artois and Sancerre, the former started at 10.00 a.m. sharp! The latter could last until the early hours…

I met some amazing people with Kim, unfortunately most of them are now deceased including Diana Dors, Alan Lake, Sir Mark Birley, Omar Sharif and Charles Gray (who played Blofeld in the James Bond movies) apart from

Michael Medwin and Eddie Richardson, who I believe are still around.

Kim has often been portrayed as a playboy, a chancer, a thief and a womanizer for over six decades, so much tittle tattle has been written about him, but he was always one glass of wine ahead of the gossip columns.

I hope the chapters contained in this book will reveal the kind, generous, soft albeit somewhat vulnerable side of his charming charismatic personality.

Kim had an incredible presence, charisma and a 'silver tongued' voice that afforded him the ability to mingle with both Royalty and aristocracy as well as villains and gangsters. The two extremes of society could never meet, so he was the ideal conduit to initiate deals and schemes, almost a modern day 'Robin Hood'!

The majority of well-known characters referred to in this book have had their stories told in many previous publications. Kim's life links many of them together like pieces of a jigsaw puzzle, but his was far more interesting than theirs.

I have had mixed emotions whilst writing this biography and if it is published, I sincerely hope that it doesn't wind up on the fiction counters!

This is the first book written solely about Kim and I duly dedicate it to his memory.

# CHAPTER ONE

## AEROPLANES ABDICATION & ADVENTURE
## (1935 - 1938)

Michael was born into a world of glamour and intrigue with a 'silver tongue' as opposed to a 'silver spoon'. Michael's mother, Yvonne was one of the very first and youngest female pilots to qualify in England at Brooklands after World War I and she held her own Private Pilot's Licence. It was his parents' mutual interest in flying that brought the couple together originally.

Michael's parents were Anglo Irish Catholics living in Richmond, although his father spent most of his time in America and Canada, where he had established many influential and powerful contacts, including the immensely wealthy Sir Harry Oakes.

Vivian Conrad George Colnaghi Caborn-Waterfield was a highly capable pilot and a successful businessman specialising in gold mine investment. He worked closely with Sir Harry Oakes, who was thought to be the richest individual in the British Empire and known for his lavish lifestyle. By the 1930's his Lake Shore mine in Ontario was the most productive in the Western Hemisphere, and ultimately proved to be the second largest gold mine in the Americas. Oakes had become a British citizen.

In 1935, he moved to Nassau in the Bahamas in an attempt to escape the massive Canadian taxes that the ruling Conservative Government had levied against him. According to Sir Harry, it was costing him $17,500 in taxes per day to live in Canada. The government wanted 85% of Oakes' immense wealth in taxes and was taxing his mine so extensively that it amounted to as much as 25% of the gold mined at Lake Shore Mines.

He resided in the Bahamas until his gruesome murder in 1943. Oakes proved to be a dynamic investor, entrepreneur and developer in the Bahamas. He had a major role in expanding the airport, Oakes Field, in Nassau. He bought the British Colonial Hilton Hotel in Nassau, as well as building a golf course and country club. He also developed farming and new housing on the island. All this activity greatly stimulated the struggling economy in what had been a sleepy backwater, with only about 70,000 inhabitants in the late 1930's. This activity took place mainly on the principal island, New Providence, and it was estimated that Oakes owned about one third of that island by the early 1940's.

Oakes had become the colony's wealthiest and most important resident and he was a close friend of the Duke and Duchess of Windsor.

Oakes was invited to the British colony by Sir Harold Christie, a prominent Bahamian real estate developer and legislator, who became his close business associate and friend. Oakes was created a baronet during 1939 as a reward for his philanthropic endeavours in the Bahamas, Canada and Britain. He had donated $500,000 in two bequests to St George's Hospital in London and gave $1,000,000 to charities in the Bahamas ($30,000,000 in today's money).

Michael started school when he was five years old at the Sacred Heart Catholic Primary School in Teddington, it was a very strict religious school and most of the teachers were nuns. Michael was not a religious boy but he did become an altar boy.

When he began the Christmas term in September 1936 both the teachers and pupils were full of the news about the King and his scandalous relationship with the then still married Wallis Simpson. Michael had always admired Edward VIII for his style and elegance.

Edward was the eldest son of King George V and Queen Mary. He had been honoured with the title of Prince of Wales on his sixteenth birthday, nine weeks after his father succeeded as King. He served in the British

Army during the First World War and undertook several overseas tours on behalf of his father.

Edward became King upon his father's death in early 1936. He showed impatience with court protocol and caused concern among politicians by his apparent disregard for established constitutional conventions. Only months into his reign, he caused a sensational constitutional crisis by proposing marriage to Wallis Simpson, an American, who had divorced her first husband and was seeking a divorce from her second. The Prime Ministers of the United Kingdom and the Dominions opposed the marriage, arguing that the people would never accept a divorced woman with two living ex-husbands as Queen consort.

Additionally, such a marriage would have conflicted with Edward's status as the titular head of the Church of England, which at that time opposed the remarriage of divorced people if their former spouses were still alive. Edward knew that the British government, led by Prime Minister Stanley Baldwin, would resign if the marriage went ahead. This could have forced a general election which would have ruined his status as a politically neutral constitutional monarch.

Choosing not to end the relationship, Edward abdicated on December 11th 1936.

A young Michael listened to the King's broadcast to the nation.

**_"You all know the reasons which have compelled me to renounce the throne...."_**

The nation, as it turned out, did not know all the reasons. With a reign of just 326 days, Edward was one of the shortest reigning monarchs in British history. He was succeeded by his younger brother Albert, who chose George VI as his regnal name.

Although the nuns at Michael's school were appalled at their King's behaviour, Michael perceived Edward as a buccaneering romantic hero, little did he know about

12

various facts concerning the Duke of Windsor's (Edward VIII's new title) personal life that would save him serving a further four years in a French jail in later years!

During 1937, Michael's father Vivian had been spending more and more time in the States, he had also been travelling to Dutch Guiana (now called Suriname) a sovereign state on the north eastern Atlantic coast of South America. He had been involved in funding a new gold mine there with Sir Harry Oakes, the mine was highly successful and Vivian made a handsome profit.

After the disastrous Florida hurricane and the great depression, Oakes had bought 2,600 acres of partially developed land in northern Palm Beach County, Florida from Harry Seymour Kelsey, who lacked the finances to rebuild his shattered development.

Oakes spent a great deal of money on the improvement of this property, which was later bought by John D. MacArthur who completed its development. It included most of North Palm Beach, Lake Park, Palm Beach Gardens and Palm Beach Shores. Oakes' home in North Palm Beach was like a castle and became the club house for the village country club. On the strength of his continuing business relationship with Oakes, Vivian decided to live full time in America, which he preferred anyway, and he started to organise the relocation of his family to Miami, Florida.

On a cold sunny October morning in 1937, Michael was with his mother, Yvonne, they were on their way back home from Brooklands airfield in Surrey. Michael was elated as he had finally taken the controls of Yvonne's beloved Tiger Moth aeroplane while in flight, but Yvonne was sad as it was the last flight they would make together before the aircraft was sold prior to the family's migration to the United States.

Yvonne asked Michael:

**"Michael, what do you want to do when you grow up?"**

The seven-year-old boy replied:

***"I want to be much richer than you and Daddy and fly faster than both of you."***

As Yvonne's elegant Lagonda convertible drove through the wrought iron gates at the family's house just off Richmond Hill, the estate agents 'for sale' sign had been erected and the Pickford's lorries had already arrived. The trucks were being loaded with their furnishings and wooden tea chests, containing the family's chattels.

Mildred, the Caborn-Waterfield's resident housekeeper welcomed Yvonne and Michael home with 'Johnny', who was Michael's brother, two years younger. His real name was Edward John, but he was always referred to by his nickname, 'Johnny'.

Because of their forthcoming relocation to America, Michael didn't return to the Sacred Heart Catholic Primary School that September for the Christmas term. Michael hated the school and didn't really excel in any particular subject although he was always competitive on the games field. The two boys were very excited about the adventure that they were about to embark upon.

Two days later the family boarded the R.M.S. Aquitania in Southampton and began the transatlantic voyage to New York via Cherbourg. Michael was spellbound by Cunard White Star Line's magnificent four funnelled liner and especially it's opulent first-class dining saloon designed by architect Arthur Joseph Davis, modelled on the Ritz Hotel in London, a venue that he would become very familiar with later, in his adult life.

On board, white tie was expected to be worn for evening dinner. The two boys accordingly wore bow ties. On the third evening at sea, mid-Atlantic, the Caborn-Waterfield family were invited to dine on the 'Captain's Table'. The immaculately dressed young boys enthralled the Captain (Capt. J. C. Townley, R.D.R.N.R). He duly invited them to view both the ship's bridge and boiler rooms with him the following morning. The view of the ocean from the Bridge and the heat from the steam boilers fascinated the boys. It was to become a day that Michael would remember forever.

On the fifth day at sea Michael stood on the promenade deck, mesmerised by the tugs pulling the great steam ship up the Hudson River to dock in Manhattan. They passed the symbolic Statue of Liberty and Staten Island.

Having only ever seen photographs before, he marvelled at the sight of the Empire State Building (the World's tallest building in 1937) and the beautiful art deco spire on top of the Chrysler Building.

The family booked into the luxurious Pierre Hotel on Fifth Avenue for a couple of days before flying down to Florida, to the new home that Vivian had previously purchased.

Those first few days in New York had a massive impact on Michael, he marvelled at the architecture and visited the top of the Empire State Building. He saw Broadway shows as well as dining at Sardi's restaurant, best known for the hundreds of caricatures depicting show business celebrities that adorn its walls.

It was the first time the family had spent time together for ages. Again, little did Michael know that he would return to New York thirteen years later, under very different circumstances.

Their new home was a magnificent art deco villa on South Beach off Collins Avenue in Miami. It was literally a stone's throw from the golden beach and Atlantic Ocean. The family were thrilled with their new property, and over the next few weeks, they explored the sun-drenched state from Palm Beach down to the Florida Keys, whilst they awaited the arrival of their belongings from England.

Michael and Johnny had started having daily private lessons from Mrs Stevenson (an elderly ex-pat widow) and unusually she seemed to have gained Michael's attention during the tutorials.

Michael walked along the shore every day and was fascinated by the riding school on the beach, he yearned to ride across the sands in the hot sun himself. Michael's parents encouraged him to begin riding lessons. A few months later when the house in Richmond was finally sold, Vivian bought a new Lincoln convertible. This car initiated Michael's interest in American automobiles, many of which he purchased in later life, he loved the wide whitewall tyres and big chrome 'fenders'.

His father also purchased a Chris Craft Barrel Back speedboat, this mahogany launch was just about the most fashionable day boat on the market at the time and as far as Michael was concerned, it was the perfect opportunity for him to learn to water-ski.

Michael had no idea how much these new interests were going to influence his future life and ambitions.

Sir Harry Oakes was based in Nassau, but he was unhappy with the Island's educational facilities so he enlisted his son, also named Harry, to a relatively new school in Miami, named, St. Patrick's Parish School. It was founded in 1926. This religious school was highly regarded by Oakes, and he recommended it to Vivian, who consequently enlisted Michael to commence in January 1938.

Although Michael detested school life, he excelled in the new gymnasium, and started to learn the intricacies of polo, he was fascinated by the polo ponies at the school and tried to ride one every day.

This was the school where Michael was 'rechristened'. The nuns named him 'Kim', why?

To quote Kim:

*"Happenstance, simply, there was already a Michael and a Mike. The name Kim was carefree, appropriate and Mik spelt backwards"*

It was to remain with him for the rest of his life.

Although his parents still referred to him as Michael, everybody else called him Kim especially at school. The name Kim was originally an American name meaning noble or brave, qualities which the Catholic nuns of Miami obviously recognised in the young Michael Caborn-Waterfield!

**A De Havilland Tiger Moth similar to the aircraft flown by Kim's mother, Yvonne**

**Kim's School, St Patrick's Convent Miami**

Kim's Chris Craft Barrel Back 19 speedboat

**I WILL REFER TO MICHAEL AS 'KIM' FROM HEREINAFTER.**

# CHAPTER TWO

## MIAMI MAFIA & MILLIONAIRES
## (1939 - 1943)

Back in Britain, Prime Minister Stanley Baldwin had retired from office in May 1937, Neville Chamberlain took his place, but his premiership was dominated by the question of policy toward the increasingly aggressive Germany. When Adolf Hitler came to power, he wanted to unite all Germans into one nation.

In September 1938, he turned his attention to the three million Germans living in part of Czechoslovakia called the Sudetenland. Sudeten Germans began protests and provoked violence from the Czech police. Adolf Hitler claimed that 300 Sudeten Germans had been killed. This was not actually true, but Hitler used it as an excuse to place German troops along the Czech border.

During this uneasy situation, Prime Minister Chamberlain, flew to meet Hitler at his private mountain retreat in Berchtesgaden and attempted to resolve the crisis. He returned proclaiming that any possibility of war had been averted.

In the early hours of 30th September 1938, Prime Minister Chamberlain signed the Munich Treaty with the Nazi leader, Adolf Hitler, giving Czechoslovakia over to German conquest but bringing, as Chamberlain promised:

*"Peace in our time."*

Kim's father had no confidence in the Prime Minister's words. He felt that war with Germany was inevitable.

On September 1st 1939, peace was shattered by Hitler's invasion of Poland. Chamberlain declared war against Germany on September 3rd 1939. During the next eight months, he showed himself to be ill equipped for the daunting task of saving Europe from Nazi conquest. After

British forces failed to prevent the German occupation of Norway in April 1940, Chamberlain lost the support of many members of his Conservative Party.

On May 10th 1940, Hitler invaded Holland, Belgium and the Netherlands. The same day, Chamberlain formally lost the confidence of the House of Commons. Winston Churchill, who was known for his military leadership ability, was appointed British Prime Minister in his place. He formed an all-party coalition and quickly won the popular support.

On May 13th 1940, in his first speech before the House of Commons, Prime Minister Churchill declared that:

*"I have nothing to offer but blood, toil, tears and sweat."*

He offered an outline of his bold plans for British resistance. In the first year of his administration Great Britain stood alone against Nazi Germany, but Churchill promised his Country and the World that the British people would:

*"Never surrender."* They never did.

At the outbreak of war, the Military Training Act was overtaken by the National Service (Armed Forces) Act and the first intake was absorbed into the army. This act imposed a liability to conscription of all men aged between eighteen and forty-one years old.

Although Vivian Caborn-Waterfield was now successful and happily living in Miami with his family, he still felt patriotic and wanted to contribute to the British war effort. He always wondered if he would be 'called up', but he did not join up for a further three years.

Kim was now just nine years of age, he had never shown much interest in World War II, mostly because he'd been protected and sheltered from the harsh realities of war, and partly because he was living a carefree outdoor existence in the hot sunshine. He had become exceedingly fit and suntanned.

During 1940, the family would often drive up the Atlantic Coastal Highway 95 to Fort Lauderdale or Palm Beach for the weekend in their gleaming new white Cadillac Lasalle convertible. Vivian often felt a sense of guilt that he was not aiding the R.A.F. back in England.

Vivian was always at the 'beck and call' of the mighty Sir Harry Oakes who would require and literally demand his company when he visited the American mainland from Nassau, the Capital of the Bahamas. Oakes often extended the invitations to include Vivien's family. His son Pitt, was of a similar age to Kim. If Kim was on school holidays, he would occasionally accompany his parents to some very 'educational' social occasions. They would have to meet Oakes either for business or pleasure in various locations including New York, Miami or Palm Beach, where Oakes had considerable property interests. Oakes even invited them to Havana, Cuba, where he was meeting with the newly elected **President Fulgencio Batista of Cuba** to discuss banking and finance, he always wanted Vivian's presence and commercial input.

The Caborn-Waterfield family stayed in the famous Hotel Nacional de Cuba for two days. The hotel stood out due to its refined elegance and its ancient splendour, which since 1930, had attracted a large number of famous personalities including the newly appointed British Prime Minister, Winston Churchill.

The chance of meeting President Batista was to serve Kim a tremendous 'business' opportunity eleven years later. He would see both the hotel and Batista on many future occasions, but under very different circumstances.

Vivian could never refuse Oakes' invitations because he had become his major source of income, by both obtaining funding and consulting him in the mining industry.

The family also stayed occasionally at Westbourne, his home in Nassau. Oakes was known to be a very difficult man to work with, he was direct and very abrasive at times. He was a person subject to sudden temper outbursts. On the other hand, he could be a tenacious, brilliant and very generous man.

On one occasion in 1940, the Caborn-Waterfields were invited to dinner by Oakes to the famous Joe's Stone Crab Restaurant in Miami which was founded in 1919, it was the haunt of politicians, actors and socialites. The restaurant was reputedly referenced in Ian Fleming's novel, Goldfinger, as 'Bill's on the Beach' in which James Bond ate the best meal he had ever had in his life.

When the family arrived at the Washington Street venue, they were shocked to see their friend, Sir Harry, holding court with his wife Lady Eunice, Charles Bedaux and amazingly one of the era's most notorious gangsters, Meyer Lansky. Lansky was a diminutive Jewish immigrant who was rumoured to be the Mafia's accountant. He was well-known everywhere in Miami and operated many of the local rackets.

'Maier Suchowljansky' was born during 1902 in Grodno, a Polish city which was annexed by Russia. His family emigrated to the United States in 1911 and his parents allegedly couldn't recall Suchowljansky's birth date so he was assigned the birthday of July 4th for his immigration records. Suchowljansky's name was eventually changed to Meyer Lansky, and he became a naturalized citizen in the late 1920's. Growing up on Manhattan's Lower East Side, Lansky eventually became an organised crime figure, instrumental in the development of a national crime syndicate in the United States. He started up a street gambling business and became a mentee of Arnold Rothstein, nicknamed 'the Brain'. Rothstein was an American racketeer, businessman and gambler who became a king pin of the 'Jewish mob' in New York City.

Lansky had befriended Benjamin 'Bugsy' Siegal and 'Lucky' Luciano. The men formed a partnership linking together various mob factions across the country, while also incorporating more reputable spheres of power into their dealings. Lansky was deemed to be the financial mastermind behind this system, with his earnings reputedly reaching hundreds of millions of dollars, although this figure has since been disputed. They were known for hiring out men who doled out violence and murder for other organisations.

With wealth earned from bootlegging, Lansky ventured into other illicit arenas, maintaining gambling as the cornerstone of his operations. It was during this period that Lansky wanted to extend his casino operations and gain a foothold in Cuba and the Bahamas. He had engineered the 'chance' meeting in the restaurant that night with Sir Harry Oakes for two reasons, firstly, he knew that Oakes was the most influential person in the Bahamas and had the trust of the newly appointed Governor of the Bahamas... none other than the Duke of Windsor, who was staying at Oakes' house, Westbourne, while the termite ridden official residence in Nassau was being refurbished.

Wallis Simpson, now the Duchess of Windsor, devoted her energies to the renovation of Government House. Improvements included modern decor with regency accents, wallpapers imported from New York, a fresh coat of paint including a room painted the colour of the Duchess' favourite face powder. The Bahamian House of Assembly authorized £2000 for the work on Government House but the costs far exceeded this amount and the royal couple personally funded many of the renovations.

Secondly and far more importantly, Lansky wanted Oakes to use his influence to initiate an introduction to the newly elected President Fulgencio Batista, who Kim and his family had already met.

The purpose of the proposed introduction was to establish a lavish playground in Havana to include casinos, hotels and nightclubs.

America's Office of Strategic Services worked with Lansky in World War II to curtail saboteur activities at the New York docks, Lansky was very proud of this and dropped it into the conversation with Oakes as if to buy himself respect and credibility.

Sir Harry Oakes' other colleague, Charles Bedaux, had been introduced to him by the Duke of Windsor on a fleeting business visit to Nassau. He had dropped out of school as a youngster and moved to the United States, where he became a United States citizen.

He became a multi-millionaire by pioneering work management systems which interested Sir Harry Oakes.

Bedaux had purchased the sixteenth century Chateau de Cande, in France; he lived there with his American second wife, Fern.

On June 3rd 1937, Bedaux had hosted the wedding of Wallis Simpson and the Duke of Windsor. Bedaux then arranged the couple's 'honeymoon' to the Third Reich in Germany, where they publicly met the Fuhrer, Adolf Hitler.

***(This meeting will be addressed later on in the book.)***

When Paris was occupied by the Germans during World War II, Bedaux became acquainted with leading Nazi figures. After the fall of France in 1940, he was appointed as an economic advisor to the Third Reich. Bedaux's wife, Fern, was interned briefly in Paris during the war but was soon released through their connections to the German government in France.

It was quite well known that Bedaux handled a number of gold bullion movements, and on one occasion, he had asked for Sir Harry Oakes' assistance in shipping a delivery to the emergent State of Israel. When Sir Harry discovered that it was actually Nazi looted gold bound for South America, he refused.

Kim was spellbound by the conversations he had heard that evening in the shellfish restaurant. He was beginning to realise that his father Vivian was in a far more distinguished and important position than he had previously given him credit for.

Kim also began to learn the art of staying silent, he could hardly tell the nuns and fellow pupils at St Patrick's what he had listened to, when he had to recite his news in the classroom each week.

The next two years were quite uneventful for Kim, as he progressed with his studies at St Patrick's, while his father spent much of his time taking the short flight from Miami to Nassau for meetings with Sir Harry Oakes. Kim had used the time to learn how to be a spectacular water skier, and he was now taking extra lessons in horsemanship, which was his true passion.

It was on one of these visits that Vivian Caborn-Waterfield actually met the Duke and Duchess of Windsor who had now settled into the newly decorated Government House. Vivian was not impressed with the Duke because, although he found him very charming and debonair, he knew that the Duke was widely regarded as a Nazi sympathiser. His ties with Nazi Germany had made him a liability for Britain during World War II, which was the reason for his appointment as Governor of the Bahamas in the first place, as it removed him from Europe for the war.

The Duke and Duchess of Windsor had continued to cause anxiety for the British Government during their time in the Bahamas, as their visits to the United States attracted an enormous amount of publicity. They displayed wealth and hedonism in what was a very austere time for Great Britain. The Duke of Windsor had publicly expressed pessimism about a British victory, which really angered Winston Churchill, who the Duke thought of as a war monger.

There were even rumours that the Duke was willing to deal with the 'Fuhrer' in order to win back his throne. Apparently, Adolf Hitler wanted to install the Duke of

Windsor as a Nazi puppet. These rumours were not helped by the numerous visits made by the Duke to Germany, prior to the war and his eventual abdication.

Vivian found the Duchess to be extremely elegant although somewhat aloof and louche. She undoubtedly held a grudge against the British and resented the way in which her poor husband had been treated by the establishment. Kim was fascinated by his father's words, he had always held the Duke in great esteem, not for his politics, but for his wonderful taste in clothes and lifestyle. He could never have imagined that his life would be caught up with the Windsors thirteen years later.

Sir Harry Oakes had obviously obliged Meyer Lansky and introduced him to the Cuban President because he was now busy starting to develop Havana into a City that would make Las Vegas look tame.

**The Duke & Duchess of Windsor in the Bahamas 1940**

The Duke and Duchess of Windsor - Governor of
the Bahamas 1940

Meyer Lansky

# CHAPTER THREE

## MURDER IN NASSAU
## (1943 – 1943)

On July 8th 1943, Vivian received some terrible news, Sir Harry Oakes had been found murdered in his bedroom at his mansion, Westbourne, in Nassau, he was sixty-eight years old. He had been brutally battered to death, his corpse was smothered in blood and partially burned, the crime scene was similar to that of a ritual voodoo massacre, his testicles had been speared and the remains of his body was strewn with feathers. The Bahamas' Governor, the Duke of Windsor (formerly H.M. King Edward VIII), who had become a close friend of Oakes during the previous three years, took personal charge of the investigation from the outset.

The Duke vainly attempted to enforce press censorship, but this was completely unsuccessful. Oakes' vast wealth, fame and British title, combined with the grisly nature of the crime, generated worldwide interest in the case.

Etienne Dupuch, the colony's foremost newspaper publisher was a friend of Oakes and he ensured constant coverage of the case for several months.

The Duke of Windsor 'believed' that the local police lacked the expertise to investigate the crime, then contrary to Colonial Office convention, he called in the Miami police department which had very close Mafia connections especially with Meyer Lansky, instead of calling Scotland Yard for assistance. The Duke turned to two particular American policemen he knew on the Miami force, Captains Melchen and Barker.

Melchen had previously guarded the Duke in Miami and both policemen were suspected of being on the Mafia's payroll. It was a very strange decision, the

Bahamas was a British Crown Colony at that time, and there were British security personnel stationed in wartime New York and Washington D.C. who could easily have had travelled quickly to Nassau to carry out a full investigation. The two American detectives were, in theory, called upon to assist Bahamian law enforcement, but to the dismay of the local police they completely took over the investigation. By evening on the second day of the investigation, thirty-six hours after Oakes' body was discovered, they had arrested Oakes' son in law, Count Alfred de Marigny.

The Duke's blunder fed the rumour that he was part of a plot to frame an innocent man and have him hanged for Sir Harry Oates' murder.

De Marigny had eloped and married Oakes' daughter, Nancy in New York City, without her parents' knowledge. She was eighteen and no longer needed her parents' consent to wed. De Marigny, fourteen years her elder, had met Nancy at the Nassau Yacht Club, where he was a prominent and competitive sailor. The two had been dating for a couple of years before their marriage, without her parents apparently fully realizing the seriousness of their relationship. De Marigny was thought to have been on bad terms with Oakes, due to de Marigny's cavalier attitude and playboy existence. The fact that he had been married twice before for short periods to wealthy women and that he had not asked Oakes' permission to marry his daughter seriously tainted their relationship. Oakes and de Marigny had quarrelled publicly on several occasions in front of witnesses.

When Nancy was informed of her father's death and her husband's arrest, she was in Miami on her way to study dance with Martha Graham at Bennington, Vermont. It was her great friend Merce Cunningham who gave her the tragic news. She then travelled to Bar Harbour Maine, the family's summer home, to join her mother, Lady Eunice, at her husband's request. However, Nancy soon returned to

Nassau and began to organise her husband's defence. She was convinced that de Marigny was innocent and stood by him when many others, including her family, believed him guilty.

The young Countess soon became a favourite with the press worldwide for her auburn hair, deep set eyes, fine figure and a mild resemblance to Katherine Hepburn.

The murder managed to knock the war off the front pages temporarily. Nancy spent heavily, hiring a leading American private investigator, Raymond Schindler, to dig deeply into the case, and a prominent British trained Bahamian lawyer, Godfrey W. Higgs, to defend her husband. They eventually found serious flaws in the prosecution's case.

Alfred de Marigny was committed for trial, and a rope was ordered for his hanging however, he was acquitted in a trial that lasted only several weeks, after the detectives from Miami were suspected of fabricating evidence against him. The chief piece of evidence was a fingerprint of his, which Captain Barker claimed had been found on a Chinese screen in Oakes' bedroom, where the body had been found. Later, it was discovered that the print had been lifted from the glass of water that de Marigny had used during his questioning by the Miami Police captains. Immediately after Oakes' funeral had been held in Bar Harbor Maine, Captain Barker, told Nancy and Lady Eunice Oakes that he had already positively identified de Marigny's fingerprints on the Chinese screen, justifying de Marigny's status as the main suspect. It was obvious that de Marigny was being framed.

By very detailed and thorough cross examination at the trial, de Marigny's lawyer showed that Captain Barker had not in fact positively identified the single fingerprint as belonging to de Marigny, until several days later than he had originally claimed, after he had returned to Miami and that Barker had taken several dozen other fingerprints from Oakes' bedroom, many of which were still unprocessed weeks later. An American fingerprint expert witness, testifying for the defence, called into question the professionalism of the techniques used by Captain Barker during the investigation. The expert testified that the de Marigny print could not have come from the Chinese screen, since none of the background pattern design from the screen appeared on the de Marigny print photograph, although other photos of fingerprints lifted from the screen showed this pattern.

De Marigny testified that he had not visited Westbourne, Oakes' home and the murder site, for two years before Oakes' death, because of on-going conflict with Oakes. Several of de Marigny's dinner party guests from the fateful night testified at the trial and strengthened de Marigny's alibi that he was hosting a party, and later drove several guests to their homes, late that night, with a witness in the car, at the time when the murder was committed. The approximate time of the murder had been determined by two Bahamian medical examiners. Significantly, but perhaps not too unsurprisingly, the Duke of Windsor arranged to be away from the Bahamas while the murder trial was in progress. Therefore, he was unable to be called as a witness.

After the trial, Nancy went with de Marigny to Cuba to stay with their old friend Ernest Hemingway. De Marigny was deported to Cuba after a recommendation by the murder trial's jury, because of his supposedly unsavoury character and frequent advances towards young girls in the Bahamas. The ruined de Marigny and Nancy eventually separated in 1945 and divorced in 1949.

No one has ever been convicted of Sir Harry Oakes' murder and there were no further court proceedings after de Marigny's acquittal. The case received worldwide press coverage at the time, with photos of the beautiful and charming Nancy in court. It has been the subject of continuous interest, conspiracy theories, including several books and films, and remains one of the most prolific unsolved crimes of the twentieth Century.

Lansky was building up his empire in Cuba, thanks to the introduction by Oakes to President Batista. Lansky wanted to further his interests in Nassau.

It was generally suspected that Meyer Lansky was behind the killing of Oakes, due to Oakes' resistance to casino gambling in the Bahamas.

After meeting with the Duke of Windsor in Miami, Lansky had obtained approval for his plans to develop gambling on the islands. Lansky was working with Harold Christie, a property developer and Stafford Sands, who was the jury foreman at the de Marigny murder trial.

Oakes had earlier apparently given his approval for the casino project, but then changed his mind by the time of his murder, strongly opposing it. Lansky sent several henchmen including his sidekick **Frank Carbo** to meet Oakes on the night of the murder to 'persuade and if necessary, intimidate' him to approve the project, but not to kill him. During a late-night meeting with Harold Christie held aboard a fast powerboat that had travelled from Miami to Nassau earlier that day, Oakes was punched severely several times on the head and died.

This was covered up; Oakes' body had then been taken back to his home by Christie, who was spotted as a passenger in his own station wagon by a Nassau Police Captain late that night. A fake voodoo slaughter involving castration and feathers was then staged in Oakes' bedroom at his home.

This directly contradicted Christie's statement that he had not left Oakes' home that night and in fact claimed he was asleep in the room next to Oakes' bedroom where the slaughter was supposed to have taken place and he claimed to have only woken the following morning to discover Oates' battered body. His body was left on the actual bed that previously been slept upon by the Duke of Windsor.

It had troubled Bahamian legal authorities in the lead up to the de Marigny trial, that Oakes' body had apparently been moved, confirmed by forensic examination of his blood data.

It was said that Lansky later privately punished his henchmen who had been involved with the murder.

But there is another theory. For reasons which I will reveal later in this book, Adolf Hitler had an incredible hold and power over the Duke and Duchess of Windsor, who had introduced Charles Bedaux, the Nazi ambassador, to Sir Harry Oakes.

When Sir Harry Oates, quite correctly and understandably, pulled out of the looted gold bullion deal, the Duke's business associate, Harold Christie, was staying at Oakes' home, Westbourne on Cable beach. He was sleeping in the next room. Christie was the most powerful of the 'Bay Street Boys', which were a gang of thieves that had their hands around the throat of the finances in the Bahamas. It was known that he and the Duke, together with the pro-Nazi Swedish banker Axel Wenner-Gren were under investigation by the U.S. Internal Revenue Service for serious breaches of wartime currency control regulations. All three were also being investigated by the U.S. Intelligence Service under the supervision of Mark Roland for possible Nazi collaboration. The implications were devastating. Sir Harry, alarmed and disillusioned over the gold bullion affair with Charles Bedaux was potentially a witness for the prosecution which would have led to further scandal for the Duke and a charge of treason could not be ruled out.

If either of these theories are correct, it begs the question as to whether the Duke of Windsor had prior knowledge of the planned murder. Firstly, Lansky was in contact with the Duke who had already given his seal of approval to the casino project that Oakes no longer wanted to proceed, secondly, why had the Duke instructed only two useless officers to investigate the crime and why would they in turn fabricate evidence if not instructed to do so by their superior, who in this case was solely the Duke of Windsor. Thirdly, why didn't the Duke seek the assistance of the British government and Scotland Yard, which would have been the correct protocol. It is also interesting to note that the Duke literally ran away and left the Island during the farcical trial for fear of being called as a witness.

Vivian Caborn-Waterfield took the slaughter of Sir Harry Oakes very personally, not only had he become very friendly with the legendary tycoon, but he had also lost his main source of income. He was also uncomfortable and almost slightly paranoid about his closeness to Oakes' business affairs, he felt he knew too much and was even surprised that he had not been questioned by the Duke of Windsors dubious detectives, who were based in his home town, Miami.

There were obviously suspicious characters in Miami and the Bahamas who had their own reasons for wanting Oakes dead, if he wasn't going to 'play ball' he was a danger to a number of unsavoury characters who would stop at nothing.

It was time for Vivian to go home and fight for his Country.

The Duke and Duchess of Windsor left the Island at the end of World War II in 1945 and returned to France. The Duke never worked again, but he would become an integral part of Kim's future.

By The Associated Press.

NASSAU, Bahamas, July 8—Sir Harry Oakes, American-born mining engineer who discovered one of the world's richest gold mines, was found dead in his bed today and the presence of injuries on the body caused an extraordinary investigation.

Two Miami police officers who specialize in solving homicides were summoned by airplane to reinforce Nassau authorities.

The body of the 69-year-old British baronet was discovered by a friend who called to keep an early appointment.

A coroner's inquest was called behind locked doors. (British censorship prevented the transmission of additional information concerning the investigation.)

Sir Harry, reputed to have a fortune worth as much as $200,000,000, had an appointment to take his friend for a tour of his 1,000-acre sheep farm, latest of the many enterprises which made him Nassau's leading business man.

He had planned to go to the United States Tuesday, but delayed his trip to show the farm to Nassau newsmen this afternoon.

The body will be sent to Bar Harbor, Me., where Mrs. Oakes and three of the couple's five children received word of his death.

The Duke of Windsor, Governor of the Bahamas, canceled appointments to take a personal hand in the investigation.

Capt. E. W. Melchen of the Miami homicide squad, a personal friend of the Duke, who has been

Continued on Page Thirty-six

The Duke of Windsor with Sir Harry Oakes, Bahamas
1941

Kim with his Dalmatian dog.  Sir Harry Oakes

Charles Bedaux          Alfred de Marigny

The Duke of Windsor & Sir Harry Oakes at the Polo,
Bahamas 1941

# CHAPTER FOUR

## ANNUS HORRIBILIS
## (1943 - 1944)

In the latter part of 1943, Vivian Caborn-Waterfield was in a quandary, he wished to leave the United States immediately and return to Great Britain and serve his Country.

There were no civilian ships operating on the transatlantic run, the mighty liners had all been requisitioned and utilised as troop carrying vessels. The World was at war and the German U boat threat in the Atlantic was very real.

He felt uneasy because of his association with Sir Harry Oakes, who was murdered, most probably at the behest of either Royalty, a president, or gangsters. He just wanted 'out'. He decided to contact some of Oakes's old associates in Canada (the late Oakes' name still carried a great deal of weight in his native Country). After much research, he found out that Canadian Vickers in Montreal had just finished building a new frigate for the United States Navy, but in fact the new ship was going to be transferred and delivered to the British Royal Navy under the established lend lease program.

The new ship's name was H.M.S. Evenlode (Pennant: K300) and it was being fitted out at the Norfolk Naval Shipyard in Virginia and about to set sail to Great Britain under the command of Lt. Commander Alfred Laurence Turner.

After pulling many strings and paying various bribes, Vivian negotiated a safe passage for his family and himself back to Great Britain. He instructed lawyers to dispose of the house, boat and several cars in his absence and gave notice to his son's schools.

The Caborn-Waterfield's were driven from Miami to Portsmouth, Virginia and after three overnight stops and very few belongings; they finally arrived at the Norfolk Naval Shipyard, which was the U.S. Navy's largest military base on the Eastern Seaboard.

There was a big problem... how to stowaway an attractive middle-aged woman on a Naval ship fully crewed by male seamen on a delivery mission. Mrs Caborn-Waterfield was luckily wearing trousers, she put her husband's overcoat over her head and when it was all clear, she was escorted to the captain's quarters, where she remained for the next five days. The captain slept in the crew's quarters claiming he would rather be 'hands on' with his crew. Vivian was given a uniform and the two boys became the youngest ever falsely designated 'ships boys' in British Naval history.

The Caborn-Waterfield's returned to a war-torn England from the United States during the autumn of 1943, in time for their sons to begin the Christmas term at new schools.

Kim, now aged thirteen was placed at Cranleigh Public School as a boarder, whilst Johnny, being a year younger was placed at Cranleigh Preparatory School as a day boy. They had wanted to move to Central London but after the 'Blitz' and destruction of the City; they felt it would be less dangerous and more appropriate to purchase a modest house in Weybridge Surrey and a 1938 Riley Kestrel motor car, which wasn't quite the same as the family's beautiful old Lagonda LG 45 convertible.

On a damp September morning, the time had come for Kim to begin his new school. He loaded the Riley up with his school trunk and new tuck box stuffed with confectionery. Kim sat in the front of the car dreading the thought of leaving his mother.

Upon arrival at the school, the name 'Caborn-Waterfield' was up on the school's notice board. He was allocated to boarding house 'North One' under the supervision of the housemaster, David Loveday.

Kim knocked on Mr. Loveday's study door with Yvonne in order to make his acquaintance and waited to hear the words "come in".

When it came to judging people and situations, Kim had a particular flair, relying on his 'gut feeling' as opposed to just common logic. He confidently held out his hand to Mr Loveday and more or less instinctively knew that this was not going to be an easy relationship. He had a horrid little moustache, very bland clothes, old unpolished 'Oxford Occasional' lace up shoes and a harsh abrupt voice, furthermore his handshake was limp, and his body language was common... all the attributes Kim hated.

Having explained his nickname to Loveday, he said a very emotional and tearful goodbye to Yvonne, Kim felt totally destitute, he had never been alone like this before.

That evening, he unpacked his pyjamas and slippers in the austere and miserable dormitory, he climbed into his archaic tubular metal bed and cried himself to sleep.

The next morning, after very little sleep, Kim realised that he must 'shape up'. He had to make the best of this ghastly chapter in his life or he would sink.

After the morning lessons and a dreadful 'school stew' for lunch, it was time for him to be assessed on the playing fields. Being autumn, Rugby was on the agenda, a game that Kim had never played before but had always been fascinated by. Kim's slight physique made him an ideal 'hooker' in the scrum and he was chosen to represent the school's 2nd XV team.

Little did he know how relevant the word 'hooker' would become, albeit with a very different meaning!

Rugby really enabled Kim to survive that first term at Cranleigh, he also joined the Combined Cadet Force and was very proud of his olive-green army uniform.

He had made a few friends, in particular a highly refined young man by the name of Michael Reynolds. He was different from the other pupils, his family lived in a large Georgian house in Kensington, and his parents were obviously wealthy and worldly. Like Kim, he had travelled widely. Kim associated with Michael, they were on the same 'wavelength', both the lads' fathers were pilots, and they even shared the same Christian name. They were both far more stimulated by sex, girls and making money rather than learning English Literature, Mathematics or Latin. They would spend many evenings discussing Michael's life in London and Kim's in Miami.

After all the conversations with Michael, Kim yearned to see the 'bright lights' of London, and all the famous sights in the Capital city that he had never seen during his childhood in the United States.

Kim had matured considerably during his first term at Cranleigh and his voice had now started to break. This was going to be one of his greatest assets in the future, his accent and delivery were like a sophisticated mixture between Sir David Dimbleby's and Richard Burton's tonations. Everyone noticed what an educated distinguished voice he had acquired.

As the school 'broke up' for holiday, Kim returned home to Weybridge for Christmas with his family. Kim's parents had two Christmas surprises for him.

The first, was that his father had signed up with the Fleet Air Arm and was going to be redeployed from his station at Detling in Kent and posted to Bermuda. He was to be stationed on Darrell's Island in the New Year. Vivian had done some brief training a few weeks before aboard H.M.S President which was a converted gunnery training ship. It is still permanently moored by the Embankment on the Thames in London to this day.

The second, was a course in horse riding at a local Weybridge stable, he was thrilled with their gift. During the first lesson, out in the woods, Kim showed the rest of the pupils and the instructor what he had learnt in Miami, his horsemanship was far more advanced than theirs. This really sowed the seed in Kim's mind that he would like to become an amateur steeplechase jockey one day.

The family happily celebrated the arrival of 1944 at The Cricketers Inn at Bagshot. Vivian was preparing for military service and Kim was preparing for his return to Cranleigh.

They were all unaware that 1944 would become their 'Annus Horribilis'. Imperial Airways had built an air station on Darrell's Island which is a small island within the Great Sound of Bermuda. This operated as a staging point for the early scheduled transatlantic flying boats of both Imperial Airways and Pan American World Airways. At that time, no conventional aircraft could operate from Bermuda as there were no airfields. Darrell's Island was taken over by the Royal Air Force at the beginning of World War II because Bermuda's location made it an important strategic naval station.

There were two command units on it being:

RAF Transport Command who operated large multi-engined flying boats, carrying both freight and passengers between Europe and the Americas.

RAF Ferry Command which was responsible for delivering aircraft from manufacturers to operational units. The requirements of the RAF and Fleet Air Arm could not be fulfilled by the output of British factories alone and the Air Ministry had placed orders with aircraft manufacturers in the United States, including flying boats like the Catalina which were designed for long range maritime patrols and were capable of being flown across the Atlantic, albeit in stages.

Under his Commanding Officer, Major Cecil Montgomery-Moore, Lieutenant Commander RN Vivian Caborn-Waterfield was responsible for training Bermudian volunteer pilots from the local territorial units for the Royal Air Force and the Royal Navy using Luscombe seaplanes. The pilots who passed their training were sent to the Air Ministry and assigned to the RAF or the Royal Navy's Fleet Air Arm.

Vivian found disciplined active service a far cry from the cushioned life he had enjoyed in Florida and was beginning to question why he had ever signed up.

While much has been written about the secrecy that surrounded the D-Day landings, Kim and the boys at Cranleigh were among the first in the country to know the invasion had started on June 6th 1944.

The first indication that something was about to happen came when Dunsfold aerodrome, which was built in 1942 as a base for the Canadian Air Force, was put out of bounds. Up until then, it had been common for boys to cycle there, cadging sweets and chocolate and, on occasions, ammunition to explode at a later date.

It had also been one of the responsibilities of the Cranleigh Home Guard to provide sentries for the aerodrome. In the days before the invasion, the lower field was put out of bounds and used as a base for hundreds of Canadian military vehicles. On June 5th 1944, they all disappeared.

On the evening of June 5th 1944 after a quiet day, the skies suddenly filled with planes. There were Lancasters, Liberators and Stirlings. They all knew the invasion was about to begin. Throughout that night the planes poured over, Kim and Michael stayed awake all that night. In the morning, boys crowded around radios, which were only allowed to the few who had their own studies, for any news. The few daily papers that arrived were grabbed within seconds.

The most senior boys were taken out of lessons and were all put on standby to help offload the wounded from the hospital trains as they were brought back. In fact, this never happened because fortunately the casualties were nowhere near as bad as had been expected.

On the morning of August 13th 1944, Yvonne went to her letterbox to collect the mail, there was a telegram on the floor, subconsciously she knew that something was very wrong, she opened the telegram which simply stated:

> *"We regret to inform you that on the August 10th 1944 your husband, Commander RN Vivian Caborn-Waterfield died after a brief and short illness."*

In a total state of shock, she collapsed on the floor, but she had to quickly compose herself knowing that she had to break the tragic news to her two sons, who were on their summer school holidays.

Kim took the news very badly; he could not accept that Vivian had died from a non-specified illness especially as his thirty-eight-year-old father was such a fit and healthy man.

Kim knew that he had to demonstrate responsibility and help his grieving mother through the next two weeks waiting for Vivian's body to be repatriated and making the necessary funeral arrangements. It was a ghastly time and a time Kim would never forget.

Six years later in 1950, Kim was twenty years old and had made sufficient monies to fund his own enquiry into Vivian's death. He located his father's Commanding Officer Major Cecil Montgomery-Moore who was living in Connecticut U.S.A. He had since retired from the forces and returned to civilian life. He had a very different explanation of what had happened that day in Bermuda.

Apparently, Vivien had started a routine training flight on the morning of August 10th 1944 piloting a Luscombe Model 8B powered by a single Lycoming 0-145 engine. The aircraft sped down Great Sound of Bermuda and became airborne climbing to about 1,000ft. As the plane started to change course, there was a violent explosion and the aircraft immediately broke up mid-air killing both the occupants

There was an immediate investigation by the Air Ministry, which was supposedly inconclusive at the time, but recorded engine failure as the cause of the accident, all records of that investigation either don't exist or have been destroyed.

Kim always remained convinced that his father had been killed because of his previous dealings involving Meyer Lansky, Sir Harry Oakes and the Duke of Windsor.

Having researched the Armed Forces war records myself, Vivian's death is recorded on the August 10th 1944 and surprisingly only states one word:

*'Illness'.*

No one will ever know...

**Cranleigh School**

**Luscombe M-62A as flown by Kim's father, Vivian in Bermuda 1944**

# CHAPTER FIVE

## SCHOOL & SEX
## (1944 – 1946)

When the adolescent Kim returned to Cranleigh that autumn in 1944 he was a different person, he was grieving for his father and felt he had outgrown schooling, he did not really excel in any particular subject and with the exception of rugby. He was becoming increasingly bored by the whole disciplined environment. Mr Loveday was becoming less and less impressed with the young Caborn-Waterfield, although their relationship had never been comfortable, it was now becoming fractious. Kim thought Loveday was provincial and petty. Loveday thought Kim was rebellious, arrogant and spoilt.

The situation between them became worse when Kim was caught buying and selling items, mainly wrist watches, between fellow pupils. This enabled Kim to earn small amounts of money, but enough to exist better than anyone else in his school house and indulge some of his newly acquired expensive tastes. Unfortunately, one day, a younger boy sold his watch to Kim which had been a birthday present from his parents, when the parents asked him where his watch had gone, he lied, and said it had been stolen by Caborn-Waterfield rather than telling them the truth that he had received money for it. This resulted in Kim being reported for theft to Mr Loveday.

Kim tried to explain that he had paid for the watch but Mr. Loveday chose to believe the younger boy and ordered Kim to return it, luckily Kim had not sold it yet. A few weeks later Kim took part in his first raid… the tuck shop! He was caught 'red handed' and severely thrashed. Mr Loveday warned him that if there were any more problems or antics, he would ask his mother to remove him from the school.

This incident was not going to be the only time that Kim Caborn- Waterfield was accused of theft, the next time would prove far more serious!

May 1945 saw the end of World War II; the Germans had unconditionally surrendered at Reims. A very tarnished Great Britain struggled to recover, the Country was broke and rationing was implemented everywhere.

Michael Reynolds' father had been discharged from military duties and had returned to 'civvy street' in Kensington. The Reynolds family asked Kim to stay with them in London for a week during that summer holiday; Kim was thrilled by the invitation and duly boarded a train from Weybridge to Waterloo.

Kim disembarked from the old green steam train and saw Big Ben and the Houses of Parliament for the first time, he was awe inspired. Michael's parents were a delight, their modern outlook reminded him how great his own parents were when they were based in Miami a few years earlier. They showed Kim many of the famous London sights including St Paul's Cathedral, the Tower of London and Buckingham Palace. Evenings were spent at their beautiful Georgian house in Phillimore Gardens near Kensington High Street.

The rest of 1945 was very boring as far as Kim was concerned and after a very quiet Christmas and a miserable sixteenth birthday, he duly returned to Cranleigh for the Spring term of 1946. Kim had started preparing and revising for the 'School Certificate Examination' (the equivalent of 'O' levels today) which he was due to sit in July at the end of the summer term.

Kim was very aware of his sexuality; several people had even asked him if he was still a virgin at sixteen. As the school term progressed, it was really beginning to play on his mind, some of the boys pleasured themselves or each other, this was not an option for Kim, one thing was for sure, he was not gay. The bursar in the school office had

47

already tried to seduce him on a number of occasions...
without success!

Something had to be done. One evening, as half
term was looming, Kim attended a senior school prefect's
hilarious briefing and advice on venereal disease, half
listening and half giggling, he devised a plan, he asked
Michael Reynolds:

*"Michael, I may need your help, I want to tell
my mother that I am staying with you and your family
in London for half term, will you please cover for me
if there are any dramas?"*

*"Why's that?"* asked Michael.

*"Because I want to go to London and visit
Shepherds Market."*

*"What for?"* said Michael.

*"Don't you know? Shepherds Market is famous
for prostitutes and ladies of the night,"* replied Kim.

*"So what?"* asked Michael.

*"I really want to try one and I've now saved
enough money, I've read it costs about a fiver for a
fuck!"* said Kim.

*"You're crazy, but OK,"* said Michael.

Kim signed the exeat book and stated that he was
being collected by his mother for the half term break. He
then contacted his mother and explained he would be
staying with Michael Reynolds's family in London for a
couple of days over the school holiday. She suspected
nothing was wrong as Kim had legitimately stayed with
them during the previous summer. He had created two
days of freedom... or so he thought.

On the Saturday afternoon, Kim walked to
Cranleigh station and boarded a train to London, changing
at Guildford and arrived at Waterloo with £25 in his
pocket (about £300 in today's monetary terms), the money
he had saved from his precarious deals at the school. He
took a bus to Hyde Park Corner and wandered down
Curzon Street, turning right into the alley that leads to

Shepherds Market which is a small square in the Mayfair area of central London, developed in 1735-46 by Edward Shepherd on the open ground used for the annual May fair from which Mayfair gets its name. It had been associated with prostitutes ever since the eighteenth century.

It was still daylight and to his surprise everything was very quiet. He was expecting a bustling area full of bars and clubs and of course an available girl to satisfy his curiosity and desire. He quickly realised that the whores worked out of the flats above the shops with door bells marked with a girl's name followed by 'French lessons taught here' or 'Professional massage available'.

Full of adrenaline and realising how naïve he was, he decided to return after nightfall, and walked around Hyde Park Corner to Grosvenor Crescent Mews, where the famous Lilo Blum riding stables were situated.

He loved horses and he had read about these stables from various gossip columns in the newspapers. Up until World War II, Hyde Park was ringed with livery stables, some had as many as five hundred horses, most of the stables did not survive the war but against all odds the German born Lilo Blum had opened her business two years previously in 1944 funded by the proceeds from the sale of her racehorse named 'Pickup'.

As Kim approached the stable doors at the front of the mews house, he came across a feisty lady who casually acknowledged him; it turned out to be Lilo Blum herself.

They started talking and Kim explained that he had learned to ride in Miami. Miss Blum was fascinated listening to Kim; she was so impressed that this young man had such an immaculate voice and showed such striking mature confidence. She took an immediate liking to him and suggested he should return early the next morning and join her on the Sunday morning ride through Hyde Park, but she did add, "the charge is ten schillings an hour my dear". Kim agreed to meet her at 6.a.m the following morning and made his way nervously back to Shepherds Market.

After walking several 'circuits' of the square, contemplating whether he could actually go through with this crazy idea, Kim finally summoned enough courage to ring the doorbell on the front of a house marked flat 4C followed by 'Jean-qualified French teacher'. Awaiting an answer, a highly made up blonde young woman with bright red lipstick pushed her head out of the upstairs window above the front door and shrieked:

*"Second floor, luv!"*

Kim pushed open the front door and climbed up the shabby staircase with unopened letters strewn all over the floor. The girl opened the door of the dimly lit apartment clothed only in a cheap flimsy pink housecoat.

*"Well, hurry up luv and come in."*

Kim, surprised at her Geordie accent quietly said politely:

*"Good evening, Jean."*

Kim was not aware that prostitutes used false names.

Jean, obviously surprised by Kim's young age but articulate voice replied:

*"Any special or unusual requests, luv?"*

Lost for words, Kim sheepishly said:

*"What do you mean?"*

*"Anal, oral or anything else?"* she replied:

Not understanding the question, Kim answered:

*"I will leave it to you."*

*"Well, you're a shy one, aren't you, luv? 'urry up and get undressed,"* said Jean.

Kim handed over five guineas and started to strip down, Jean removed her housecoat revealing her slim tanned naked body to Kim, the rest is history.

Kim apparently had the audacity to ask Jean if he could stay for the night, she replied: *"Time for you to go luv, I'm a busy lass."*

Feeling very macho and yet somewhat sordid, Kim found himself a cheap bed and breakfast in Lower Belgrave Road that night. He asked the night porter to be woken early at 5.a.m in order to join Lilo Blum's early Sunday morning horse ride in Hyde Park.

He went to sleep with the satisfying knowledge that he had finally lost his virginity.

Having showered and dressed the next morning, Kim knew that he still had enough cash left to afford a taxi back to Grosvenor Crescent Mews and meet up with Lilo Blum.

As Kim entered the stables again, he noticed how attractive Miss Blum's stable hand girls were, young fresh and natural, a far cry from his encounter with Jean the previous night.

Having been introduced to the riding master and groom, Kim mounted his allocated horse and the party crossed over Hyde Park Corner next to the Duke of Wellington's stately old house known as 'No1 London'. Kim had never ridden in a city centre before, riding alongside motorcars was an unusual experience, he thought the horses must have been amazingly well-trained by Miss Blum. Once in the Park, the pace quickened and Kim accelerated his horse into a gallop alongside the Serpentine. His fellow riders were aghast at his riding techniques and abilities.

For the first time in ages, Kim felt free and invigorated, it was as if all his worries were fading behind him as he rode faster and faster. Kim decided that he wanted to become a steeplechase jockey more than anything else in the world… an ambition that would stay with him for many more years.

Having paid the ten shillings riding fee, Kim thanked Miss Blum and said that he hoped to return soon.

In later years, Caroline and John Kennedy rode at Lilo Blum,'s mews stables, as did their cousins the Radziwills. Zsa Zsa Gabor, Muhammed Ali, Englebert

Humperdink and many other celebrities were amongst Miss Blum's customers.

Kim went back to Waterloo in order to catch a train back to Cranleigh, he really didn't wish to return to the school, he had just had his first taste of freedom…and sex.

Little did he know, what catastrophes would lay ahead for him that afternoon.

As he arrived back at North One, his school house, the housemaster, David Loveday was looking out of his study window when he noticed that Kim was walking down the drive alone on foot carrying an overnight bag.

Loveday remembered that Caborn-Waterfield had signed the exeat list stating that he was staying in London with Michael Reynolds' family for the weekend; he was therefore very surprised to see Kim on foot alone.

Half an hour later, Loveday casually put his head around Kim's door and said:

*"Caborn-Waterfield, please come into my study, I would like a word with you."*

*"Yes sir,"* replied Kim,

*"Where have you been this weekend?"*

*"With Reynolds, Sir."*

*"Really, well, I have just spoken to the Reynolds' housekeeper who tells me Michael Reynolds is on his way here now with his parents in their car and nobody stayed with their son this weekend. I then telephoned your mother who confirmed that you told her that you were staying with the Reynolds' as well. What do you have to say Caborn-Waterfield?"*

Kim stared at the study ceiling, blushing, not knowing how to reply.

*"Well sir….er….er…. I went horse riding."*

*"What for 2 days?"*

Kim knew he was in big trouble.

*"This school does not tolerate liars, I warned you last term that you would be expelled from here if I*

*had any more trouble with you, I have asked your
mother to meet us here tomorrow and I have reported
you to the Headmaster who wants to see you in his
study after roll call and prayers in the morning. Now
bend over that armchair."*

Kim bent over and the first of six firm strikes with a
cane landed on his backside, it was bloody painful, but
Kim's pride and arrogance wasn't going to demonstrate
the pain to Loveday.

*"Now tell me where you have been at once."*
*"London sir,"* replied Kim.

Smarting and humiliated Kim knew that David
Loveday hated him and he was not going to let this matter
go un-investigated.

The next day, Kim reported to the Headmaster, who
not only gave him a further 'six of the best', but also
informed him that upon his housemaster's
recommendations, he would be removed from Cranleigh
School. Kim was told not to attend the morning classes
and to remain in North 1 house until his mother, Yvonne
arrived.

Yvonne arrived at Cranleigh shortly after lunch time
and had a private meeting with David Loveday in a
desperate attempt to reverse the school's decision, but
unfortunately neither the headmaster nor housemaster
could be persuaded. Kim packed his trunk and walked
outside to Yvonne's waiting Riley.

On the way, back to Weybridge, Yvonne was
beyond furious with Kim, she didn't understand why her
son would go to London, stay in a bed and breakfast just
in order to go horse riding, and even if that were true,
surely, he would rather go horse riding in the countryside?
Her instinct told her that there was a lot more going on in
Kim's head than he was telling anyone.

She was just relieved that she had sent Johnny to a
different Public School because Kim had gained such a
bad reputation at Cranleigh.

53

Kim hated school and especially his housemaster, David Loveday, who eventually became the headmaster of Cranleigh.

Kim was just sixteen years old with no qualifications behind him, just an obsessive dream to become an amateur steeplechase jockey.

**Lilo Blum's Stables**

# CHAPTER SIX

## NEWLEY & NYLONS
## (1946 – 1948)

The underlying atmosphere in Kim's household was not good during the summer and autumn of 1946. Yvonne was coming to terms with the loss of her late husband and being a very attractive woman, she was now being pursued by a couple of potential suitors, one of whom Kim hated with a vengeance. She had also become very frugal since becoming a widow but she was still supporting Kim with food, clothes and occasional horse rides at the local stables. Kim had promised his mother that he would continue his studies at a local college but frankly he had no intention of taking his education any further. He had become very unhappy and frustrated at just being in the small house doing nothing.

By November, the situation had reached boiling point. Kim had no money whatsoever, he knew that he either had to find employment or go back college, which wasn't really an option as far as he was concerned. He was desperate to live in central London and kept reminiscing the previous summer in his mind. He would somehow have to find a career that would enable him to rent a small apartment in the Capital.

Kim had remained in contact with Michael Reynolds who was still at Cranleigh studying for his school certificate. As he pondered his problems he wondered if the Reynolds family could be of any assistance to him.

During December when all the schools broke up for the Christmas holiday, Kim contacted Michael and politely asked if he could come and stay with him in Kensington for a few days prior to the festive period, Michael asked his parents. They obliged, although they were a little apprehensive about seeing Kim again after his very public expulsion from Cranleigh earlier in the year.

A few days later, Kim arrived in Phillimore Gardens with his suitcase. The following day Mrs Reynolds took Kim and Michael shopping and they ended up in Fortnum & Mason. It was the first-time Kim had ever seen Jermyn Street and all the wonderful men's outfitting shops. Mentally, he had purchased the entire street and this was definitely where he wanted to live.

Over dinner that evening, Kim practiced his natural charm and salesmanship. He explained to the very understanding Mr Reynolds that he needed to come to London in order to find work.

Kim was incredibly surprised when the affluent Mr Reynolds offered to sponsor him to rent a small flat while he hunted for suitable employment, but only if he explained why he had been expelled from Cranleigh School. Kim amusingly told Mr Reynolds the story of coming to London in order to go to Lilo Blum's stables in Grosvenor Crescent Mews and take a ride through Hyde Park. Michael was still a virgin; he had never told his parents the true reasons for Kim's truancy and his parents accepted the whole of his plausible explanations without question.

Kim later said:

**"I felt like a fucking orator on stage, they totally believed me, thank God!"**

The next day Kim caught a bus with Michael to Piccadilly and started to look for local estate agents in order to rent a studio. They found a small estate office in Duke Street and enquired if there was anything suitable in the area. A tall austere pin striped gentleman at the front desk greeted them and asked:

**"Aren't you a little too young to be taking a flat, son?"**

Michael chipped in and explained that his family lived in Phillimore Gardens and they had offered to guarantee the rental payments while Kim looked for employment. The agent accepted the explanation and marched them around the corner to a small studio on the first floor of a Victorian building at the junction of Jermyn Street and Duke Street St James's. The studio was very small but clean and freshly painted, the bed folded down from the wall.

*"How much is this then?"* asked Kim:

*"Five guineas a week, son."* replied the agent.

*"Would you accept four and a half guineas a week sir, if so we will take it?"* questioned a confident young Kim.

*"I will have to take instructions and let you know later on today."* replied the estate agent.

The agent shook hands with both the boys and they spent the rest of the day window shopping in the St James area.

Later that day the agent contacted Mr Reynolds to confirm the lower figure had been accepted and asked him to visit his office as soon as possible in order to sign the necessary documentation. Mr Reynolds was quietly impressed by Kim's power of bargaining.

The formalities were concluded during the following day and having thanked the Reynolds family profusely for all their kind support and hospitality, Kim returned to Weybridge with a new front door key in his pocket. He was worried about how he was going to tell his mother that he was going to leave home before he was seventeen years old and live in town.

Kim was very affectionate towards Yvonne over the next couple of days and gradually summoned up the courage to tell her that he was going to leave Weybridge. To his surprise, she took the news very calmly and even offered to drive him to Jermyn Street with his small quantity of personal belongings. Kim seriously wondered if she was actually relieved by him leaving.

They arrived at the tiny studio in St James's and Yvonne helped Kim carry the cases up the old staircase before she gave him a kiss goodbye, the farewell reminded him of his first day at Cranleigh.

Yvonne drove home worrying about her young son's future, but Kim was unfazed, believing that now was the time life could really begin. All he needed was to earn plenty of money and prove to himself that he could become an amateur steeplechase jockey.

With very little cash, he walked down Duke Street to the Red Lion pub, which was formally a gin palace, and ordered his first pink gin which consists of Gordon's Gin with a touch of Angostura Bitters, only to be questioned about his age and eligibility to purchase alcohol. Having coaxed the busty blonde barmaid into believing that he was twenty-one, he duly asked her around to his new studio after she finished her shift, she accepted, and the flat was duly 'christened' on his first night in residence.

Kim could never remember her name although he continued to frequent the pub.

Kim subconsciously had already realised that no job or sensible career that a seventeen-year-old lad could gain would ever make him wealthy enough to achieve his ambitious goals.

Yvonne sent Kim some money that Christmas, hoping he would come home for the break, but he actually spent all the funds from his mother in the pub alone.

At the end of 1946 Kim was seriously broke, he couldn't even pay Mr Reynolds the rent that was due and he felt terribly guilty when he considered the trust and faith he had shown in him.

On a very cold evening in February 1947, Kim wasn't able to top up his gas meter with coins in the studio, he was frozen. With the last few 'coppers' he possessed, he made his daily pilgrimage down to the Red Lion and took a seat in the saloon bar contemplating his future. With only a half pint of beer for company, he was even wondering if he could obtain credit in the pub that he had become so well-known in.

There was a scruffy and yet interesting young man drinking alone who acknowledged him as if to say:

*"Would you like to join me?"*

Kim reacted immediately hoping the lad would buy him 'the other half'.

*"Good evening, I'm Michael Caborn-Waterfield, but everyone calls me Kim,"* he replied.

*"Watcha mate... my name is Anthony Newley, have you 'eard' of me? I'm an actor."*

A startled Kim politely answered in his perfect 'stiff upper lip' voice, that he had not.

The lad replied:

*"Jesus Christ, you're a toff aren't ya, I've been playin' a small part in a show around the corner, look at me, I'm still 'wearin me' stage clothes."*

Kim had always been interested in anything theatrical and would have chosen acting as a second choice after his preferred career as a jockey. He was also highly entertained by Newley's Cockney accent and slang so he decided to take the conversation further.

Newley kept topping him up, and the evening eventually became a major drinking session during which they formed a highly unlikely early friendship.

Kim knew he had to start making money immediately and confided his dire financial circumstances to Newley, who happened to be born in the same year as Kim and was nearly always broke as well.

Newley said:

*"Very easy to earn a few quid mate, everythin' is black market 'ere' these days, if I wasn't actin', I'd get in on the game myself, all the theatres in London need stockings and you can't get them mate, I could let 'ya' meet some theatre managers if you could get the gear, see what 'ya' can do... got to go now, I'm*

*working in the morning, here's my number, stay in touch."*

Kim climbed into his bed that night with a thumping headache but he was still sober enough to wonder if his new-found friend had an idea worth exploring.

Anthony Newley was born in Hackney, he was Jewish. His parents, who had never married, separated during his early childhood. During World War II, he was evacuated to a foster home in the countryside, safely away from the aerial bombing attacks on London and the ghastly Blitz.

Although recognised as very bright by his teachers, he was uninterested in school, and by the age of fourteen was working as an office boy for an insurance company. When he read an advertisement in the Daily Telegraph headed 'Boy Actors Urgently Wanted' he applied to the advertisers, being the prestigious Italia Conti Stage School, only to discover that the fees were too high. Nevertheless, after a brief audition, he was offered a job as an office boy on a salary of thirty shillings a week plus free tuition at the school. While serving tea one afternoon, he caught the eye of producer Geoffrey de Barkus, who cast Newley as 'Dusty' in the children's serial 'The adventures of Dusty Bates'.

During the next few days Kim strolled around the more sordid parts of town and realised there were many street traders, commonly known as 'spivs' selling different types of nylon stockings and other unobtainable items at premium prices.

He contacted Newley again and suggested he invest into the first deal as he had no cash himself, Newley agreed to put his month's wages into the first purchase that Kim made from a very suspect character simply called 'Jim', who was trading on a street corner off Portobello Road, Notting Hill.

Kim bought a 'parcel' of black nylon stockings from Jim for £6 in cash, and that night was introduced to the manager of the Victoria Palace Theatre by the street-wise Newley. They sold them all very quickly by the backstage entrance and received £10 in cash. The pair were thrilled with their £4 profit which they split between themselves and this became the first of many much larger transactions that would take place over the following few months. Kim had found his first serious friend in the big city.

Unbelievably, Kim began to pay his rent to Mr Reynolds on time every month. He kept the studio immaculately, but used it as a 'bordello', clocking up as many conquests as possible. He was still always short of money due to his expenditure on clothes, clubs and gin.

Kim's day never started before lunchtime, he would tour the stage doors at night time with his wares and then usually head for a 'clip joint' to find a 'floozy'. He had developed his powers of seduction down to a fine art.

He regularly went horse riding in London and he had renewed his acquaintance with Lilo Blum at the riding stables in Grosvenor Crescent Mews. After a ride one afternoon, Lilo Blum asked him join her at the Hyde Park Hotel where she was meeting Tommy Rayson for a drink. Rayson had trained the winning horse, Lovely Cottage, ridden by jockey Captain Robert Petre at the previous year's Grand National at Aintree. Lilo praised Kim's horsemanship to Rayson and Kim was overwhelmed when Rayson invited him down to Epsom the following weekend for a trial. Kim had now obtained his driving license, and bought a second-hand MG TC painted in dark blue, out of his profits. He accepted the invitation.

After arriving at Epsom racecourse on the Saturday, he was shown to a very large horse by Rayson, which he mounted, but within seconds the frisky horse threw Kim to the ground breaking his right wrist severely, he was rushed to a local hospital and plastered up. Although he still yearned to be a steeplechase jockey, this ambition was to be illusive, especially after the accident.

He did however tell Michael Reynolds to spread the rumour that he had run away to Tommy Rayson's National Hunt stables to his old classmates back at Cranleigh. Hence the stories that still fly around today.

By the end of 1947, Kim had no less than about twenty stage managers and ten hotel concierges on his payroll, each one receiving weekly 'back handers' from Kim to encourage greater sales of the nylon stockings.

Kim would drive the same circuit most evenings around Soho and Shaftsbury Avenue. The MG's boot would be laden with stock and once sold, he would often meet up with Newly for a nightcap.

During the Spring of 1948, Kim's new venture had expanded and he started to frequent some of the more affluent clubs and watering holes of Mayfair and Chelsea, the major problem was that whatever he earned on the black market would nearly always be spent by nightfall. He was usually accompanied during this period by Anthony Newley, whose acting career was really beginning to prosper.

Kim was thrilled to hear that Newley had been chosen to co-star in Peter Ustinov's new comedy movie Vica Versa starring Petula Clark, he yearned to be associated with show business and asked if he could be involved in anyway.

*"See what I can do,"* replied Newley.

A few weeks later Newley contacted Kim and asked:

*"Ello mate, fancy being an 'extra' on set next week?"*

Kim couldn't believe his luck, he seriously had 'visions of grandeur' imagining that he could become a film star. He rapidly applied for an equity card and actually kept it valid for the rest of his life.

The next day, Kim drove to the film studios and Newley, cast as Dick Bultitude, introduced him to both

Peter Ustinov and Petula Clark who was already a very well-known singing star at that time.

Unfortunately for Kim, the part he was offered involved a two-minute non-speaking 'walk on walk off' roll.

Kim drove back to the West End early evening, fascinated by the experience and yet disappointed that 'stardom and fame had eluded him, but at least he could always say that he had been in a movie.

**Anthony Newley in the 1948 British comedy film, Vice Versa directed by Peter Ustinov & on his wedding day to Joan Collins in 1963**

# CHAPTER SEVEN

## SEX & SILK STOCKINGS
## (1948)

One evening, Kim and Newley were sitting having a quiet bottle of champagne at Bertie Green's Astor Club which was littered with prostitutes, politely called 'hostesses', in Berkeley Square.

Newley was in a great mood, having just been awarded the part of 'Artful Dodger' in David Lean's new film Oliver Twist. He was telling Kim all about Lean's cinematographic background.

Sir David Lean's first work as a director was in 1942 in collaboration with Sir Noel Coward, the film was called 'In Which We Serve'. He later adapted several of Coward's plays into successful films. These films were 'This Happy Breed' in 1944, 'Blithe Spirit' in 1944 and 'Brief Encounter' in 1945 starring Celia Johnson and Trevor Howard as quietly understated clandestine lovers, torn between their unpredictable passion and their respective ordinary middle-class marriages in suburban England. The film shared the Grand Prix honours at the 1946 Cannes film festival and earned Lean his first Academy nomination for directing and screen adaptation. Celia Johnson was also nominated for Best Actress. It has since become a classic and one of the most highly regarded British films.

One could only imagine how proud the young Anthony Newley felt that night.

They were later interrupted by two impeccably dressed men who could hear their conversation standing at the bar:

**"Hey aren't you that new young fellow that's in Peter Ustinov's new movie with Petula Clark?"**

*"Yeap, I am Anthony Newley, and I'm about to start another new movie with Alec Guinness."*

*"What's the film called, son?"*

*"Oliver Twist, it's directed by David Lean, I'm the artful dodger."*

Replied an excited Newley:

*"May we buy you fellas a drink?"*

*"Thank you, kind sir."* humbly replied Kim.

The two gentlemen introduced themselves to Kim and Newley, as Bobby McKew and Michael Eland (also known as Mike Eaton-Eland).

Turning to Kim, Eland asked:

*"Well, what game are you into dear boy, are you an actor too?"*

Kim was a little thrown by the question, he was not going to own up as being a 'black market' trader to a complete stranger and he didn't want to appear upstaged by Newley.

*"No, actually I'm heir to the Colnaghi Aviation empire (one of his late father's Christian names), my trust matures on my 21st birthday."*

Anthony Newley choked on his drink. He couldn't believe what Kim had said and later remarked that Kim was quick-witted when it came to 'getting out of the shit'.

Kim then reversed the question on Eland and he was equally surprised by his answer.

*"Bobby and myself work with Billy Hill, do you know who he is? He runs this city you know, if ever you need anything, and I mean anything, it can be organized."*

Kim paused and spontaneously asked:

*"Can you supply nylon stockings worth the money in large quantities?"*

Eland replied:

*"Let's not talk here, come and meet me in my office tomorrow after lunch, it's in South Audley Street, I might be able to help you, here's my card."*

The four men had a few more drinks before choosing which of the hostess' they fancied and would take home with them for the night.

Kim was fascinated by the two men and he was determined to do his homework to find out who Billy Hill was prior to his meeting the following day. Early the next day Kim went to the local library to study previous newspaper articles in order to learn about Billy Hill's empire. After more investigation, he discovered that William 'Billy' Hill was born in 1911 and that he was a criminal, linked to smuggling, racketeering and violence.

He was one of the foremost perpetrators of organised crime in London. He began as a house burglar in the late 1920's and then specialized in 'smash and grab' raids targeting furriers and jewellers in the 1930's.

During World War II, Hill moved into the 'black market', specializing in foods and petrol. He also supplied forged documents for deserting servicemen and was involved in London's West End protection rackets with fellow gangster Jack Spot. In the 1940's, he was charged with burglary, and fled to South Africa. Following an arrest there for assault, he was extradited back to Britain, where he was convicted for the warehouse robbery and served a little time in prison. After his release, he met Gypsy Riley, better known as 'Gyp Hill', who became his common-law wife, who Kim would meet some years later in Tangier. The memories of Meyer Lansky flashed in Kim's mind.

As Kim approached the entrance to Eland's office that afternoon, he was intrigued, but somewhat frightened and apprehensive. He had been dealing with spivs and stockings for nearly a year, but he had never been involved or exposed to London's serious underworld before.

Kim was shown into a small office, and Eland's first remark was:

**"Dear boy, you seem to have been very busy, my scouts tell me that you have Soho and the theatres**

*'sewn up', I am very impressed, but I'm not too sure about your story concerning the Colnaghi aviation fortune. What would you say if I told you that I can supply you the stockings for 20% less than I think you're giving the street traders? But you would have to commit to buying far more stock than you're currently, purchasing off the streets. We buy from the States and have all the stewards on the Queen Mary 'sorted out'."*

Kim thought very carefully, wondering if the chance meeting at the Astor Club the night before had in fact been orchestrated by Eland, McKew or even Billy Hill himself.

*"Mr Eland, make it 25% and I'll give you my commitment."*

As he said this, he wondered where the hell he was going to find the necessary cash to enable him to honour these purchases. Eland agreed the deal, Kim perhaps a little naively, left Eland's office believing that he was now climbing the ladder.

He immediately telephoned Anthony Newley and suggested they should meet at Churchill's Club in Bond Street later that night for a celebratory drink.

Although he had dealt with Michael Eland, Kim eventually became much closer to Bobby McKew. Little did Kim know how significant Bobby McKew would become in shaping his future, they would both serve time together in a filthy French jail, just six years later.

On many occasions, Kim managed to sell his stock before he had to pay Billy Hill's lieutenants, this created great cash flow, he was making more and more cash.

Kim would often tease Newley about his dreadful Cockney voice and his terrible table manners really believing that he could create an 'English Gentleman' out of his pal.

Kim had amassed a large wedge of 'readies' (Cockney slang for cash) one week and decided to take matters in his own hands, he telephoned Newley and said:

*"Hey chum, I feel like I'm Al Capone during prohibition, I've had a great week, are you working this weekend?"*

*"No mate,"* replied Newley.

*"Listen, you've done enough for me this year, especially when I was skint, I've decided you need some further education so we're going to Paris on the Golden Arrow boat-train tomorrow, I'm booking the Georges V Hotel, Michael Eland tells me it's a great place to stay, it'll be fun, see you on platform two at 10.00 am at Victoria station, I'll have the tickets, it leaves at 10.30am, don't be late."*

*"Can't wait, when will we be back,"* replied a very surprised Newley.

*"Monday afternoon,"* said Kim.

*"Ok, but I have to be on the Oliver Twist set at the studios on Tuesday, otherwise David Lean will kill me."*

*"You'll be there, don't worry,"* replied Kim.

The pair met on platform two at Victoria station the next morning, Kim's pockets were stuffed with rolls of white fivers, which you couldn't legally take out of the Country in those days. He was determined to enjoy himself.

Amazingly, the pair of young men were not approached by Customs at Victoria that morning. They boarded the first class 'Pullman' coach which travelled the entire journey to Gare du Nord in Paris. Once aboard they started drinking pink gins in the Trianon Bar, and then enjoyed a wonderful lobster lunch, washed down with a bottle of 1945 Puilly Fuisse white Burgundy.

They arrived in Paris and made their way to the famous hotel, albeit somewhat pissed.

That evening, Kim suggested they visit some of the clubs in Place Pigalle. Kim knew Toulouse Lautrec, Pablo Picasso and Vincent van Gough once had studios there and was eager to explore the area. They actually ended up in the Saint-Germain-des-Prés, at a newly opened club aptly named the Saint-Germain-des-Prés Club, where the legendary jazz musician, Miles Davis, had just performed. Once they had settled at the bar, Kim noticed a pair of 'floozies' sitting in an alcôve, not one to waste time, he went straight over to them and performed his now perfected script :

**"My God darlings, you both look so magical. I'm Kim Caborn-Waterfield."**

Without going into too much crude detail, the pair of lads took the blonde and the brunette back to the Georges V hotel that night and barricaded them in the room for two days. While they were sampling ALL 'the goods', room service delivered an endless supply of Perrier Jouet Belle Epoque champagne. The final account rendered by the hotel was horrendous.

Newley returned to London a day late, minus his virginity and the displeasure of David Lean. Kim returned back to London… broke!

During the autumn of 1948, Newley had a whirlwind romance with Joan Shandell, a model and an aspiring actress, who he had met a few years before while studying at the Italia Conti school, they rapidly become engaged despite the fact he wasn't practicing monogamy.

Newley really wanted to marry his co-star, Diana Dors, and falsely boasted to his friends that he had lost his virginity to her a few weeks earlier while filming Oliver Twist. Kim obviously remembered their recent antics in Paris and knew that Newley's claim was bullshit. It was merely a brief encounter as far as Dors was concerned, but Newley was secretly besotted with her and was always jealous of her subsequent boyfriends.

During mid-December Kim received a call from Newley to inform him that he was getting married to Joan in a few days' time and asked him to be his best man at a small informal wedding organized in Chelsea. Kim naturally thought she must be pregnant because Newley had organised the wedding so quickly, but he was wrong, this was not the case, a simple reception was arranged and the couple married. They were unfortunately divorced in 1955 and Newley later married Joan Collins in 1963.

Kim returned to Weybridge to celebrate a very quiet, and last Christmas with his mother, his brother 'Johnny' and their Dalmatian dog which was called, Caesar.

Just after Boxing Day, the newly married Newley telephoned Kim back at the studio in Jermyn Street and asked:

*"Whatcha doin' New Year's mate?"*

*"Celebrating my nineteenth birthday, why, what have you in mind?"* replied Kim.

*"Do ya know the Cross Quays boozer near the river?"*

Kim replied, *"Yes"*, but he didn't actually know the venue.

*"See ya in there around ten o' clock for a few jars before the bell strikes, my co-star Diana Dors will be there but before you ask mate, I've already given her one, but that's between us, Joan, my new wife will be there."*

Kim asked if it would be alright to bring along his other best friend, Michael Reynolds. He had no idea how this particular evening would influence his own future.

Kim put on his dandiest suit, splashed on the Guerlain L'heure Bleue, his favourite cologne, and set off to the Cross Keys in Lawrence Street, which was built in 1708 and was the oldest pub in Chelsea. Hundreds of years previously it had been the watering hole of William Turner, the famous artist and regular visitors had included the writers Agatha Christie and Dylan Thomas.

Newley was holding court at the bar with his new wife, Joan, and several other friends including a beautiful young Rank starlet blonde actress who had played 'Charlotte' opposite him in Oliver Twist. Kim had immediately clocked the gorgeous blonde sitting on a bar stool, it was Diana Dors, she was seventeen years old and gorgeous.

Kim already knew a little of Dors' history, through Anthony Newley. At sixteen-years old she had signed to the Gordon Harbord Agency and that during the signing of contracts, she changed her contractual surname to Dors, the maiden name of her maternal grandmother at the suggestion of her mother Mary Fluck.

She would later say:

*"They asked me to change my name. I suppose they were afraid that if my real name Diana Fluck was put up in lights and the L bulb blew...."*

In 1947 she had won the London Films Cup, awarded by Sir Alexander Korda. and then she signed a contract with the Rank Organisation and joined J. Arthur Rank's 'charm school' for young actors and actresses.

Kim approached her with a fire burning inside him, but he was not going to make it obvious that he fancied her like crazy; he thought it more appropriate to play hard to get.

She had a wonderful ability to tell stories against herself which instantly enthralled Kim.

To quote Dors about Kim:

*"I glanced away from my friends to see a boy with the most disturbing eyes that seemed to pierce right through me, his dark good looks were almost beautiful... I half-smiled in his direction, but he abruptly turned away as if he hadn't seen me. As he had expected and anticipated, his lack of interest intrigued me and we immediately became lovers."*

To quote Kim about Dors:

*"She had a golden swing of tawny blonde hair with wicked blue eyes, bee stung lips and an astonishing hour glass figure, radiating personality, exerting an almost imperious magnetic pull on all around her. For me it was a 'Coup de Foudre."*

To quote Dors about Kim:

*"Borrowing a few pounds here and writing more post-dated cheques there, it would have seemed incongruous if anyone had prophesied the vast fortunes we would make separately in the years ahead. If only we could have accumulated all those millions at the time we were still in love and knew what we wanted to do with our lives, there would no doubt be a different story now."*

Diana Dors & Chelsea's oldest pub, The Cross Keys, where she met Kim on his 18th birthday.

# CHAPTER EIGHT

## DANDY & DORS
## (1949 – 1951)

Kim and Diana Dors made love the night that they met... all night.

Dors would always joke that it was her nineteenth birthday present to him, he would always joke that the New Year should start with a bang. It was literally 'love at first sight' and the lovers became inseparable from the moment they met in Chelsea. Kim had enjoyed more than many brief liaisons, but he had never embarked upon a serious relationship before.

He saw less and less of Anthony Newley, who was quietly jealous of the new tempestuous relationship that had blossomed. He was not only infatuated with Dors himself, but he was also becoming increasingly bored with his recent marriage to Joan Shandell.

A few weeks later, Kim and Dors had their first serious row. There had been a few incoming telephone calls at the small flat for Dors, Kim was convinced she was whispering to a possible suitor, or even possibly having an affair. When he confronted her, she confessed that the calls had been coming from the influential film director David Lean, who had tried to give her some 'very private' rehearsals while shooting Oliver Twist the previous year. She willingly played along with him, flirting as always, hoping for the next starring role.

Kim went out that evening on his usual deliveries around Soho in the old MG, slightly inebriated, muttering under his breath about that 'Fucking Fluck'. Dors' original surname.

Kim had become increasingly intrigued by fashion, and wanted his style to emulate his hero, the Duke of Windsor. Money was awash at that time, so he commissioned Huntsman in Saville Row to cut some very unusual collarless 'dandy' suits for himself in both Prince of Wales checks, various Scottish tartans and plain pastel colours. His shirts were made by Turnbull & Asser in Jermyn Street. They differed from convention with flamboyant cuffs that folded back on themselves and onto the sleeves of the jackets, he also loved roll necks sweaters. Kim would only wear suede boots which he called his 'Chelsea boots' and exquisite Patek Philippe watches, which despite costing a fortune from Garrards, the Crown jewellers in Regent Street, he would lavish on young girls around the town.

Kim would always refer to Diana Dors as simply, 'Dors', a nickname that Kim would call her for the rest of her short life.

Dors found Kim's new dress style very natty and dapper but also highly amusing, she therefore nicknamed him: 'Dandy Kim'… a name that would stay with him and haunt him forever.

Kim loved socialising and boozing with Dors and the Rank show business crowd in London. The Rank Organisation's acting school was called The Company of Youth but was often referred to as 'The Charm School'. It was founded by John Davis, the chairman of Rank in 1945 and the school's main acting teacher was Molly Terraine. It's pupils, or more appropriately prodigies, included: Christopher Lee, Honor Blackman (Goldfinger 007), Claire Bloom, Patrick McGoohan (Danger Man), a very young Joan Collins (she married Anthony Newley three years later) and of course, Britain's answer to Marilyn Monroe and Jayne Mansfield… Diana Dors.

Because of his eccentric and expensive taste in clothing, mixed with his charming voice and well-rehearsed manner, 'Dandy Kim' was creating quite a name for himself around the town as a wealthy, hedonistic showman, an image which he thoroughly relished. It was around this time of his life that he had started appearing in the gossip columns of the national newspapers, more by his association with Dors, than anything else.

One day, Kim received a massive order for nylons and on the security of this transaction, thought it was time for the little MG sports car to be upgraded; it no longer suited his newly acquired status. He part exchanged it for a massive 1932 Rolls Royce Phantom II Sedanca de Ville with coachwork by Gurney Nutting, one of the most prestigious coachbuilders during the 1930's. It was beautiful, elegant and nearly twenty feet long.

Kim became acquainted with Captain Hartman, the owner of Lendrum & Hartman Ltd in Albemarle Street who was a dominant figure, he was the sole importer for the ostentatious American Cadillac cars in Great Britain which were mainly sold to flamboyant or theatrical people. Kim loved these automobiles, it reminded him of all his happy days in Florida when his father was alive, driving to Palm Beach.

Needless to say, he purchased a brand-new white Cadillac convertible for Dors, she was seventeen and didn't even have a driving licence.

Their spending and eccentricities became worse; Kim even created and commissioned 'The Waterfield Tartan', which he used to trim the headlining in his old Rolls Royce. He was happier than ever, great sex, a famous blonde actress, a new Cadillac and an old Rolls Royce.

Kim used to laugh:

**"I'm a triple sandwich; I have sex before, during and after lunch."**

They had achieved flamboyant notoriety as a couple that would always create a show wherever they went, this showmanship suited the Rank Organisation and kept Dors in the press, but Dors' parents were not impressed with Kim, Mr and Mrs Fluck named him the 'snooty opportunist'.

To gain further respectability and interest, he would often insinuate that he came from an aviation dynasty and that he was the sole beneficiary of the 'Colnaghi Trust' and that he would also inherit the title, 'Count Colnaghi'.

During this period, Kim decided to follow his family's tradition and learn to fly properly. He often showed off and told people that he had started flying when he was eight years old. He wanted to take to the air again and hold a licence. He started taking lessons with London Aero and Motor Services Flying School based at Elstree Aerodrome. The flying club, operated two Piper PA-17 Vagabond's which featured dual controls, enabling them to be used for pilot training. Kim flew solo after eight hours training and quickly notched up the mandatory thirty-five hours needed to enable him to qualify for a full Private Pilot License; he took the theory examination in London, which involved understanding weather conditions, cloud formations and aeronautical maps.

He had no idea what this British licence would enable him to do in Cuba, the following year.

On a serious note, Kim had never believed his father had simply died of a 'non-specific illness', in Bermuda. He often thought of the powerful characters that he had met when he was a mere child with Vivian, his father. Sometimes he wildly thought that the trio, being, Meyer Lansky, Bedaux or even his hero the Duke of Windsor had something to do with it, he usually just dismissed these crazy thoughts as a far-fetched conspiracy theory, but now he had enough money to instruct an agency in New York to locate the whereabouts of his late father's Commanding Officer.

One morning Kim received a telegram that read:
*Attention Kim Waterfield:*
*Located Commanding Officer Major Cecil Montgomery-Moore in Connecticut U.S.A... ret'd forces... returned civilian life...*
*explanation...Commander RN Vivian Caborn-*

*Waterfield started routine training flight... morning...*
*August 10ᵗʰ 1944... Luscombe Model 8B... single*
*Lycoming 0145engine... Aircraft... Airborne... Climb*
*to 1,000ft appro... Change course... Violent*
*explosion... Aircraft broke up mid-air... Both*
*occupants killed... Investigation Air Ministry...*
*Inconclusive... Recorded engine failure... Cause of*
*accident... All records of investigation... don't exist*
*or have been destroyed... Await your instructions.*

Why do British Naval records read just 'illness'?
Kim wondered.

Kim never told his mother, Yvonne, about this, and
after very careful consideration didn't think he should take
matters any further, one, he couldn't bring his father back,
two, if it was sabotage, the culprits concerned were
certainly powerful enough to take him out as well if
necessary.

Dors made her leading role breakthrough in 1949,
winning the part of 'Dora' in the new film 'Diamond City'.
It was a drama set in South Africa based on the true story
of Stafford Parker who was elected president of the
Diamond Diggers Republic in 1871 directed by David
Macdonald and starring David Farrar and Honor
Blackman. Filming began at Denham studios and moved
on to South Africa for location shooting. Dors had to
travel to South Africa, but agreed, prior to her departure,
that it was time to move from the small Jermyn Street
studio and find somewhere more befitting their newly
acquired success.

One morning, Kim found a beautiful new apartment
in Hamilton Terrace in St John's Wood; it had three
bedrooms, two bathrooms and plenty of space. He agreed
to sign a new lease.

That afternoon Kim went to Cartier in Bond Street
and purchased a solid gold lighter for Mr Reynolds, as a
gesture of thanks for all the kind support he had
previously shown him and a gold ring for Dors. He

proudly paid using a cheque drawn on his new Hoare & Co bank account. He telephoned his old chum Michael Reynolds and invited him to dinner that evening with his parents at the Savoy Grill to explain that he was moving and would no longer need his father's guarantee for the rent payable on the Jermyn Street studio and that it was becoming too difficult to park both the Rolls Royce and Cadillac in St James'.

During the lavish dinner, Kim learnt that his old friend was going to study business at Yale University and was relocating to the United States that autumn.

When a very suntanned Dors returned from South Africa, she found that Kim's crazy hedonism and spending had spiralled totally out of control, he had completely furnished the new flat with expensive items from Waring & Gillow and furthermore he had purchased a unique Delahaye 175S motor car for her. It later became known as the 'Dors Delahaye'. This astonishing roadster was a 'one off' built in Paris by Saoutchik and was painted in bright turquoise, its interior was remarkably contemporary, incorporating a stylized eagle's head on each door panel and an expansive dash panel that seemed aircraft inspired with its rows of knobs and a stunning transparent Lucite steering wheel.

(This automobile recently sold in auction for £3 million)

The fact was that in reality he was totally broke.

Dors insisted that the Cadillac was sold immediately in a useless attempt to restore his finances. He couldn't even afford to pay for his stock and that could have had some serious consequences with Billy Hill's lieutenants.

The whole situation became far worse; they were evicted from their new home and even had to spend a couple of nights on a friend's living room floor before finding enough cash to rent a bedsit at Collingham Road in Kensington. Dors found a new role and went on a south coast tour with the musical comedy, 'Lisette'.

She suddenly discovered she was pregnant on the eve of her eighteenth birthday. She returned to London immediately, being sick all the way, and met Kim. They had to find somewhere the pregnancy could be terminated because neither of them could afford a professional Harley Street abortionist. Kim borrowed £10 on the strength of his inheritance that he would never receive, to pay for the operation from an amateur female butcher; she performed the procedure on a kitchen table in Battersea. For Dors the whole episode was a nightmare, it took many months before she recovered physically, and dramatically changed their relationship.

Having just undergone her first abortion, she then learnt that Rank was £18 million in debt, they had closed the Charm School and furthermore made her redundant.

After a while, Dors appeared with Barbara Murray in 'The Cat and the Canary' at the Connaught Theatre in Worthing. She was then contracted to Elstree Studios who cast her in a play called 'Man of the World', starring Lionel Jeffries. It opened at the Royal Shakespeare Theatre in Stratford-upon-Avon and capped her works that year to win her the Theatre World Magazine's Actress of the Year Award.

Kim and Dors spent a very quiet Christmas in Kensington. He cancelled his twentieth birthday party at Murray's Cabaret Club, which was, incidentally, where Christine Keeler met Stephen Ward prior to the 'Profumo 'Affair'.

Kim and Dors both believed that America held the key to their future, business in New York for Kim, the movies in Hollywood for Diana but their relationship was beginning to dwindle partly because Kim's career was waning and Dors was no longer receiving any major film offers.

1950 was a quiet year; Dors' parents were becoming increasingly concerned about their daughter, both for her career and for her choice of partner. Kim was licking his wounds and wondering what to do next, he had become bored with the black-market trade and realised that post war rationing was coming to an end, therefore ending his racket. He always believed there would be another deal around the corner, but it was not happening this time. He even contemplated trying to buy and sell petrol or whisky and he regularly met up with Billy Hill's lieutenant Bobby McKew, trying to find a new lucrative scheme. Kim and Dors were both borrowing money, mainly from Yvonne, to survive and yet they still continued to entertain friends extravagantly in their tiny home.

Kim rarely spoke to Yvonne, but he still hoped that there might be a small inheritance due to him from his late father's estate on his twenty first birthday but after another miserable Christmas, he found out there was nothing forthcoming.

Yvonne was broke herself, but she managed to send Kim £50 for his twenty-first birthday.

Dors started to receive film offers again, including a major role in 'Lady Godiva Rides Again' (released in the United States as 'Bikini Baby') which she started filming in early 1951. The film was most notable for the presence of actresses who were later to become famous. Diana Dors appeared as a beauty queen and was later marketed as the film's star. It also featured Joan Collins in her film debut as an unaccredited beauty contestant and Ruth Ellis, who was the last woman to be executed in England after being convicted of the murder of her lover, David Blakely.

The film was temporarily banned by the American Board of Film Censors on account that Diana's navel was deemed too risqué. While on set, she met Dr Stephen Ward, who had a minor role in the film, he became besotted by Dors and tried to befriend her at any opportunity, she eventually accepted an invitation for a drink from him, she told him that she had a boyfriend, being Kim, and surprisingly Ward suggested that they all meet up in Wimpole Mews, where Ward lived. Kim hit it off with Ward mainly because they both liked discussing women, but Kim did wonder about Ward's sexuality because he seemed to collect beautiful girls but never actually performed with any of them himself, Kim thought he must have been a voyeur.

Dors would later state:

**"He looked devious and he was something of a show off, I didn't want to be suspected of being one of his call girls."**

Ward would later be part of Kim's circle and gain notoriety in the Christine Keeler, Mandy Rice-Davis and John Profumo scandal.

Dors met a 'salesman' in the local pub called Dennis Hamilton, he also lived in Collingham Road and knew Kim's brother Johnny. Hamilton was a conman, a violent, filthy tempered and unpredictable playboy who had been the protégé of homosexual actor Eric Portman. He had a dazzling smile that charmed everyone, regardless of what they thought about him, his motives or principles. Dors strangely became attracted to him, and finally conceded to his obvious advances.

Kim always had a good instinct, he sensed Dors' affections were being given elsewhere and by May 1951, the usually alcohol induced rows had become more and more frequent. Dors wanted to end the relationship and take her chances with the foul Dennis Hamilton. To make matters worse again, Kim was arrested over a shady deal and sentenced to a month in jail, giving the loathsome Hamilton the perfect opportunity to make his play on Dors which he did successfully. He took her to see Danny Kaye at the London Palladium on their first date, Dors stayed with Hamilton that night and duly left Kim, taking the beautiful Delahaye with her.

Kim was devastated and inconsolable; the only solution was either heavy drinking binges with his Chelsea friends or copious fucking. Despite pleading with Dors to return, he knew it was over, the game was up and the good times were gone.

He started preparing his next chapter and thought it would be prudent to create distance between Dors and himself. Although he had very little money, he sent the old Rolls Royce for restoration, not knowing that he wouldn't see his beloved car for the next four years, when it would become part of a much greater caper.

Dors married Dennis Hamilton five weeks later at Caxton Hall, London on Monday July 3rd 1951, her parents were not enamoured with the proposed union and decided not to attend the ceremony. Diana, who was still under the then, legal age of twenty-one, had to forge their signatures on the form that gave permission for their daughter to be married. It was even rumoured that Hamilton had threatened to smash up the vicar, if he didn't perform the service.

Dors was later to find out that Hamilton was a mean drunk and took to beating her up on a regular basis. He boasted about her earnings, most of which he stole for his nefarious schemes, thus indirectly getting her into trouble with the UK taxman.

To quote Kim:

*"Diana Dors was a darling and I always swore to protect her. She was naughty and wild, for her, sex was a game she loved to play. That was why she agreed to Hamilton's suggestion that they have a two-way mirror in their house and watch others making love. She loved to tell me about the well-known people in the mirror going at it in the most bizarre ways."*

To quote Diana Dors:

*"I am the only sex symbol Britain has produced since Lady Godiva!"*

Kim later said:

*"I knew I had to pique her curiosity, above all to be different. Neither of us could have known that we*

82

*were to become inseparable lovers for the next sublimely wild sixteen months, a sort of freewheeling, free booting madness where we alternated as catalysts sparking mayhem around us. When that unquenchable loving fire inevitably burned itself out, we parted. No ashes, no embers but a spark that lit a deeper love that was to last another thirty-five years, until that moment when I held Diana's hand as she lay dying."*

When Dors married Hamilton on July 3rd 1951, Kim was sipping a pink gin at the bar in the '21 Club' in New York. Kim was only twenty-one years old and had made over £100,000 (£1.5 million in today's money) by this time and spent all of it.

**Diana Dors with the 'Dors Delahaye'**

**Diana Dors with her new Cadillac convertible at Pinewood Studios.**

# CHAPTER NINE

## THE WALDORF & THE WINDSORS
## (1951)

Kim had come of age, he was just twenty-one years old and he decided to spend some time in Paris, hoping to find a new scheme or scam to relieve his severe case of financial cramp. He had a crazy notion that his clothes were unique and the French couturiers would flock to buy his designs, he was very hurt to find out that nobody was interested so he borrowed some more money from his mother, Yvonne, and not wanting to return to London, purchased a first-class ticket to New York.

He landed in New York for the second time in his life in May 1951. He had flown on the TWA Constellation service from Paris to Idlewild Airport (now JFK).

As his yellow Checker taxi crossed the bridge onto Manhattan, he had mixed emotions.

Firstly, he was still devastated and yet humiliated by Dors' rejection.

Secondly, the drive into the city brought all the happy memories of his childhood days when he made the same journey with his parents.

Thirdly, most importantly, he wondered what the bloody hell he was going to do. He only had limited funds with him, he needed a break... and quickly. Kim booked into the Plaza hotel at the top of Fifth Avenue, unpacked his crocodile luggage and took a shower.

He contacted his old friend Michael Reynolds, who was by now studying business at Yale University in New Haven, Connecticut. Kim needed to borrow money quickly, Michael obliged, and suggested that Kim should contact and meet up with socialite Patrick de la Poer Horsley-Beresford (a direct descendant of William the Conqueror) who was now living in New York and engaged to the heiress, Marion Morton. Patrick's family knew the Reynolds family back in London very well. Kim was sincerely grateful for any fresh social leads he could find.

A few days later, having contacted Patrick and explained he was alone in New York, they arranged to meet for lunch at Sardi's restaurant situated just off Broadway, famed for its 1,200 portraits of show business caricatures hanging on the walls. The pair hit it off immediately, both being gregarious and hedonistic; Patrick was six years older than Kim and obviously knew everyone worth knowing in the city. Every sentence he uttered included the name of a famous actor, actress or socialite. Kim was so thankful and relieved that Patrick paid the bill.

A merry go round of party invitations began to appear, all the aspiring New York beauties loved Kim's immaculate English voice, cavalier attitude and of course the unique 'Dandy' suits. He was already carving his own identity.

He had also found out that the Duke and Duchess of Windsor retained a permanent suite at the Waldorf Towers, part of the Waldorf Astoria Hotel.

The Duke of Windsor had been photographed in all the gossip columns that Spring, vacationing, yet again, this time in Portofino, Italy, wearing a very camp pink jacket, Kim immediately sent a telegram to his tailor, Huntsman, in London, requesting a replica be made for himself and sent to New York. Kim was becoming the toast of the town, holding court in either El Morocco, known as 'Elmo's,' or Copacabana, the two best nightclubs in New York at that time. These clubs were the perfect settings to find gorgeous new women and wealthy new business contacts. Kim's debts were spiralling out of control again.

El Morocco was Kim's favourite haunt, there was nothing quite like it in London, he loved the modern bohemian atmosphere and its famous blue and white zebra skin walls. He even commissioned a special pair of boots in blue and white crocodile to match and later claimed the colour combination was the inspiration of his registered racing colours.

Everyone in New York thought he was a British multi-millionaire, heir to an aviation dynasty and his image was further enhanced when he was described by a New York journalist as: *'**The young British millionaire who looks like Peter Lawford'**.* The Plaza hotel suite had now become his own personal bordello.

One evening, at Elmo's, Kim met the famous lesbian party organiser, Elsa Maxwell, who was an American gossip columnist and professional hostess, renowned for hosting lavish parties for royalty and the socialites. Kim found her somewhat pompous, self-important and very ugly, but he was fascinated by her claims that she had introduced the Duke and Duchess of Windsor to American society, she talked about the Windsors as if they were her family and it was very clear that she especially adored the Duchess.

She also bragged about her close relationship with the movie mogul, Jack L Warner, who had just purchased the famous La Villa Aujourd'hui at Cap d'Antibes on the French Riviera. Despite her ugliness, Kim realised Elsa Maxwell was an important new contact and worth knowing.

There were many rumours surrounding the Duchess of Windsor. It had been suggested that she was in fact a hermaphrodite. She had an unfortunate mole on her square jawed and masculine face, her voice had an unpleasant rasp and her idea of wit was raucous American wisecracks. The Duke, apart from collecting teddy bears, was apparently sexually inadequate and prone to premature ejaculation, he liked to be dominated and had no body hair. The word had spread that the Duchess was in fact a femme fatale between the sheets with legendary talents.

She supposedly, had the ability to make a matchstick feel like a cigar and a Chinese skill at which she was apparently adept, involving a prolonged and carefully modulated hot oil massage of the prostate. Indeed, it was well known that Wallis had spent a good deal of time in China, where she later admitted that her first husband, Earl Winfield Spencer, had taken her out for drinks in many bars of ill repute. There was even rumoured to be a dossier, which detailed the intimate techniques she had perfected called the 'Baltimore grip', the 'Shanghai Squeeze' and the 'China Clinch'.

None of these rumours, however, had ever been conclusively proved. Whether the Duchess ever mastered the 'Shanghai squeeze' or not, there was no doubt that she was unusually experienced for a well brought up young lady in the early twentieth century. The likelihood was that she knew a variety of sexual techniques, including oral sex, which would not have been standard education for most British or American girls of the day.

The rumours further abounded, when on the May 24th 1950, the Cunard liner 'Queen Mary' sailed from New York with the Windsors on board. Also travelling was Jimmy Donahue. By the time they reached Cherbourg, the Duchess was in love with Donahue. She was fifty-four years old, he was two decades younger. The Windsors were the guests of honour when he celebrated his thirty-fifth birthday on June 11th 1950 at Maxim's restaurant in Paris. His affair with the Duchess was just getting into its stride, for both of them, fellatio was the main attraction. Donahue once said, on leaving a restaurant with the Duchess:

*"I am now going to have the best blowjob in all America."*

The other attraction for her, of course, was that he was witty. No one who ever met the Duke of Windsor ever thought he was anything but dim, he just passively relied on the adoration of strangers, as if he were still a King. Some who saw Donahue often with the Windsors assumed it was the Duke who was involved with him, with the Duchess merely operating as their smokescreen. It was true that when he was at Oxford as a younger man, the Prince of Wales had been subjected to speculative gossip about his relationship with his tutor, Henry Hansell. He was similarly connected with his cousin, Lord Louis Mountbatten. The Duke was too passive and masochistic, possibly too under endowed, for the Duchess' tastes. Although she once said, during a row with Donahue:

*"And to think I gave up a king for a queen."*

She knew she could rely on Donahue, and his mother for the things she enjoyed. However, both the Duke and the Duchess eventually tired of his boorishness, and when that happened they cut him and his mother out of their lives. The end came in Baden-Baden in the autumn of 1954, when the Duke simply said:

*"We've had enough of you, Jimmy, get out."*

That was that.

Donahue was a high school dropout. Following his expulsion, he took lessons with the tap dance master Bill 'Bojangles' Robinson. Having been born into a very wealthy family, Donahue never felt the need to earn a living, he lived lavishly, travelling the World with a valet in tow and staying at the most expensive hotels. He was known within his circle by the nickname 'Jeem'.

What was so strange was the way in which all three travelled around the world together as a 'threesome'. The big question was; whether Donahue was the lover of the assumed bisexual Duke or had they formed a 'ménage-a-trois'? Jimmy Donahue was the grandson of Frank Winfield Woolworth, founder of the Woolworth retail chain. He was also the first cousin first and confidante of the American socialite Barbara Hutton, who Kim would meet very shortly and then some years later in Tangier.

Donahue later confessed that he had enjoyed a four-year affair with the Duchess of Windsor, but their sexual acts did not include penetration. This fact was endorsed by Lady Pamela Hicks, daughter of Earl Mountbatten of Burma and a cousin of the Duke of Windsor.

Kim would later find out some of these rumours were true and others were nonsense, he knew that she was perfectly capable of bearing a child… he just found out in the most extraordinary way.

(Madonna directed a film named W.E. depicting the life of the Duchess in 2011. The opening scenes illustrate Wallis having a miscarriage on them bathroom floor, having been beaten by her first drunken husband, Earl Winfield Spencer. This would not be feasible had she been a hermaphrodite.)

Elsa Maxwell was fascinated by Kim, they stayed in touch, and she later introduced him to many well-known people including the Vanderbilts, the Spencer-Churchills, Barbara Hutton, Greek ship owners such as Niarchos and Livanos, Hollywood stars such as, Judy Garland and Merle Oberon. The exotic and glamorous Merle Oberon ranked among the most striking performers during the early years of sound cinema, she was so mesmerised by Kim's impeccable manners and style that the Indian born film star invited him to join her for dinner at the Roosevelt hotel with Laurence Olivier. Kim put on one of his 'dandy' jackets, it was a mistake, Olivier presumed he was gay, and spent the rest of the evening flirting with him. Kim dodged his glances, needless to say, they did not meet again.

Michael Reynolds contacted Kim at lunchtime on July 3rd 1951. He had just been speaking to his parents in London on the telephone, they had informed him that the news bulletin on television included the story Dors had married Dennis Hamilton that afternoon at Caxton Hall in London. Naturally Kim was very upset. He took a cab to the '21' Club on West 52nd Street that evening and got totally smashed on pink gins. He went on to meet Patrick de la Poer Horsley-Beresford and in a drunken stupor, confessed his precarious financial position to Patrick.

He left the Plaza hotel the following day, without fully paying his account and with the financial help of

Patrick de la Poer Horsley-Beresford, who appreciated Kim's dilemma, booked into a suite at the Waldorf Astoria hotel.

His funds were running out, he desperately needed a deal or a scam.

It was September 1951, Kim's life had always been wild, but now it was going to take on an added edge, danger. For perhaps the first time in his life, Kim just happened to be in the right place at the right time.

Kim was standing in the Waldorf Astoria hotel foyer, by the concierge's desk, when he overheard a conversation regarding a fellow hotel guest, none other than the ex-Cuban President Fulgencio Batista, Kim couldn't believe his ears, surely this was not just a coincidence that both the Duke of Windsor and the Cuban leader, both lived part-time in the Waldorf Astoria?

The truth was that in early 1944, Batista handpicked a puppet, Carlos Zayas as his successor, in order to keep the relationship with the mob in America alive and continue developing casinos and hotels, but he had been defeated at the election in by Dr. Grau. Batista had intended to discomfort the incoming administration in every possible way, particularly financially. Batista made a systematic raid on the Treasury with the result that Dr. Grau found empty coffers when he took office. When Grau was inaugurated, Batista left Cuba for the United States.

*"I just felt safer there,"* he later said. What an understatement!

Batista had divorced his wife, Elisa, in 1945 and married Marta Fernández Batista and he spent the next eight years in America, between, his home in Daytona Beach Florida and his permanent suite at the Waldorf Astoria hotel in New York City. Two of his four children were born on American soil.

Kim was always enterprising and ingenious; he had a wild thought, could an association with the Cuban leader help him in gaining financial status?

He was aware of the relationship between Batista and the Mafia, namely Meyer Lansky, and he remembered the evening back in Miami eleven years previously with his late father, Vivien. Kim was totally unaware that Batista was planning to build an arsenal in order to lead a military coup which would return him to power as a dictator.

How could he conjure a meeting? His first port of call was Patrick de la Poer Horsley-Beresford. They lunched at Delmonico's the next day and pondered the question. The answer was simple... bribe and befriend the hotel concierge and let him suggest to Batista that an associate of Meyer Lansky was staying at the hotel and would like to make his acquaintance. It worked, and unbelievably the hotel's internal phone rung in Kim's suite two days later. A deep Hispanic voice said:

*"I understand you know Mr Lansky and would like to meet my boss."*

Nervously, Kim replied that he would. He was duly invited to Batista's suite the following morning which was situated a few storeys above his own.

Kim knocked on the door, not really knowing what he was going to say, it opened and he was ushered to a large sofa, the bedroom door opened and the imposing authoritative leader entered:

*"So, you know Meyer Lansky, do you? What do you know about Meyer Lansky?"*

Kim recited the story of the evening in Miami with his father, Sir Harry Oakes and Meyer Lansky, the Cuban listened and stared into Kim's bright grey eyes intently:

*"You were just a kid. I've had you checked out, what do you do?"*

Kim paused and used his now famous line:

*"I am the sole beneficiary of the 'Colnaghi Trust' and I will become Count Conalghi."*

Batista screwed up his face and dismissively said:

*"Kid, you're a liar. You're full of shit. Your parents just flew aeroplanes and your father was a prospecting consultant for Harry Oates. You're just a small-time chancer trying to make a name for yourself here, having failed in your own country."*

*"But sir, do you remember meeting me with Sir Harry Oakes with my family ten years ago?"* Kim replied:

*"Shut up and listen, kid."* boomed Batista.

Kim hung his head in shame, praying for the meeting to end.

*"Do you have a plane, a valid flying license, a British passport and an American bank account?"* Batista asked.

*"I have all those things except the plane sir."* humbly replied Kim.

*"Do you have money?"* asked Batista:

This time Kim knew that he had to tell the truth and quietly said:

*"No sir."*

*"So do you really think you've got balls?"* asked Batista:

*"Yes sir."* answered Kim.

Batista looked around to one of his henchmen and said:

*"Get the kid $500."*

He glared at Kim and merely said:

*"Here's my number in Florida. Meet me there in two weeks. I will arrange an aircraft. I have a job for you, but you keep your mouth shut about this meeting. Let's see what you're made of."*

Batista made a physical gesture as if to say that the meeting was over, Kim left the room with his knees shaking and returned to his hotel suite knowing that he was $500 better off, but also sensed that there was danger around the corner. He also knew that by taking the cash, he had to go to Florida shortly.

Kim, naively, had no idea what he was becoming involved in or where it would take him.

**Elsa Maxwell.  President Batista of Cuba**

# CHAPTER TEN

## FLYING FORNICATING & BATISTA
### (1951 – 1952)

With very little of the $500 he'd received from Batista left intact and suffering from severe financial difficulties, Kim caught a Greyhound bus from Union City, New Jersey to Daytona Beach, Florida. He never forgot that ghastly twenty-hour journey, with kids screaming all the way. Kim wasn't used to buses. When he arrived, with very little luggage, he found a cheap motel and duly telephoned the number Batista had given him back in New York.

Although he didn't speak to the Cuban leader personally, the man who answered the telephone was obviously expecting his call and instructed Kim to make his way to Daytona Beach Airport the following morning at 10.00 a.m.

Daytona Beach Airport was a county owned airfield, three miles southwest of Daytona Beach, it was much smaller in those days than it is today. Batista chose to live in Daytona Beach because he wanted to have contact with Cuba. He didn't want to live in Miami because the location was far more of a security risk and it was also to close to where the mob leader Meyer Lansky was based. He also wanted to be far enough away from Cuba so that it was not easy to get to him, but close enough for him to maintain regular contact with his Cuban followers.

When Kim arrived at the small airport, there were three dubious looking suited gentlemen waiting for him. They beckoned him over and led him to their large black Lincoln limousine.

To quote Kim:

*"It was like a scene from a fucking mafia movie."*

They drove around the airfield and into a small aircraft hangar.

Kim, being a keen aviation enthusiast, instantly recognised the aircraft sitting majestically on the hanger floor. It was a Lockheed Model 10 A Electra. Lockheed built a total of 149 Electras powered by two Pratt & Whitney R 985 engines, it was similar to the aeroplane flown by aviator Amelia Earhart, who had disappeared during an attempted around the world flight in July 1937.

Kim, confidently, climbed aboard the aircraft quietly worried that he had never flown a twin-engine aeroplane before, his British licence only permitted him to fly single-engine aeroplanes and he wasn't even sure that his licence was recognised in the United States. Most Countries have different laws and regulations regarding flying licences.

He was involved past the point of no return, so he said nothing, he thought they were going to ask him to fly somewhere. Thank God, the three men, who were obviously working for Batista, showed him back to the car and the four of them took a short drive to a beautiful house on the coast, a couple of miles away.

Kim's head was bursting, what was he getting himself into? He almost feared for his life.

When Kim walked into the house, he couldn't help noticing the beautiful paintings hanging on the walls, he was shown into a large living room where Batista was sitting on a buttoned leather sofa and asked:

*"Well kid, you got here, what do you think of the plane?"*

*"Beautiful aircraft Sir."* replied Kim, wishing he wasn't there.

*"This is the deal, you will fly on Tuesday nights to Havana with cargo. You have to land at 02.30 hrs sharp at the Aeropuerto Militar de Ciudad Libertad where you will be met. You will then fly back with further cargo on Thursday nights. You will land here at the local airfield at 06.00 hours until further notice.*

*You will be paid $2000 each week upon your return.
You will keep your mouth shut and this meeting
between us never happened. As you are very aware,
one call to Meyer Lansky finishes you in this Country,
or any other for that matter! You understand me, kid?
Now let me see your passport."*

The Cuban was precise and showed no emotion.
Kim nodded as if everything was normal, but it wasn't.

Kim questioned his own ability to fly the twin-
engine aircraft and what the hell was the cargo? He was
scared out of his mind.

He asked if he could practice flying a few circuits
around the airfield first, to accustom himself to the
aircraft's controls before venturing out across the Atlantic
Ocean. Batista agreed with no hesitation and Kim was
taken back to the airfield.

Although Kim was worldly for his age, he was
completely out of his depth at this stage. He had the
intelligence to guess that the cargo must firstly, be illegal,
and secondly, it would most likely be arms.

The next day Kim, still worried about the validity of
his licence, sat at the controls and nervously started the
aircraft's engines. He jerkily taxied to runway number six
and waited for clearance from the control tower.

*"NC 1129, you are clear for take-off."*

Kim pushed the two centre throttles fully forward
and thundered down the runway, gradually pulling on the
joystick. He became airborne and headed out towards the
ocean. All the tuition he received at Elstree the year
before was paying off. The plane, although quite old,
handled beautifully.

As Kim used to say:

*"I took to that old plane like a 'fly to the turd'."*

For the following few weeks Kim settled into his
new role and thought of himself as a modern day 'Biggles'.
He amassed a huge pile of cash. He remained at the motel

in Daytona Beach, and he stayed at a very cheap hotel in Havana on Wednesday nights.

It was time to start exploring. One day he was walking down the Malecon, which is a broad esplanade roadway and seawall. It stretches for five miles along the coast in Havana. It was the well-known home for many of Havana's prostitutes. Kim was in his heaven and would scout for new 'talent' every week.

To quote Kim:

*"It was the Thailand of the Caribbean, I honestly can't think of a Country where prostitution is so ingrained and pervasive into the culture, you fuck, you pay. All the Cuban women you meet at night are whores. Even the good-looking Cuban women you meet during the day also expect money for sex. Every Cuban girl I banged, blew my flute. By the way, in my experience, Cuban girls always gave head without request, and they were so damn good at it. Argh!"*

Somehow in Kim's mind, he saw himself as a modern-day buccaneer, not the gun runner he had become. He still hadn't worked out what he was bringing back onto mainland America soil upon the return journeys to Daytona Beach.

As it turned out, 1951 was financially Kim's most successful year ever. He worked hard for Batista, who had doubled the number of flights to Cuba to two per week. He was now earning $15,000 each month which in today's terms equates to about $200,000 every month.

With fresh money in his pockets, Kim checked out of the motel and signed into the beautiful Ormond Beach hotel, six miles north of Daytona Beach. He then bought a brand-new silver Jaguar XK 120 Roadster, which was a massive status symbol in those days, especially in America. Some weekends Kim would drive along the coast to Palm Beach, he loved walking along Worth Avenue and flirting with all the glamorous wealthy wives and the 'wives in waiting'. Kim was never one to miss an opportunity.

Kim no longer walked along the Malecon searching for Cuban whores. He stayed at the Hotel Nacional de Cuba in Havana, where he had stayed with his family as a child. It was where he had met Batista for the first time ten years previously with his father, Vivian. This time it was different, he entertained a number of 'ladies of the night' in the hotel for company, he even had his favourite whore called 'Alise'.

Now it was time to finally visit the nightclub that he had heard so much about for the last few years, The Tropicana. However, it was closed, having been subject to a major expansion and refurbishment program, which was being funded by the mob, and namely, someone who Kim had met before, Meyer Lansky. Lansky had become the top syndicate figure in Cuba.

Kim secretly knew that the wooden chests loaded on the Lockheed Electra each week contained guns and ammunition, but he was in self-denial. Now the question in his mind was, what the hell was he flying back from Cuba each week in the large sealed sacks? One Thursday night, while flying the plane back from Havana, he leant over behind his captain's seat and pulled one of the sacks forward onto the empty co-pilot's seat. He broke the seal, pulled the sack open and realised that there were literally hundreds of thousands of dollars in cash.

It didn't take much intelligence to realise that not only was he fuelling and abetting Batista's weapons arsenal on the island each week, prior to the Cuban leader's eventual return, but he was also bringing Batista and Lansky's ill-gotten gains from gambling and prostitution back to mainland America to be laundered. The more Kim analysed his position, the more frightened he became. He was earning fantastic wages, but how could these larger-than-life characters ever let him go? He knew too much.

It was Christmas time and Kim had been told that he was not needed for a few weeks. He decided to spend the festive season back in New York with his old friends.

Times had changed, he was returning with plenty of money, albeit that he had earned it under very dubious circumstances.

He drove his new Jaguar up the coastline to New York with the hood down, it was a long drive, although a far cry from the Greyhound bus that he boarded from New York just a few months before.

When he arrived back in New York, he booked into the Waldorf Astoria with his pockets bursting at the seams with money. He immediately contacted Patrick de la Poer Horsley-Beresford and paid him back all the money that he had borrowed earlier in the year. The usual round of partying started again with Kim, using his risqué image and 'dandy' suits to clock up as many sexual partners as was physically possible. After an amazing birthday party at the Copacabana night club, he returned to the hotel with his birthday present to himself, two beautiful American models. Kim had turned twenty-two years old and was enjoying his first ménage-a-trois. He spent an absolute fortune that Christmas and New Year in New York.

It was February 1952, Kim had returned to the Ormand hotel in Florida and resumed his bi-weekly missions to the Aeropuerto Militar de Ciudad Libertad in Havana, for Batista.

He always wondered why his flying credentials and licence had never come under scrutiny. One Thursday night, while flying back across the ocean to Daytona Beach airfield ladened with 'sacks', the weather was closing in and the clouds were becoming darker and darker. The flight was becoming more and more turbulent and Kim was in the midst of a violent storm with thunder and lightning. Suddenly he saw a fork of lightning appear to strike the starboard wing simultaneously igniting the engine into a ball of fire. Kim rapidly pulled on the switch marked 'right-hand engine fire extinguisher', while struggling to control the plane on the remaining port side engine.

He was approximately eighty miles out of Daytona Beach airport and the Lockheed was veering from side to side. Kim wanted to fly as low as possible under the heavy storm, but not too low, as the aircraft was unable to climb powered by only one engine and it would most likely stall if he tried to climb. With the wipers on the maximum setting and half the instrumentation not working, he genuinely had visions of crashing into the rough sea. Thankfully the plane levelled out and he managed to make a very bouncy landing back at Daytona in the torrential rain.

To quote Kim:

**"Fucking hell, I thought I was fish food that night and going to meet my maker."**

Having handed his 'sacks' over to two of Batista's 'heavies', he drove back to his hotel.

It was 4.30 am, when he returned to his room and he remembered that he had a half bottle of brandy in the desk, he drank the lot and retired to bed and prayed to safely extract himself out of Batista's clutches and survive to tell the tale.

Soon after this incident, Patrick telephoned Kim to inform him that he had heard several disturbing rumours concerning his 'employment' down in Florida and he questioned Kim, as to whether they were true or not. Kim felt his credibility was being questioned and he felt uncomfortable. He was addicted to excitement, but even his nerve was starting to evaporate, the gun running operation had become too risky, surely Batista had stockpiled enough ammunition by now?

Kim's prayers were answered by luck and coincidence as he still didn't know that Batista no longer needed his flying skills, as he had decided to return to Cuba in order to run for the presidency again. At the beginning of March 1952 one of Batista's minions telephoned Kim at the hotel and informed him that his services were no longer required. Kim packed his bags and drove the Jaguar back to New York and checked back into the Waldorf Astoria to enjoy a few quiet days of relaxation.

Batista knew he couldn't win the forthcoming election in Cuba. In fact, he was considered the least likely candidate out of three nominations. On March 10th 1952, he staged a military coup, three months before the elections. He seized power with army backing, heavily armed with the guns that Kim had been delivering. He ousted the outgoing President Carlos Prio Socarras and cancelled the elections. He took control of the Cuban government as 'provisional president'.

Kim didn't have to question how Batista's army had been so heavily armed or how the arms had been paid for on the mainland.

Meyer Lansky had even offered the acting President, Carlos Prio Socarras, a bribe of U.S. $250,000 to step down so that Batista could return to power. Once Batista took control of the government, he quickly put gambling back on track. The new dictator contacted Lansky and offered him an annual salary of U.S. $25,000 to serve as an unofficial gambling minister.

By 1955, Batista had changed the gambling laws once again, granting a gaming license to anyone who invested $1 million in a hotel, or U.S. $200,000 in a new nightclub. Unlike the procedure for acquiring gaming licenses in Las Vegas, this provision exempted venture capitalists from background checks. As long as they made the required investment, they were provided with matching public funds for construction, a ten-year tax exemption and duty-free importation of equipment and furnishings.

The government would get U.S. $250,000 for the license plus a percentage of the profits from each casino.

Shortly after the coup, the United States government recognized Batista's government. Arthur M. Schlesinger was later asked by the U.S. government to analyse Batista's Cuba.

His report stated:

*"The corruption of the Government, the brutality of the police, the government's indifference to the needs of the people for education, medical care, housing, for social justice and economic justice is an open invitation to revolution."*

Back in power, Batista did not continue the social policies of his earlier presidency. He wanted recognition by the upper echelons of Cuban society, who had never accepted him in their social circles.

Batista's increasingly corrupt and repressive government then began to systematically profit from the exploitation of Cuba's commercial interests, by negotiating lucrative relationships with the American Mafia, headed by Meyer Lansky, who by then controlled the drug, gambling and prostitution businesses in Havana.

For several years, up until 1959, the Batista government received financial, military, and logistical support from the United States.

He was finally overthrown by Fidel Castro's July 26th movement which led to an urban and rural based guerrilla uprising against Batista's government. It culminated in his eventual defeat by rebels under the command of Che Guevara at the Battle of Santa Clara on New Year's Day 1959. By which time, Kim would be languishing in a filthy French jail.

Batista immediately fled from Cuba, having amassed a huge personal fortune, to the Dominican Republic. He eventually found political asylum in Portugal, where he lived until dying of a heart attack on August 6th 1973.

He donated his impressive art collection from his home in Florida to the town of Daytona Beach, where they now hang in a museum.

Kim never saw or spoke to Batista again. He would never see Florida, Cuba or anywhere in the Caribbean ever again.

He was lucky to be alive.

**Kim's Lockheed Model 10 Electra**

**Kim's Jaguar XK 120 Roadster**

# CHAPTER ELEVEN

## BEWITCHING BARBARA
### (1952)

Kim was back in New York enjoying his earnings and wallowing in his own illegitimate success. He was up to his old habits, constantly spending.

One sunny June morning, Kim and the wealthy Patrick de la Poer Horsley-Beresford, went to buy a pair of new Rolls Royce Silver Dawns, from J.S Inskip, the renowned Rolls Royce and Bentley distributor and coachbuilder in New York City. They purchased one white two door convertible, for Patrick, and one dark blue saloon, for Kim, part exchanging the Jaguar, that he had purchased in Florida. They took delivery of these two cars across the bridge and into New Jersey, to avoid paying New York State tax.

On one summer's morning Kim woke up in Waldorf Astoria, having just clocked up yet another conquest, the previous night. He needed some 'blotting paper' to cure his hangover, a stodgy lunch was the order of the day. He wondered who to have lunch with and telephoned Elsa Maxwell to find out if she was free that day, Elsa, never one to turn down a free lunch hastily accepted and Kim booked a table at his favourite haunt, Sardi's restaurant. Kim arrived at the restaurant first and naturally ordered a pink gin. A few minutes later Elsa arrived, she was never attractive, but she looked worse than ever on this occasion, both harassed and furious. Kim duly stood up, welcomed her and asked:

*"Are you alright Elsa? you don't seem to be yourself."*

*"I've had a terrible morning Kim darling,"* replied Elsa.

*"What's the problem?"* asked Kim.

*"The Duchess of Windsor has described me as looking like a 'cook on her night out' in an interview with another magazine. How could she do this to me? It was me who made them film stars in this City, how dare she, I will make sure she gets her just reward."*

Kim wanted to smirk but thought better of it as Elsa had obviously lost her best social 'trump card'. She was ageing, obese and vengeful. Perhaps, being a lesbian, she had 'come on' to the Duchess and this was Wallis' way of distancing herself from Elsa. Kim paid very little attention to what Elsa was saying for the rest of the lunch. He was more interested in wining and dining beautiful young girls and getting laid than listening to Elsa's endless boring stories about the Windsors.

Towards the end of lunch, Elsa Maxwell invited Kim to a party in the Hamptons, which he duly accepted, for the following week.

It was a beautiful sunny day during May. Elsa made her way by taxi to the Waldorf Astoria. Twenty years before her imprimatur of social acceptability carried so much weight, the hotel even gave her a suite rent free when it opened in New York in 1931 at the height of the depression. They were hoping to attract rich clients because of her patronage. Elsa was hoping that Kim would be driving his new Rolls Royce that day.

She was looking forward to the scenic drive ahead of her in the elegant blue automobile to the Hamptons.

They arrived at the Hamptons and after driving through the magnificent black and gold gates of the palatial Palladian mansion, the resident valet parked the beautiful car in prime position next to all the chauffeur driven American limousines.

The ballroom was filled with some of New York's wealthiest and most affluent socialites. It was like an American 'who's who' get together. Elsa was working at what she did best and she cased the room like an animal cornering its prey, but in her profession, the prey was intrigue, gossip, drama and spice to print in her revealing weekly gossip column.

To quote Elsa Maxwell:

*"Someone said that life is a party. You join in after it's started and leave before it's finished. I make enemies deliberately; they are the piquant sauce to my dish of life. A bore is a vacuum cleaner of society, sucking up everything and giving nothing, bores are always eager to be seen talking to you. I did not feel fit to be married. I belong to the world. I knew it instinctively when I was quite young. Certainly, I am one of the best-known people in the entire world today. Why, because I did not marry and I felt that I was not for marriage. It wasn't my ... thing to do."*

Elsa Maxwell was a closeted lesbian who publicly condemned homosexuality despite enjoying an almost fifty-year romantic partnership with the Scottish singer Dorothy "Dickie" Fellowes-Gordon. The two met in 1912 and remained together until her death in 1963.

Kim smiled to himself, if only they knew he had been a black-market nylons dealer and then been promoted to an international gun runner!

The seventy-year-old Elsa navigated the room with Kim trailing behind her sipping his flute of champagne. She stopped by the side of a large fearsome Jewish gentleman.

*"Kim, I would like you to meet Jack L. Warner, this is his wife, Ann, and his daughter, Barbara."*

Kim was spellbound, was this the omnipotent owner of Warner Brothers, the largest film studios in the World?

*"How do you do, sir."* Kim nervously offered the film mogul a handshake.

Kim had read enough to realise that he was meeting a man who was so powerful that he had the ear and confidence of President Franklin D. Roosevelt during

World War II. Furthermore, Warner's daughter, Barbara, was gorgeous and Kim could feel all those same sensations he felt when he had met Dors, a few years previously in Chelsea.

It was unusual for Barbara to be in the States, she was on a rare visit from Europe. She had been to finishing school in Switzerland and settled in Paris, rather than return to her home in California. Kim was immediately smitten and during conversation, she told him that she would be in New York City for the next ten days.

To quote Kim:

**"She was magic, a teenage 'Lolita', a breath of fresh air."**

Always seizing the moment and knowing what a catch the World's most important film producer's daughter could be, Kim invited her for lunch in the city that week.

He organised a wonderful lunch at the Pierre hotel and brought a vast bouquet of flowers with him to the grill room.

Kim used every technique he had learnt in twenty-two years with vigour to make Barbara feel the most important girl on Earth. He only had a week operate and he either pounced now, or the moment would be lost. He took the young eighteen-year-old out every day, visiting different parts of the city, in the Rolls Royce filled with flowers, dressed in his renowned 'dandy' suits and 'Chelsea boots'.

They were having lunch one day in Little Italy when Barbara asked Kim where he received his income from to enable him to have such an extravagant and hedonistic lifestyle. He gave his usual reply:

**"I'm the heir to the Colnaghi Aviation empire."**

Barbara, now nicknamed 'Bar' by Kim, believed his answer. Kim was very surprised when Barbara then asked:

**"Kim, I have a problem. Although my father is a multi-millionaire, he is a tyrant and he purposely gives me very little money. It's his way of gaining**

*power and control over me. I'm leaving New York for Paris in a few days and I owe $5000 over there. I have tried to request a loan from my father, who as usual, just dismisses me, saying that he came from nothing and had to make it for himself, and I should do the same. I hate to ask you, but please, could you help me?"*

Realising why Bar had questioned his monetary position before asking for a loan, he agreed to the loan, hoping that it would further cement their relationship.

He still had plenty of money left anyway.

To quote Kim:

*"It was just a bloody good job that Bar didn't know where my money had come from."*

Kim pursued Bar with great tenacity. He took her to an exclusive restaurant for lunch each day, followed by shopping and then dinner. After dinner, he would take her to El Morocco, where he was now a well-known figure. It was finally working out. Two nights prior to her departure, instead of dropping Bar back to her family's suite at the Plaza after another boozy night, they started kissing and cuddling. As the Rolls Royce steamed up, Kim suggested that she stayed with him in the Waldorf Astoria. She enthusiastically agreed.

They made love all night. Kim knew that he now had her in the 'palm of his hand'.

Kim later said:

*"It was never going to work, I was Catholic, she was Jewish, Jack would never have approved."*

Barbara's mother, Ann, was a much softer person by nature than her husband, Jack. She suggested to Barbara that she should invite Kim to their farewell dinner at the Oak Room in the Plaza hotel. They were returning to Hollywood and Barbara was returning to Paris.

The evening was an absolute delight and despite Jack's gruff dismissive attitude, the Warners suggested that Kim might like to join them the following year at their villa on the French Riviera. The Warner family spent their summers at Cap d'Antibes, where Jack bought the famous Villa Aujourd'hui a few years prior. Kim was incredibly flattered and said he would love to see them again.

After Bar's departure from New York, Kim felt the same emotions as he had done when Dors left him in St John's Wood a couple of years before, he still often thought about Dors. Kim was becoming moody, depressed and bored.

New York wasn't going to provide him a living, let alone indulge him in the opulent lifestyle that he had become accustomed to.

The lure of London, and in particular Chelsea beckoned, along with the wish to be nearer to Bar in Paris. Kim was in constant contact with Bar which was costing him a fortune in long distance calls from his hotel suite.

Kim was still young and viewed most beautiful women as potential targets and conquests. The relationship with Bar was very different. He had fallen for her and although their relationship was very embryonic, she rapidly became Kim's 'soulmate and confidante'.

Kim decided to leave America in November 1952 and return to London. According to Kim:

***"I quit while I was ahead. I'd had two years of debauchery, been paid incredibly, and lived to tell the tale!"***

Kim sold the blue Rolls Royce back to J.S. Inskip at a considerable loss and promptly spent most of the proceeds on settling his numerous restaurant accounts and a huge bill at the Waldorf Astoria, mainly consisting of champagne, caviar and overseas telephone calls to Bar. The concierge at the Waldorf Astoria arranged a first-class ticket on the Pan Am Stratocruiser transatlantic 'Blue Ribbon' service to London.

Kim had often wondered what his family were doing in England, it was time to find out. Kim never returned to America again. Kim was still only 22 years old and had earned about $200,000 (£1.5 million in today's money) but yet again had spent most of it.

**The Waldorf Astoria Hotel.  Jack L. Warner**

**Jack Warner arriving in London with his daughters, Joy & Barbara**

## CHAPTER TWELVE

## ROBBERY ON THE RIVIERA
## (1952 – 1953)

It was November 1952 when the Pan Am Stratocruiser touched down at London Airport (now Heathrow Airport). Kim had enjoyed a fabulous fourteen-hour flight on the presidential upper deck of the aircraft. His dinner, at 30,000 feet, had consisted of 'Boeuf Braise Bourgoise' washed down with a couple of bottles of 1948 Chateau Palmer. After a good sleep, he was happy to be home.

He immediately booked into the Dorchester hotel on London's Park Lane and concentrated on finding a new apartment. Kim quickly found an elegant new residence in Egerton Gardens, just off Knightsbridge. The property would give him the stage set that he was looking for.

He then asked Commander Hugh Keller, who was a director of Paddon Bros in Cheval Place, to return his newly restored Rolls Royce. Kim was shocked at the bill for all the work carried out and the storage charges, but he was thrilled to see his old car again.

He contacted Bobby McKew, who he hadn't seen for a couple of years, the pair met up and Kim told him some of the antics that he had been up to in the States. He also told him that he needed to get back to work.

London had moved on from post war austerity and rationing. Most black marketeers had ceased to exist, but many illegal gaming houses had arisen under the control of Billy Hill working with John Burke and Bobby McKew.

Billy Hill liked to be known as the 'Bandit King' and would say:

*"They say Humphrey Bogart could go for my twin brother, and he looks like what a gangster is supposed to look like."*

By coincidence, Kim's younger brother Johnny was now living in Central London and making a prosperous living. He worked with John Burke who was a university educated unscrupulous charmer. They were running illegal 'Chemin de Fer' parties for the wealthy elite, including Ian Fleming, Lucian Freud, Lord Lucan and the Duke of Devonshire.

There were three popular variants of 'Chemin de Fer'; Punto Banco, Baccarat Banque and Baccarat Chemin de Fer, known as 'Chemmy'. Punto Banco was strictly a game of chance, with no skill or strategy involved. Each player's moves were forced by the cards the player is dealt. In contrast, Baccarat Chemin de Fer and Baccarat Banque, both players can make choices, which allows skill to play a part.

Baccarat is a comparing card game played between two hands, it first appeared in nineteenth century France and was introduced to London by an underworld character known as 'The Vicar'.

McKew was aware that Billy Hill had masterminded the famous 1952 Eastcastle Street robbery of £230,000 from a Post Office van. It had been the largest robbery ever recorded in British history, and Hill's girlfriend Gypsy insisted on being one of the getaway drivers. They counted out the money together in a suite at the Dorchester hotel. The stolen cash needed to be laundered and illegal gambling was an ideal vehicle.

Bobby McKew suggested that Kim should use his social skills to attract both aristocracy, villains and beautiful girls to the tables. Kim was never a casino gambler but he could see the potential in meeting some of the characters involved.

To quote Kim:

*"It was simple; villains, aristocracy and show business people all have one thing in common… lust. All I had to do was find the crumpet."*

Kim had returned to his old habits, networking

various deals and now introducing the 'socially correct' people to the illegal gaming parties held in London's Belgravia and Mayfair.

It was Christmas time and Kim's twenty third birthday. Kim flew to Paris and Bar was waiting at Le Bourget Airport for him in her new Jaguar sports car, which was similar to the roadster which Kim had purchased in Florida the year before. He had been visiting her regularly and usually stayed at her magnificent apartment, which was presumably owned by Jack L. Warner, on the Avenue Foch in Paris. The couple celebrated Christmas with lunch at the Georges V hotel and after a sumptuous meal Kim pulled out a small velvet box from his pocket and passed a flawless four carat diamond ring across the table and asked for her hand in marriage. She accepted, but no set dates were arranged. There was something Kim did not know; he was being played at his own game.

The main reason that Barbara had chosen to stay in France after her schooling had finished was that she had met Claude Terrail, who was born in 1917 and seventeen years her senior. Tall and elegant, Claude Terrail was gloriously matched to his restaurant, La Tour d'Argent, his family's celebrated Parisian restaurant on the Quai de Tournelle, across the Seine from Notre Dame, in the fifth Arrondissement. He took over from his father, André, in 1947, and maintained the traditions of haute cuisine and a touch of snobbery that kept the venue very special.

Under Terrail's omnipresent stewardship, the restaurant served a procession of important customers, including the H.M. the Queen, Sir Winston Churchill, John F. Kennedy and Dwight D Eisenhower. Errol Flynn and Orson Welles were among patrons who became his friends.

The attraction was its most famous dish, 'Canard Au Sang' or 'Bloodied Duck'. Not for the squeamish, the recipe involves a bird slaughtered by strangulation in order to preserve all the blood, and the use of a special press to extract all the fluids for the rich sauce. The restaurant also had one of the finest wine cellars in the World, hidden under the banks of River Seine, and valued at millions of dollars even in those days.

Kim flew back to London in early January 1953, he was now engaged to the World's largest movie mogul's daughter.

On New Year's Eve 1952, the Duke and Duchess of Windsor were finally 'crowned' with makeshift paper hats, while they attended a New Year's gala dinner at the Sherry-Netherlands Hotel. After the formal dinner, they went on to celebrate at El Morocco. Whether in Monte Carlo or sipping Bellini's at Harry's Bar in Venice, the Windsors were always the 'toast of the town'.

Kim worked hard during the Spring and saw a great deal of both his brother Johnny and Bobby McKew, they were doing very well out of the 'Chemmy' racket, although Billy Hill always received the lion's share of the profits. Kim loved driving around the town in his Rolls Royce and meeting all the heiresses and debutantes. He also travelled to France fortnightly to see his fiancée, Bar. He was looking forward to the summer holiday with Bar and her family at La Villa Aujourd'hui on Cap d'Antibes.

Although Kim had been invited to join the Warner family for the summer break, he was not sure if the invitation actually included staying in the villa. He asked Barbara where he was sleeping when he arrived, she explained that she'd asked her father if he could stay with her in the villa, but Jack had apparently refused on the basis he felt Kim was a 'spiv' and a 'social climber'. He suggested if she still wanted Kim to join them, he should book himself into a local hotel in Antibes or Nice. Kim was very hurt by this decision and invited Bobby McKew to join him on the trip, as he didn't want to spend time alone there when he arrived. He also thought that he would drive the Rolls Royce down to the Riviera in a vain attempt to impress Jack L. Warner. In late July, they motored to Paris and having frequented some familiar old haunts, drove on to the South of France. They booked into the Martinez Hotel in Cannes.

The journey was to change Kim's life and his destiny. It was not going to be a happy holiday. Jack L. Warner spent most summers in the south of France, firstly attending the Cannes Film Festival, and then staying for the rest of the season with his wife Ann and his daughter Barbara at the famous villa where he had previously entertained both Charlie Chaplin and Ava Gardner. This year he had invited his old friend Elsa Maxwell from New York to join them.

Kim and Bobby McKew met the Warner family and guests for dinner that Saturday evening at the villa. The dinner was very strained, Barbara and her father were not close, but he had educated her impeccably in Europe, he was both distant, dictatorial and mean to her. She resented him. Barbara was always short of money and being young, was bored by her parent's constant round of business meetings and dinner parties.

Elsa Maxwell had already arrived from New York and asked to deposit various documents and jewellery in the villa's safe which was in Jack's bedroom.

Over the previous few days, Jack had been losing large sums of money in the Monte Carlo casino and was not in the best of moods.

Things became worse. Kim had been told in London about 'Gigi', a young French call girl who operated out of a luxurious private apartment behind the Negresco hotel in Nice. She had the reputation of captivating every man she met. Kim could not resist; it was a warm Sunday morning and he drove the old Rolls Royce from Cannes to Nice and parked in a backstreet. He rang Gigi's doorbell and after a considerable wait, the front door opened. To Kim's horror and surprise a very hot and sweaty Jack L. Warner stampeded out. Both men were highly embarrassed, but obviously, Jack couldn't tell Barbara because she would then tell Ann, his wife. Warner now knew that his future son in law was a cheat and Kim knew the movie mogul's reputation as a philanderer was true! They finally had something in common. They both had to endure Sunday lunch together as Barbara had invited Kim over to the villa. The two men had enjoyed the same girl that morning before lunch. It was not the most comfortable way to spend the rest of the holiday.

There was another problem on the horizon, as usual; Kim was running out of cash. He asked Bar if she could pay back the $5000 which he had loaned her in New York the previous year.

Over the next few days, Jack had a surprisingly lucky break at Palm Beach Casino in Cannes. He won 250,000FF (about £25,000 then and £400,000 in today's money). He placed the cash into his safe in the bedroom, prior to leaving on a ten-day trip to the Venice Film Festival with his wife, Ann and Elsa Maxwell.

On August 24th 1953, Barbara was now alone at the villa and only had the resident staff for company. She unsuccessfully tried to coax Kim into opening the safe on the pretext that Jack had promised her a percentage of his winnings as she had brought him good luck in the casino, and her share would more than cover her indebtedness to Kim.

Kim would not open the safe without Bobby McKew's help, being one of Billy Hill's 'boys' he had far more experience than Kim in this field, and more importantly, his presence would help elude Kim's guilt.

On August 25th 1953 at about 10.00 p.m., Kim and Bobby McKew arrived at La Villa Aujourd'hui after enjoying dinner in Juan Les Pins. The villa's staff had that evening off duty and Barbara had a few female friends over for dinner. The staff had prepared dinner for Barbara and her friends before leaving, but the soiree had really just become a drinking session. She was so relieved that her father had left for ten days in Italy.

The three of them had a drink and nervously talked about the money in the safe.

Barbara, quite drunk, again tried to talk Kim into opening the safe. McKew, knowing Kim's cash flow problem agreed that taking the money was their only option. They walked up the staircase and into Jack's bedroom, Bobby McKew opened the door of the safe very easily with the key which Barbara already had in her possession.

Kim was nervous, he was about to steal from the most powerful movie mogul in the World, a man who once had the 'ear' of the US President Eisenhower.

They found a stash of cash made up of five small sealed packs of 50,000FF in ten thousand French franc notes each, which was the highest denomination possible. A few empty Cartier presentation boxes and several buff-coloured files underneath, being a few movie scores, and a large brown coloured file marked 'Strictly Confidential' with Elsa Maxwell's name on it.

Kim would later say:

**"Bloody hell, they made me out to be the 'Riviera Robber'. The actuality of it was that I didn't even open the safe that earned me that dubious renown."**

Kim opened the brown file which contained the most explosive information ever that would literally have changed the course of modern history had it ever become public knowledge.

The file contained an alleged diary of events in the form of a timeline concerning King Edward VIII and Mrs Wallis Simpson, their affair, their allegiance to the Nazi party in Germany and the son who was born to Wallis in 1937 and subsequent adoption of this child organised by Adolf Hitler. It even alleged the promises of the Third Reich to make Edward President of Europe and their son to succeed him, should Germany have won World War II.

It detailed the scam of Edward sending Wallace to the South of France in 1936 on the pretext of alleviating pressure from the press on her, but in fact it was to conceal her pregnancy, which would have changed the whole bloodline of the British Monarchy. She was not a hermaphrodite as rumours would have it. She always wanted a child but believed she could not conceive since being attacked and abused by her first alcoholic husband Earl Winfield Spencer Jr, and subsequently miscarrying her baby. She was therefore determined to give birth to this child, even though Edward was reluctant, she was totally dominant within their relationship.

The two, after all, gladly met with Hitler during their highly-publicized tour of Germany in 1937, and neither of them displayed much compunction about associating with figures suspected of being pro German, if not outright fascist. Even in the midst of World War II, when England was fighting for its life against the Reich, the Windsors were passing the time in the Bahamas, where the Duke was made Governor.

Neither of them worked overtime to dispel the notion that, in the end, it didn't much matter to them whether or not Germany won the war.

Kim could not believe the contents, he crammed everything into his flight case that he always carried, full of adrenaline.

The two men left the villa and nervously drove back to the Martinez in Cannes and headed to the bar for a much-needed drink.

The next morning Kim read the film scripts that accompanied the deadly file, and realised they were a film outline of Elsa Maxwell's factually based story entitled 'The Boy Who Should Be King'. Not only was she secretly trying to coax Jack L. Warner into making her dossier into an action-packed movie but she was transparently 'pointing her finger' at the Duke and Duchess of Windsor who, she was determined to destroy after they had upset her so much by the Duchess' remarks in New York the previous autumn.

The Windsors had been discreetly informed of Elsa Maxwell's dossier and the Duchess never spoke a bad word about her ever again. As Elsa, would say:

**"Nobody upsets me without regretting it, I have the power to make mud stick!"**

After discussing their situation, Kim and McKew decided to fly back to London immediately, leaving the old Rolls Royce in the Martinez hotel car park.

On September 3rd 1953, the telephone rang in Kim's flat in London. Barbara was hysterical. Jack had returned from Venice and opened the safe in order to read one of the film scripts in bed that night, to his horror, there was no money.

He had immediately called the French Police and there was an 'all-points bulletin' search out for Kim and Bobby McKew. Elsa Maxwell had heard all the commotion and realised her brown dossier had also been removed from the safe. She apparently had lost total logic. Certain very high-powered hierarchy were aware that she had very sensitive information and she had used the dossier as a threat in the past, or even as a passport to 'open doors' in many situations without ever revealing its contents. Elsa Maxwell now had to reveal the whole situation, including the brown dossier contents to Jack L. Warner. He then questioned himself as to whether he had made the right decision in notifying the authorities.

Barbara had lied to her father by saying that she was being blackmailed for the keys of the safe by Kim. It also seemed unclear as to who had taken what in monetary terms, but it was clear that Kim had Elsa Maxwell's all important brown dossier.

Warner was not totally convinced by his daughter's story but he thought it was best to accept it, therefore putting all the blame firmly on Kim's head. He was already out for Kim's blood after 'The Gigi Affair'.

The next morning the robbery was headline news in every newspaper in France, Kim and McKew were branded criminals. Upon her father's orders, Barbara called off the engagement, she kept the magnificent ring and they never met again. Barbara went on to marry Claude Terrail in Paris during 1955. They had a daughter, Anne, in 1959. They divorced two years later.

It was even rumoured that Alfred Hitchcock cast Cary Grant as John Robie 'The Cat' based upon Kim when he started filming 'To Catch a Thief' on the French Riviera during 1955, starring Grace Kelly.

This movie led Grace Kelly to meet Prince Rainier and become Princess Grace of Monaco upon their subsequent marriage.

**Kim's 1932 Rolls Royce Phantom II**

La Villa d'Aujourd Hui

Martinez Hotel Cannes

# CHAPTER THIRTEEN

## ELSA'S SECRET DOSSIER
### (1914 – 1952)

I felt it necessary to include some extractions from Elsa Maxwell's secret dossier which was locked in Jack L. Warner's safe at the Villa Aujourd'hui in Cap d'Antibes on the night of the robbery on August 25th 1953. Kim had two copies made in September 1953, one is still locked in an unknown safety deposit box in London, the other was lodged with his solicitors, upon the explicit instructions to publish the dossier if anything untoward or unexpected should happen to him. Kim was terrified of Jack L. Warner and was fully aware of his immense powers, he eventually returned the original to Warner during 1961, in exchange for his forty-year oath of silence. He had created his own insurance policy.

For both legal and ethical reasons, certain insertions have been removed because they are either too offensive or obscene, but its contents do explain the gravity of Kim's position with both with the establishment and certain rarefied circles. He knew too much and everybody concerned was terrified that the delicate information contained within it would become public knowledge.

To quote Kim:

*"The dossier was potentially a political volcano. It not only destroyed the bloodline of the British monarchy, but we could have had a Nazi king. If the information had been made public in the mid-fifties, it would probably have changed the course of history…and the career of Jack L. Warner! Somebody would have had my head and I wanted to live."*

Interestingly, a fair amount of speculation surrounding the Windsors is now public knowledge, thanks to the internet. There have also been various claims made that Wallis Simpson had a daughter and that the Duke of Windsor fathered a son by a seamstress, namely Marie-Léonie Graftieaux in Paris during 1912.I think that both these rumours are merely 'conspiracy' theories. The latter story has recently been written about in a book called *'The Man Who Should Have Been King'* which is highly coincidental because Elsa Maxwell's screenplay which was also in Warner's safe was entitled *'The Boy Who Should Be King'*

**This is an edited 'alleged' timeline of Elsa Maxwell's dossier:**

1914. Prince 'David' Edward had a 'homosexual liaison' with his Oxford tutor, Henry Peter Hansell.

1917. The Prince began an affair with a Parisian, Marguerite Alibert, who kept a collection of his indiscreet letters after he broke off the affair.

1918. The Prince had an affair with the wife of the Liberal Whip, Freda Dudley Ward, who later confessed that Edward was incapable of sexual intercourse.

1920. The Prince had a homosexual liaison aboard H.M.S. Renown with his cousin, Lord Louis Mountbatten, known as 'Dickie' during the Empire Tour.

1926. The Prince of Wales met Thelma Furness, Viscountess Furness (born Thelma Morgan August 23rd 1904) at a ball at Londonderry House.

1926. Charles Bedaux purchased the sixty-room Chateau de Cande estate on the Indre and Loire Rivers in Touraine, France. The Duke and Duchess would hold their marriage there later in 1937.

1930. (February) Viscountess Furness joined the Prince of Wales on an African safari. Intimacy began. He was 'sexually submissive and supposedly had a 'teddy bear fascination'.

She later said: ***"He was a strange unsatisfactory lover with homosexual leanings."***

George V was disappointed by Edward's failure to settle down in life, disgusted by his affairs with married women, and was reluctant to see him inherit the Crown.

George V said. ***"After I am dead, the boy will ruin himself within twelve months."***

Prince 'David' Edward was caught lingering in the Tate Gallery 'picking up boys and men'.

1931. (January 10th) Viscountess Furness introduced the Prince of Wales to her close friend Wallis Simpson, 'a bisexual dominatrix' with great knowledge of unusual sexual practices, learnt in Asia during her first marriage to Earl Winfield Spencer Jr.

1933. (January 30th) Adolf Hitler became Chancellor of Germany. Dr Ley accompanied him to Berlin.

1933. (April) The German trade union movement was taken over by the state, Adolf Hitler appointed Dr Ley as head of the German Labour Front. A 'close relationship' with Charles Bedaux began, he was a renowned expert in time and motion studies within large workforces.

1933. (July) Robert Vanittart, a diplomat, was at a party where there was much discussion about the implications of Hitler's rise to power. He recounted in his diary:

***"The Prince of Wales was pro-Hitler and said it was no business of ours to interfere in Germany's***

*internal affairs either with reference to the Jews or anyone else and added that dictators are very popular these days and we might want one in England."*

1934. The Prince of Wales made comments suggesting that he supported the British Union of Fascists. According to a Metropolitan Police Special Branch report he had met Oswald Mosely for the first time at the home of Lady Maud Cunard in January 1935.

1934. (January-March) Viscountess Furness visited her identical twin sister, Gloria Morgan Vanderbilt in America. The prince transferred his affections to Wallis Simpson who was asked to 'look after' him during Furness' absence. Reacting to the Prince's infidelity, Viscountess Furness had a short-lived affair with Prince Aly Khan. She openly flirted with Prince Aly Khan during her voyage back to Great Britain. It was reported to the Prince of Wales, the British and American press and the Tatler. Wallis Simpson left her husband and went to live in an apartment in Bryanston Court, London. Also, living in the building was Princess Stephanie von Hohenlohe, a Nazi spy being monitored by British intelligence. The two women soon became close friends. This was unfortunate for Simpson because of a tip off from French Intelligence, MI6 was intercepting Princess Stephanie's correspondence and tracking her movements in and out of the country since early in 1928.

The 5ft 5ins Prince 'had a small penis and could not maintain an erection'. He 'preferred to wear nappies and play with teddy bears whilst being dominated by Wallis Simpson.

Wallis Simpson was known to have socialised and collaborated with both the German Ambassador and Adolf Hitler's special envoy Joachim von Ribbentrop, the Champagne General. He would read the state secrets, then check the 'homosexual photographs' of the future King as proof of the information's authenticity.

The Commander of British Special Branch told the Metropolitan Police that Wallis Simpson was also having an affair with Guy Marcus Trundle. Charles Bedaux continued to develop relationships with government leaders of England and Germany during the 1930's. With a close friendship established over the years with Wallis Simpson, Charles and Fern Bedaux were well aware of the constitutional crisis that was about to hit England in 1936.

1935. (January) According to a Metropolitan Police Special Branch report, the Prince of Wales had met Oswald Mosely for the first time at the home of Lady Maud Cunard.

Mosely founded the British Union of Fascists which was strongly anti-communist and argued for a programme of economic revival based on government spending and protectionism.

1935. (August) Wallis Simpson was being watched by French and British special agents and a detective from Scotland Yard. In order to pass secrets, she employed a lawyer, Gregoire, who was also the lawyer for Ribbentrop, the Nazi Ambassador to London and Otto Abertz, who soon became the German Ambassador to Paris. When she couldn't get through to them, she sent crucial secrets to Anna Wolkoff, the daughter of Admiral Wolkoff. 'She was a Nazi spy sending crucial secrets to Berlin via Italy and was considered a leading figure in British fascism. Anna Wolkoff was also the dressmaker to Wallis Simpson and Princess Marina of Greece, the widow of the Duke of Kent. Five associates of Anna Wolkoff were listed by MI5 as being Nazi sympathisers. This list led right into the household of the British Royal Family.

Wallis Simpson dubbed Elizabeth, the Duchess of York:

'The Dowdy Duchess' or 'The Fat Scottish Cook'

While the future Queen simply called the American divorcee:

That woman or A certain person'.

Wallis Simpson's role, as far as the Germans were concerned, was to enmesh the weak future King Edward VIII into a sexually perverse World and then threaten to reveal reports of his sexual habits to 'high society' and the British public at large, via American newspapers if necessary. It was Edward's weaknesses as a king, his naivety around politics and his continual intoxication that made him 'non-compos mentis' most of the time. Wallis was half-American, half-German and actively spied for the Nazis.

The sessions photographed included the future King of England having a 'menage-a trois' with another man. Wallis Simpson would get up from the bed, put on her lipstick, and at the same time take a photo from her 'Kodak compact' make-up case.

1936. (January)  Edward was totally obsessed with Wallis Simpson. Edward was characterised as Mrs Simpson's lapdog and their relationship was described as: 'Sadomasochistic, relishing contempt and bullying'.

Wallis Simpson was prepared to end the relationship, she found him: 'Dependant, burdensome and claustrophobic'.

Edward's relationship with Wallis Simpson was now being reported in the foreign press, however, the British government had instructed the British press not to refer to the relationship.

1936. (January 20th)  The death of H.R.H. King George V. Edward ascended the throne as Edward VIII. The Foreign Office censored the Red Boxes before Edward received them, as they were aware that the King

127

could pass on delicate information to the Germans via Wallis Simpson.

1936. (June) 'Wallis Simpson discovered she was pregnant'. Although she understood she could not keep this child for political and constitutional reasons, she was adamant and determined to go through with the pregnancy as she previously thought she was incapable of conceiving after suffering a miscarriage during her first marriage. The King was in an impossible position.

1936. (August) Edward VIII chartered Lady Annie Henrietta Yule's yacht, 'Nahlin' for an Adriatic cruise, he had all the books removed from the library to make more room for alcohol to be carried during his cruise. Nahlin was sold to Carol II of Romania on the eve of World War II. The reason he did not use the Royal yacht was that it was operated by the Royal Navy and he was paranoid that anyone might find out that Mrs Simpson was pregnant. The King was drunk for much of the holiday.

1936. (October 27th) Wallis Simpson divorced (decree nisi) from Ernest Simpson. Case held in Ipswich.

1936. (December 1st) Two weeks after King Edward VIII first told the Prime Minister he wanted to marry Mrs Simpson, the abdication crisis built to its climax. H.R.H. King Edward VIII organised Wallis Simpson's removal from Great Britain on the dishonest pretext to the public that she could not stand being hounded by the press. He knew she had to leave before the pregnancy became obvious (she was always very slim). She was to be sent to a private villa where there could be no access before the child's birth, especially by the press. She took the £100,000 worth of recent gifts the king had given her.

1936. (December 2nd) The British newspapers finally threw off their self-imposed censorship over the affair, long played out in the rest of the world's press. The biggest news story was about to be fully out in the open.

1936. (December 3rd) The New York Times quoted a friend of an angry Mrs Simpson saying:

*"She is now determined that she will not leave the country unless the king commands her to do so. She does not want it said of her that she quit under fire. If she leaves at all she wants to go with banners flying and not creep from the country secretively like a fugitive."*

Later the same day though, that is exactly what she did.

Mrs Simpson, accompanied Lord Brownlow, the king's advisor, chauffeur George Ladbroke and Inspector Evans of Scotland Yard, they left on the seventy-mile drive to Newhaven, heading for Cannes. Despite the conditions, they made the 10.00 pm sailing of S.S. Brighton reaching Dieppe in the early hours. The press was waiting for them on the quay side. The journalists weren't sure where they were headed. They managed to shake them off until a stop at the Grand Hôtel de la Poste at Rouen at 3.00 am when a customer recognised them and took a picture. They turned towards Paris, but by lunchtime had almost doubled back on themselves to Evreux.

At the Hôtellerie du Grand Cerf, Mrs Simpson telephoned the King, shouting over a poor connection, pleading with him not to abdicate. She left some notes in the phone booth, later retrieved by the manager and kept in the hotel safe.

Fog gave way to sleet and driving snow as they passed Orleans. Unexpectedly they then turned west, seeming to confirm that Mrs Simpson was really on her way to Biarritz. They checked in to the Hotel de France at

Blois, reporters gathered outside. After a high-speed chase through the streets of Lyon, journalists finally caught up with them at a Restaurant in Vienne. Mrs Simpson left through the kitchen window. By 6.00pm they were in Avignon, 140 miles from Cannes. The final leg, ninety miles on twisted roads from Aix-en-Provence, took three and a half hours. They finally arrived at Villa Lou Viei, at three minutes to midnight on December 5th. The 830-mile drive had taken fifty-five hours.

From Cannes, she released a statement stating her readiness to withdraw from 'an untenable situation' and wrote privately to the King, urging him not to abdicate.

"*How can a reigning King have a child with a twice divorced, married American woman out of wedlock?*" she asked.


1936. (December 7th) For the next three months, Wallis Simpson, feeling sick and ill, stayed at the Villa Lou Viei, near Cannes, the home of her close friends Herman and Katherine Rogers, who were prepared to keep and protect her secret. She knew she had to make the ultimate sacrifice of giving up her baby to save the Duke from what would be the 'the scandal of the century'.


1936. (December) King Edward VIII's Abdication speech is an absolute illusion, it shouldn't have read: 'The woman I love'. It should have read: 'The woman is pregnant'. Edward VIII was already aware that Germany intended to invade Europe and he would be reinstated as the King again, once power had shifted to the Nazis.


1936. (December) The Duke of Windsor visits Vienna on official business but also to organise an alternative birthplace if necessary.

1937 (March) 'Wallis Simpson gave birth to a son'. Her London solicitor (unnamed for legal reasons) had arrived from London, with a well-known obstetrician, Dr Kirkwood from Queen Charlotte's maternity hospital and an anaesthetist. The unnamed solicitor then claimed the maternity hospital consultant was his personal physician. The reputation of the one-time head of the House of Windsor was on the line. '*Wallis Simpson knew that the baby had to be adopted*'. The Windsors both had Nazi sympathies, and powerful contacts. Charles Bedaux registered the child as the son of his secretary, Romilly, he also arranged adoption papers. Bedaux organised adoption with the German minister Dr Ley. The child was smuggled into Germany immediately with Romilly posing as his mother. Hitler was aware of the arrangements and foresaw political advantage and gain for the new 'heir' to be under Nazi care and influence. The Duke of Windsor was so entrenched in the German Nazi movement that the German Military Intelligence's Abwehr had even issued him with a 'V-Mann number' giving him special German military status. Romilly attempted to escape but was caught and held captive in Berlin.

1937 (May) Wallis Simpson's divorce was finalised. She and Edward were reunited as guests of Charles Bedaux, at the Chateau de Cande. Edward immediately proposed marriage to Wallis Simpson.

1937. (June 3rd) The couple were married at the Chateau de Cande. The famous English photographer, Cecil Beaton documented the event. Inside the wedding ring was inscribed, not only the date of their wedding but also '18-10-35' implying that they had entered into a secret engagement on October 10th 1935.

1937. Charles Bedaux orchestrated the Duke and Duchess' twelve-day visit to Germany to meet Hitler through Dr Ley, who was the couple's guide on the tour and the man Hitler had put in charge of the German labour front. He was violently anti-Semitic and was implicated in the mistreatment of slave labourers. The visit was also planned with Dr Ley to enable the Windsors to secretly see their new baby.

'The Duke even saluted the Nazi officials'.

As well as touring a mine and meeting Hitler at his mountain retreat, Edward visited a concentration camp, whose guard towers were apparently explained away as meat stores. The Duke met and dined with dozens of senior Nazis including Hitler's deputy Rudolf Hess, and his foreign minister Joachim von Ribbentrop, who knew the Duchess intimately. He also met Hitler's propaganda chief Joseph Goebbels, who was so convinced of his fascist sympathies, he described him as a:

'Tender seedling of reason'.

Hitler remarked of the Duchess: ***"She would have made a good queen."***

It was thought that they would have been installed as 'puppet monarchs' had Germany taken over Britain, but Dr Ley had other ideas. 'The newly born Prince' was in his control and would have been politically far more use to Germany than the Duke. The new Prince would be the ultimate insult to Great Britain and its citizens. Dr Ley even teased the Duke that the child would be the next British King. Edward faced numerous accusations of being a Nazi sympathiser. He was once said to have given a Nazi salute to Hitler, which he later claimed was a 'soldiers salute' and claimed the Fuhrer was 'not a bad chap'. Hitler was infatuated with Wallis Simpson and assigned a German agent to film Wallis. Hitler giggled uncontrollably in ecstatic pleasure when he viewed her on film in Obersalzburg. Both Hitler and Eva Braun were mesmerised by Wallis's hair, make-up and severe, classic, timeless clothes.

Hitler was now a speed and cocaine addict.

1939. (January 19ᵗʰ) The Duke had a major row with Winston Churchill over Spain and Churchill's call for an alliance with the Soviet Union. Lloyd George was present.

1939. When war was imminent, the Duke contacted Hitler hoping to negotiate a peaceful solution, attempting to draw upon the rapport they developed during his 1937 visit to Germany. The Duke of Windsor was willing to deal with Hitler to win back his throne.

Upon the outbreak of World War II, the Duke and Duchess fled to Biarritz in the south west of France. Wallis Simpson had informed Ribbentrop where they were going. On arrival at their secret hideaway, the location was simultaneously announced on German Radio, along with their room number. This lifted German war spirits to new levels of hilarity. Within a month they travelled to Madrid, Spain and communication with Ribbentrop was facilitated through Spanish Fascists.

A month later, they travelled to Portugal where the Duke made indiscreet remarks that Britain stood little chance of resisting a German invasion and may as well try to settle for peace with the Germans. Edward VIII was allowed to leave Spain under the direct intervention of Walter Schellenberg, a Nazi Intelligence Officer. For this favour, Schellenberg was not prosecuted for War Crimes in 1946. Schellenberg had managed the Venlo Incident for Germany but was never forgiven by the British for 'acquiring possession' of the Prince of Wales's homosexual secrets. During the Iberian sojourn, many of Edward's unguarded utterances were secretly recorded by German diplomats and pro Fascist Spanish aristocrats. They sent the material in minute detail to Berlin.

1940. (July) The Duke and Duchess of Windsor were in Lisbon, Portugal. The FBI were aware of the

Duchess' loyalties to Nazi Germany and the Duke's sexual behaviour.

They had become an embarrassing threat.

1940. (August) The Duke and Duchess travelled by commercial liner to the Bahamas, where the Duke was installed as Governor. The Bahamas was selected by Winston Churchill to prevent the Duchess from coming into contact with any British officials and from establishing any channel of communication with Ribbentrop.

An FBI memo dated 1940 also stated:

**'It was considered absolutely essential that the Windsors be removed to a point where they would do absolutely no harm'.**

1941. The Duke of Windsor, Harold Christie (Sir Harry Oakes' murder suspect) and Nazi Swedish banker Axel Wenner-Gren were under investigation by both the U.S. Intelligence Service and the Internal Revenue service for serious breaches of wartime currency control regulations. There were devastating implications and a charge of treason could not be ruled out.

1942. (December 29th) Dr Ley's second wife Inge shot herself after a drunken brawl.

1943. (January 13th) Charles Bedaux was arrested in North Africa on the personal orders of General Dwight D. Eisenhower. Suspicion is that he is heavily involved with attempting to import and organise the sale of Nazi gold in the U.S. to assist financing senior German officers' relocation to South America.

1944. (February 17th) Charles Eugene Bedaux, an intimate friend of the Duke and Duchess of Windsor as well as many of Germany's foremost Nazis, was told at a special hearing in Miami that he would have to stand trial for treason.

1944. (February 18th) Charles Bedaux committed suicide with an overdose of barbiturates in a Miami prison. He knew too much about the connections between leading American industry leaders and the industrial development in Nazi Germany in the 1930's.Bedaux's case was linked with the deaths of two FBI agents, Percy Foxworth and Harold Haberfeld who were both killed when their plane crashed mysteriously over Brazilian jungles while on route to North Africa to work on the Bedaux case. Bedaux kept being controversial after his death.

1945. The New Yorker Magazine devoted a series of three articles to Charles Bedaux, naming him a collaborator. At the same time, the De Gaulle government in France, after detailed scrutiny, granted him posthumously a Legion of Honour Award.

1945. (April 20th) Dr Ley's last visit to Hitler on his birthday, in the Führerbunker in central Berlin.

1945. (April 30th) Adolf Hitler killed himself by gunshot in his Führerbunker in Berlin. His wife Eva (née Braun) committed suicide with him by taking cyanide.

1945. (24th October) Dr Ley strangled himself in his prison cell using a noose made by tearing a towel into strips, fastened to the toilet pipe in his cell.

1952. (March) After the death of his brother, George VI, there were rumours that the Duke of Windsor was planning to purchase an English estate near London. The purpose was to make a bid for the throne on the basis that the future Queen Elizabeth II was too young to ascend. If successful, he could not only appoint himself regent, but also restore communication with his own son in Germany and endow him the future throne. There was no evidence to back these rumours.

1952. Walter Schellenberg 'suspiciously' died from stomach cancer while under British custody.

**1950 The Duke & Duchess of Windsor with Elsa Maxwell in Paris before their argument**

# CHAPTER FOURTEEN

## HEIRESSES MURDER & EXECUTION
## (1953 -1956)

Kim seemed to recover from his broken engagement to Barbara Warner reasonably quickly. He had a very quiet and peaceful Christmas, New Year and twenty third birthday in London. It was very different from the previous year in Paris with his ex-fiancé, Barbara, for company.

He often thought about Dors, she still held a special place in his heart. They were the best of friends, always offering advice to each other on the telephone or meeting each other for lunch, much to the annoyance of the despicable Dennis Hamilton.

In 1954, a group of Moroccan 'businessmen' asked Billy Hill to restore the Sultan of Morocco to his throne. The French had forced the Sultan out and exiled him in Madagascar. Billy Hill and George Walker went to Tangier. They set up a fake insurance company called The American Fidelity Corporation to cover their activities and bought a boat to go and recover the Sultan, but it all went terribly wrong. Interpol told the Moroccan police that they were 'Britain's biggest bandits', and then someone torched the boat leaving Billy Hill and George Walker fleeing to Cannes.

Obviously, Kim couldn't return to France, but he wanted his Rolls Royce back, it was still in the Martinez Hotel car park in Cannes. After a chat with Bobby McKew, Billy Hill agreed to send a couple of his junior thugs to France in order to collect the car on his behalf as long as Kim indemnified the expenses incurred. Five days later the very dirty Rolls Royce arrived in London with a bill of nearly £500 for storage costs, fuel and the lad's wages. Kim paid the bill fearful of upsetting Billy Hill and promptly sold the car to Paddon Brothers in Cheval Place for £375, he wished he had left it in the car hotel park.

The fifties in London had become a trailer for the 'swinging sixties', the grey hangover of the post-war years was finally being shrugged off, not least by budding actors, artists, musicians and young society ravers. By 1954, louche life in Chelsea became the magnet for disaffected young, their focus was the 'Chelsea Set'. Kim was firmly established as an 'honoury' member, hosting his brother Johnny's and John Burke's illegal 'Chemmy' parties.

Kim even found Tony Armstrong-Jones (the late Lord Snowdon) defacing a Grenadier Guard's dress uniform at one of his parties, which usually ended up with Kim being asked by one or more of the guests if he knew of a beautiful girl that they could take home with them for the night.

Kim was back to his old self, sleeping from 4.00a.m or later, and waking up at lunch time. In the back of his mind, he was constantly aware that the French police were mounting a criminal case against him involving the Warner robbery; he often met up with Bobby McKew, who was also running illegal 'Chemmy' games, to discuss the situation.

London experienced a complete nightlife overhaul in the mid 1950's, new clubs were opening up specifically targeting London's aristocracy as well as wealthy captains of industry and well-known show business personalities. The more exclusive, the more expensive, the better.

Kim was in his paradise.

Kim loved the Milroy Club, which was part of Les Ambassadeurs, it was owned by John Mills, a Polish gentleman who had changed his name from Jean-Jean Millstein. For £40,000, Mills had been able to secure a long lease on the ex-Rothschild home in Hamilton Place, Mayfair. Over the coming years Les Ambassadeurs became home to various venues, including The Milroy Club, The Garrison Club, Le Cercle, and Les 'A' one of

London's first gaming clubs that opened in 1961.

Interestingly, Kim's brother's colleague, John Burke, had his first meeting with John Aspinall in early 1954. The meeting seemed incidental, but in fact it was a meeting that seven years later would change the face of gambling forever in London.

Mills led a fascinating life, he was an international businessman of Polish origin, and it was rumoured that he was a government intelligence agent. However, the lines between fact and fiction are not always clear, so it was difficult to separate the truths.

The club was known as 'The night time headquarters of Society'. This was Princess Margaret's favourite nightclub in 1955. The Princess would be seen there two or three times a week with Billy Wallace or Colin Tennant. Her table, which was hidden by pillars, became known as the 'Royal Box'. The long thin P-shaped basement club had a minute dance floor but a bandstand big enough for an eighteen-piece orchestra. Kim met the Princess there on several occasions and as usual the rumours started, but for once the rumours were not true.

Kim later sued a well-known author, who claimed they had been having a long-term affair, and that Kim had landed his helicopter in the middle of Hyde Park to collect her. Needless to say, Kim won the case and the paragraph was removed and I can vouch that no affair ever took place between them.

As Kim later said:

**"I didn't know what all the fuss was about, she was fun, but fancy her, no bloody way."**

One summer's evening in 1955, Kim was with some friends at the Milroy and was introduced to the heiress Sara Skinner. Kim liked her, but she fell for Kim's charms immediately and became obsessed with him. Sara was a very wealthy woman with a beautiful luxurious house in Kensington, Kim would keep her amused for hours reciting stories filled with sexual innuendo. He knew that it was prudent to keep her around. He was right, four years later she was to show her loyalty to him on a grand scale.

Kim also spent many nights at Siegi Sessler's Club in Charles Street, which had become known as one of London's finest restaurants, a favourite hideaway for its extraordinary clientele. Privacy was assured. The code of conduct was watched over carefully by the immaculately dressed Siegi himself. Sessler had resigned from Les Ambassadeurs and started his own business after an argument with John Mills and later said of the Polish businessman:

*"We are Poles apart."*

Sessler's restaurant and bar were famous for being famous and on Monday nights provided the scene for high stakes Chemin de Fer (Chemmy) games.

Should Frank Sinatra and Dean Martin choose to entertain the lunchtime gathering with a few songs around the piano, the chances were that Sam Spiegel would have asked them to:

*"Keep it down... I'm trying to work here."*

or Groucho Marx would insist on professional singers entertaining him over his lunch saying:

*"Auditions by buskers only gave him gas."*

Sessler's restaurant was one of Stephen Ward's favourite haunts and he often launched his young prodigies in the club over a prime cut of beef, topped with Siegi's famous cognac and peppercorn sauce. The club was later purchased by Sir Mark Birley, the founder of Annabel's and renamed, 'Mark's Club'.

Kim was also a member of a strange club in Brompton Road known as 'The Little Club'. One never really discussed sex within the club but there were always girls available, supplied by the management at extra cost. The 1954 membership list was quite astonishing and included; King Hussein of Jordan, King Farouk of Egypt, King Feisal of Iraq, Douglas Fairbanks Jr, the Marquis of Milford Haven, Lord Montague of Beaulieu, The

Maharajah of Cooch-Behar, Lord Snowdon, Donald Campbell, Victor Mature, Peter Rachman, Lady Docker, Billy Butlin, Diana Dors, Dennis Hamilton, John Caborn-Waterfield, David Blakely, Stirling Moss, 'Baron' Nahum, Stephen Ward and the Duchess of Argyll, who was known for her legendry oral skills.

It was through Stephen Ward, at the incestuous 'Little Club', that Kim met Vicki Martin, formally known as, Valerie Mewes, a part-time model and mistress to the Maharajah of Cooch-Behar, whose horse racing colours, were once prominent on the British turf. Kim thought she was magical, captivating and exciting. He immediately practised his now perfected charms on her.

Kim would later say:

*"I don't know if she had a slight astigmatism, but it felt like she was always sharing a joke with you, she could be talking to someone else but Vicki always seemed to have her eyes and her smile on you. She was highly lovable, there was something terribly inviting about her look."*

Stephen Ward claimed to have met Vicki Martin in a doorway on Oxford Street during a thunderstorm. Ward produced many female prodigies and apparently, Vicki Martin was the prototype. She was best friends with the glamour seeking Ruth Ellis who managed the club. Both Vicki and Ruth had worked as hostesses at Murray's Club in Soho, where Stephen Ward, of the Profumo Scandal, later met Christine Keeler.

Vicki had an affliction for car accidents. She had been involved with twelve of them over the previous four years but was tragically killed instantly in her thirteenth crash. She was one of two people killed when the car she was driving collided head on with another vehicle on the Henley Road near Maidenhead, Berkshire on January 9th 1955. Kim was devastated and there was more devastating news to follow.

Ruth Ellis was a great friend of both Diana Dors

and Kim. Unfortunately, she miscarried her second child during January. David Blakely, her lover, fellow club member and philanderer smashed her up in a violent drunken brawl after he heard the news. Ellis suspected Blakely was having an affair with a friend's nanny. On Sunday April 10th, in a pique of jealousy and rejection, Ellis returned to Hampstead. She arrived at the Magdala public house in South Hill Park at about 9.30p.m. As she arrived, Blakely came out from the pub with a friend. He saw her and started to run in front of the car. Ruth took a .38 calibre gun out of her handbag and fired at Blakely, who was crouching in front of the car trying to hide. She ran over to him and shot him five times, the last shot from point blank range. As he lay wounded on the ground, other drinkers came out of the pub to see what had happened and Ellis was arrested, still holding the smoking gun, by an off-duty policeman. She was taken to Hampstead police station where she made a detailed confession.

On June 20th 1955, Ruth Ellis appeared in the Number One Court at the Old Bailey, London, before Mr Justice Havers (the actor Nigel Havers' grandfather). She was dressed in a black suit and a white silk blouse with freshly bleached and coiffured blonde hair. Her lawyers expressed concern about her appearance and her dyed blonde hair, but she did not alter it to appear less striking. When questioned in the dock, she merely said:

*"It's obvious when I shot him, I intended to kill him."*

She became the last woman ever to be hung in England at Holloway prison on July 13th 1955.

Kim unfortunately gained a police record in England at this time. He had met Dors with her loathsome husband Hamilton for drinks at the Embassy Club, the two men started arguing. The situation became worse when Hamilton tried to punch Kim who dodged the punch and promptly gave Hamilton a 'right hander', leaving Hamilton with a bleeding black eye. Dors tried to extinguish the commotion, but the police had already been called. Kim was arrested and bound over, this resulted in a conviction for 'insulting behaviour'. The conviction was untimely as Kim was trying to keep a low profile, law-abiding image, knowing that the law could come crashing down on him over his misdemeanours in France.

The following year, Diana Dors starred in the movie 'Yield to the Night' which was loosely based upon the Ruth Ellis murder trial.

She later said:

**"I've played my share of drunken sluts, good time girls, and whores. Being bumped off is really no novelty for me. I've been shot, hanged, strangled, gassed, burned to death, and even pushed off a cliff."**

Early in 1956, the Warner robbery case was tried 'In Absentia' (in the defendant's absence) with the most prestigious advocate (French lawyer) in France, Maitre Suzanne Blum, prosecuting on behalf of Jack L. Warner. Michel Koenig was the defending advocate. Kim was sentenced to four years' imprisonment, and Bobby McKew received a three-year sentence.

There was now a warrant out for Kim and McKew's arrest in France. The French authorities then started proceedings in the United Kingdom for the extradition of both of them.

Kim knew this would take a long time to implement if defended correctly.

Dors always fondly remembered her time with Kim and particularly their conversations about leaving England and working in America. Kim had already tried it, but returned to London, now it was her turn. Dors had pre-signed three film contracts with RKO Pictures in the States. She left Southampton on the June 20th 1956 with Dennis Hamilton aboard the Cunard liner 'Queen Elizabeth' bound for New York. She then flew to Hollywood to start shooting 'The Unholy Wife' with Rod

Steiger.

Hamilton had bought her a new Cadillac convertible upon arrival and arranged for Dors to meet the well-known and fearsome Hollywood columnists Hedda Hopper and Louella Parsons. Interviews were arranged to be held at the Hollywood home of Dors' friend, the celebrity hairdresser, Teasy-Weasy Raymond, who owned a Spanish style villa off Sunset Boulevard, formerly owned by Marlene Dietrich. To coincide with the publication of the articles, Dennis Hamilton and Teasy-Weasy Raymond arranged a Hollywood launch party at Raymond's house in August 1956, with a guest list that included Doris Day, Eddie Fisher, Zsa Zsa Gabor, Liberace, Lana Turner and John Wayne. At the pool party, full of Hollywood 'A' list celebrities, Hamilton was pushed fully clothed into the swimming pool. A drunken, bad tempered, Hamilton emerged from the pool and punched a photographer, breaking his nose, before he could be restrained. The celebrities fled and the next day's headlines in the National Enquirer read:

*"Miss Dors go home, and take Mr. Dors with you."*

The couple had agreed to purchase Lana Turner's beautiful house, but because of the resulting negative publicity, they settled for a rental property in Coldwater Canyon instead.

It became worse during October 1956 because Dors started having an affair with Rod Steiger during the filming of 'The Unholy Wife'.

In February 1957, while filming The Long Haul, Dors started yet another relationship, this time with her co-star, Victor Mature's stuntman, Tommy Yeardye. Details about their affair were reportedly leaked to the press by Yeardye himself. Dennis Hamilton discovered the relationship which led to another period of separation and eventually divorce proceedings. After Dors announced her separation from Hamilton, RKO Pictures cancelled her contract on a morals clause, naming her pending divorce as the reason but only after the movies 'The Unholy Wife' (1957) and 'I Married A Woman' (1958) were completed.

Kim had learnt that proceedings by the French government to extradite him to France in order to serve his prison sentence were well under way and that he could be arrested in the United Kingdom at any time. He knew it was going to be an uphill battle and cost a fortune to fight and overturn an extradition order in the British courts.

It was a cold November morning; Kim woke up with a splitting headache. He reached over the bed for his usual breakfast, consisting of two aspirin tablets, while nursing a terrible hangover. The anxiety of extradition to France was needling him. After a shower, he telephoned Bobby McKew and they agreed to meet for lunch at Simpson's in the Strand. Over a long roast lunch, they discussed their options; both knew that it was only a case of time before the French authorities exercised their extradition order which could lead to their immediate arrest in England. It was time to go, but the question was where to?

Bobby McKew was still working for Billy Hill. The 'boss of the underworld' loved Morocco and Tangier especially. Not only did Hill often vacation there, he also had a villa in southern Spain to be near his smuggling operation which posed as a small bar and a ski school in Tangier. Hill owned half the business, the other half was owned by his ex-employee and McKew's ex-partner Michael Eland, who used to supply Kim all the nylon stockings years before.

Michael Eland had progressed in business during the last ten years. He had married a wealthy much older woman and set up his own illegal casino on the Cromwell Road in London.

He had then divorced his wife and received a large

settlement. He left London and lived between Paris and Tangier where he was running the ski school. Although he now had his own funds, he was still backed by Billy Hill because the school and bar had a double identity, it was a ski school by day and an illegal smuggling operation by night. The employees would deliver whisky and cigarettes into Gibraltar aboard an old-World War II MTB (motor torpedo boat) which Eland kept hidden around a cove nearby. Eland wanted to sell his half of the operation and return to Paris where he had since settled.

Kim listened carefully to McKew and said:

*"What if we bought the half share from Eland and took the operation over ourselves."*

*"You want to become a smuggler,"* replied McKew.

There was one big problem, neither had the money to buy Eland's share and McKew already knew the whole place needed refurbishment. Kim asked McKew to contact Eland in Morocco and find out how much was needed to secure the purchase.

A few days later McKew called Kim and informed him that £50,000 was the best price Eland would accept. Some further £30,000 was needed to be spent on the buildings and bar area. Although, this figure sounded ridiculous, McKew knew Billy Hill was earning at least £1,000 per week from his half share of the profits in the trafficking caper.

Kim came up with a plan and that evening invited Sara Skinner to Les Ambassadeurs. He knew that he would have to perform; the heiress was in love with him. As the evening progressed, he subtly started to talk about the possibility of buying the ski school and offered Sara a 'piece of the action' if she would finance the acquisition. To Kim's surprise, she readily agreed to lend Kim the £80,000 needed. An immediate £50,000 upon completion of the purchase and some further £30,000, once the builders had finished the improvement works. All this had one condition, Kim had to spend more nights staying with her in London at her magnificent home. He knew how a gentleman should behave and readily obliged.

The following week, Kim and McKew had a meeting with Billy Hill; they needed his approval to the deal first because the pair of them were effectively becoming Hill's partners and Hill would be losing his 'first lieutenant', but as McKew explained to Hill:

**_"If I stay in this Country, I will be bloody locked up anyway."_**

Hill sanctioned the deal and Kim left with McKew for Tangier immediately. Kim was now in direct partnership with London's biggest villain, this was no game. He also realised that there were no choices, if he stayed around much longer the police could arrest him and deport him to jail in France.

He surrendered his tenancy in Egerton Gardens; it was time to head for the sunshine and new pastures.

**Michael Eland, with his actress wife Martine Carol in Paris**

# CHAPTER FIFTEEN

## THE KRAY TWINS IN TANGIER
## (1957 – 1958)

The ski school consisted of a few shoddily built bungalows, a small clubhouse and a bar on the beach. There was a pair of worn-out speedboats and an old World War II motor torpedo boat moored around the cove under camouflage. Everything needed major refurbishment.

Bobby McKew had known Michael Eland for years when they had worked together in London. But he had changed, he was more of a showman than ever, he lived his life in 'capital letters', there were no rules, just Michael's rules.

There was great rivalry between Eland and Kim, they both saw themselves as great lotharios and buccaneers. They were both were used to getting their own way. Although Kim had purchased all his nylon stockings from Michael, nearly a decade before, this time they did not get on at all well together. Kim thought Eland was 'loud, louche and a show off', Eland thought Kim was 'precious, effeminate and a snob'. The deal was finally agreed, the funds were in place, but the deal nearly floundered because Eland insisted on removing his big brass NCR cash register from the bar counter on completion, which was not in the contract. Although this was a petty situation, McKew literally, had to stand between the two men to restrain them from beating the hell out of each other.

In the Spring of 1957, after many arguments with various building teams, many of which didn't speak English, the old place was beginning to take shape. The long bar overlooked a lower level with a dance floor and an aged grand white piano on a plinth in the corner. The theme colour was washed terracotta and ficus lime.

Punkah fans revolved lazily overhead wafting the dust from the louvered shutters. Kim really believed that he had become 'Rick' from the movie 'Casablanca'. He finally named the new bar 'Dandy Kim's', an apt name for a bar in a predominantly gay area. Typically, the bar and club house were not finished in time for the grand opening,

Kim went ahead with the party anyway, giving drinks and tapas 'on the house', but he did leave an 'honesty box' by the front entrance. He opened the box in the early hours of the next morning and was surprised that such a bent crowd were astonishingly straight and honest. He also employed a sultry night club singer called Diane, she reminded Kim of Lauren Bacall.

Diane had a large ill-stitched scar down the right-hand side of her face, which Kim once enquired about. He was amazed at her reply:

*"Darling, a drunken punter started getting frisky with me at the bar one night after I'd performed, he became very rude so I ordered two large brandies and sexily poured them down his throat, most of it spilt down his sweaty shirt. He thought I was coming on to him. I just got my Zippo lighter out as if to light a cigarette and pfffff, he went up in flames. I sipped my drink and toasted him saying: "Prique Flambé." Unfortunately, he survived and slashed my left right cheek."*

Kim knew never to flirt with the tiger blond sexy singer ever again.

The smuggling operation was running at full throttle; the Costa clientele were insatiable and everyone was earning a lot of money. The old Packard powered sixty-foot-long MTB was crossing the Straights of Gibraltar most nights full to the brim with both whisky and cigarettes. It was under the command of Kim and McKew's captain whose name was Carey Fitz-Allen. The radio room on board was operated by Fred 'Sparks' Blair, both men had served in the 'Special Boats Executive'. At sea, Carey was in his element but ashore and on the piss, he was a seventeen-stone muscular monster.

One evening, Carey came into the bar with someone called Robby McRae and Charlie Kray, the Kray twins' elder brother. Kim knew of McRae through the Astor Club. He was usually a jovial character but, on this occasion, he looked serious. Carey gave a beckoning gesture for all the men to go into the kitchens, which they duly did.

Carey, who had a slice of the action in the Hill, McKew and Kim smuggling syndicate, stared intently at the others and simply said:

**"Someone's opened their fucking mouth and blown the gaff to the Beirutis."**

The problem was that a rival gang called the Beirutis had been informed about their activities including the cigarette and whisky racket. The Beirutis were not people to play with, they were the main supplier of narcotics into Gibraltar and human life had no value to them.

**"I know it's not Sparks, he knows how to keep his mouth shut."**

Kim had no real idea what Robby was going on about but he did understand the Beirutis were a serious Mediterranean mafia force, not to be underestimated. He never found out who was responsible for the betrayal, but slowly the truth emerged.

Billy Hill had undoubtedly been responsible for educating the Kray twins and making them what they had become. Hill wanted to move part-time to Tangier and had just purchased another club there called Churchill's, for his mistress Gypsy. The club was an oasis for any successful criminal.

Robby McRae had been brokering a deal codenamed 'El Minza' which in effect changed the territories within London's gangster fraternity. It also transferred power and control of some of Hill's assets, businesses and rackets to the Kray twins.

It was now obvious to Kim why Charlie Kray had suddenly turned up. He had been sent to inspect the operation and report his findings to his younger brothers, Ron and Reg, back in London. Kim was nervous enough having Billy Hill as a silent partner, but the Kray twins… that was serious, they were crazy psychotic killers.

The Krays had moved many of their activities from Bow to Belgravia and taken over 'Esmeralda's Barn' from Peter Rachman, where many illegal 'Chemmy' games were played. They had become very powerful in England and were even negotiating several contracts in Las Vegas. They had become known to the American mafia and representatives had flown to London to meet the twins.

Then there was an extraordinary coincidence. The Beirutis were becoming a real threat. Kim and his partners had even considered utilizing Sparks' knowledge of explosives to blow their boats up. At the same time, Billy King suggested that the infamous twins fly down to Tangier as soon as possible for a holiday and in order to avoid arrest in United Kingdom for hijacking armed robbery and arson.

Kim was told to look after them. He seriously thought they could look after themselves.

A couple of days later the twins arrived in Tangier. The Krays always sought publicity. They had hoped to meet the Rolling Stones in Tangier, they loved to be photographed rubbing shoulders with singers and actors.

Later, during his trial for murder, Ronnie Kray off-handily informed the judge that if he hadn't been in court he would have been:

*"Having tea with Judy Garland."*

Kim knew Ronnie Kray was homosexual and the next day organised a pair of young Moroccan boys for his pleasure upon arrival. The next morning Ronnie was in Dandy Kim's bar looking out of the window towards the souk market. He suddenly pointed his blunt finger at a frail blind beggar and turned to Kim saying:

151

*"Ere Kim, who's the Ali Baba geezer? What's 'is game?"*

Reg peered over his brother's shoulder and said:

*"Ron, go and give 'im a fiver."*

There was no way Kim was going to tell Vi Kray's favourite boy about Ahmed's caper. Kim sensed that Ronnie was about to fall for the ancient Arab's little con game. Ahmed wasn't blind, he used a seashell to tilt cactus juice into his eyes. The effect was startling, his eyes opened wide, filmed and unseeing. When he caught the attention of a 'punter', he would suddenly bow deeply, then raising his seemingly sightless face, offer a worthless Hong Kong dollar bill acting as though his victim had dropped it. Two out of three times the victim would give real money to this poor old afflicted man. Ronnie lobbed him a £5 note.

Kim wasn't going to tell Ronnie that he had just been mugged.

Francis Bacon, the controversial gay artist, was living in Tangier at the time when the Krays visited. Bacon often drank in 'Dandy Kim's bar where he met Ronnie Kray. A few days later Ronnie asked Bacon for a favour.

Ronnie, who was said to be the crueller of the twins was attracted to much younger men, as was Bacon. He said he had fallen for an African boy but he didn't think he could take him back to his hotel. He was worried about the impression it might make. Ronnie asked if he could take him to Bacon's place, where he had lots of rooms, Bacon agreed, and after that never saw the end of him.

Bacon later said:

*"You wouldn't think he'd have cared after cutting all those people's throats. People came here to lose their inhibitions, above all queers from England and America. Ronnie always seemed to be there."*

The unlikely presence of the Krays would not have gone unreported in that mecca of illicit activity. The authorities were likely to assume that the London gangsters were moving in on the contraband trade. However, another danger loomed, the word was out that the Spanish Customs agents were stepping up their efforts to obtain information on the cloak and dagger loading and sailing plans. Worryingly, they were starting to pay real money for information, but the worst danger was the incoming Beirutis who had previously operated out of Dubai. They were led by Algerian members of the FLN terrorist group. Kim would not have worried if they had come as competition, they weren't interested in whisky and cigarettes, they were heavily into the drug game and their on-going revolution against their French colonial masters in Algeria.

They had even used front men in offering to buy Kim and his partners out of the ski school.

No secret was safe in the port of Tangier and it would have been common knowledge on the waterfront that, under the cover of the ski school, Kim's operation was the only team in town with powerful speedboats and an MTB. This equipment gave them an invaluable edge on their rivals by having the option of unloading offshore, away from prying eyes. The Beirutis obviously wanted Kim's boats.

The Beirutis then tried something different, they sent a few thugs to 'Dandy Kim's' bar and announced who they were and threatened to burn the place down unless Kim agreed to sell the boats, Kim talked his way around the situation but something had to be done.

In a strange way, he felt comforted by the presence of the Krays, their reputation alone gave Kim a certain safety net and added security.

Kim was totally preoccupied with the current situation; he finally came up with a brainwave and said to Bobby McKew:

**"We're going to drop those fucking Beirutis straight into the lap of a Spanish Customs Patrol."**

McKew reminded Kim:

**"There's honesty amongst thieves."**

One of Kim's staff called Moussa had a cousin, Raoul, who worked for the harbour master at Ceuta. Raoul was privy to all the ships movements from the harbour and hated the Beirutis. Two days later Kim learned from Raoul that a cutter was being loaded around the headland, the cargo was small which meant that it was most likely to be heroin. The cutter was set to sail one hour before the patrol conducted its usual sweep. Kim's insider knowledge was better than the Customs office.

That night, Kim told Carey to wear swimming trunks and said:

**"We don't know their destination, but we're going to make sure that cutter never leaves. Wear your swimming trunks."**

Carey replied:

**"Swimming, what are you fucking talking about?"**

Kim replied: **"Underwater and lay off the sauce."**

**"Underwater... fucking hell, underwater, Jesus you're mad."** said Carey.

Carey on Spanish brandy was like balancing nitro glycerine on ice. As they swam out underwater, a shaft of moonlight on the water lit the dark hull of the Beiruti's cutter looming above them. Desperate for air, Kim kicked hard, dragging his end of the sodden fishing net, Carey followed suite. Silently surfacing, Kim pressed his cheek against the oil-stained hull.

There was no lookout and one hell of a row was taking place on board, the crew were concentrating on loading another MTB that had moored alongside the cutter on the starboard side. Raoul, creating a diversion, rowed his small fishing boat out of the dark to within a ship's length of the smugglers. Kim and Carey clung unseen to the portside gunnel before slipping underwater. Raoul had lit the fish baiting lanterns overhanging the bow. It was a perfect diversion, the lanterns created a golden glow over the millpond surface, illuminating the illicit activity and causing instant consternation. The Beirutis steamed across the deck, screaming hysterically at Raoul to pull away. He held up a basket of fish furiously protesting that he only wanted to sell his catch. Before they could react, yelling began on the starboard side where the crew were clearly desperate to complete the offloading of their incriminating cargo. Without warning, one of the Beirutis pulled out a handgun and shot a fish baiting lantern on Raoul's small boat. The echo of the gunshot and the shattering of glass brought an abrupt halt to the clamour.

The shocked silence that followed was pierced by a scream of fury from a burly figure in a reefer jacket and cap. It was the governor himself; Kim was not expecting this surprise.

*"Imbecile, fuckin cretin, do you want to alert the entire Mediterranean?"*

He barged his way to the rail:

*"You,"* he yelled at Raoul, *" You have ten seconds to fuck off before we ram you. Compris!"*

Raoul wasn't going to wait for the countdown and neither was Kim. Carey was clearly exhausted. Kim reached across the stern, Kim grabbed his end of the net and dived, within seconds, he had looped the mesh around one propeller. As Kim turned to link its twin, Kim was aware of Carey's arm reaching out to steady the line. In the same instant, the engines turned over with a muffled rumble and the power kicked in. The propellers clawed at the water, then jerked to a standstill as they fouled the net. As Kim and Carey shot to the surface, spirals of oil drifted with them. But it wasn't oil, it was blood, Carey's blood, and there was a lot of it. There was no time to examine the wound. Another engine was throttled hard as the cargo cutter attempted to free itself and pull away from the danger zone.

Renewed yelling and pounding feet running aft

spurred Kim and whatever was left of Carey to move. With the cutter's deck lights doused and clouds drifting across the moon they were able to pull themselves unseen along the length of the port side. As they rounded the bow, they were frighteningly exposed from above. Kim heard two loud splashes. They were diving in the hope of freeing the fouled propellers. They hadn't a hope of clearing the snarled mesh, but they didn't know that yet; nor did they know that within the hour a Customs patrol boat would appear around the headland.

Kim turned to Carey, but there was no point. His eyes were closed and his head was alarmingly tilted to one side. He'd crooked his good arm around the anchor chain and was attempting to tourniquet the wound with his other hand. Kim could see that the cut wasn't long but the propeller had bitten very deep and he was awash in his own blood. There was no choice, they would have to take a chance and risk exposure. If they had been spotted the whole plot would be blown and the sequel wouldn't have been pretty. But unless Carey had urgent medical attention, he would be dead anyway. Kim pulled himself to Carey's side and asked:

### *"Can you hold on? I'm going for Raoul."*

Carey nodded. Raoul had the intelligence to row towards Kim and as he came up alongside, Kim pointed to the MTB's anchor chain. Horrified, Raoul rowed towards the bow. By the time Kim and Raoul had hauled Carey's inert body onto the small fishing boat, they were both smothered in watered down blood. Luckily, they weren't spotted by any of the Beirutis aboard the cutter. They were worn out, but more was to follow.

The shriek of the Customs patrol siren paralysed them with fear, their intelligence wasn't that good, they were early. Kim threw himself into the well of the boat beside Carey's unconscious bloody body, he needn't have bothered, the Customs officers had much bigger fish than Raoul's to fry.

At dawn, Kim reached the port entrance. They disembarked the boat like three well fed raptors, the only problem was, one of them was dead.

McKew was waiting for them and the Kray twins had asked to join him after a late sleepless night. As Kim Raoul and McKew lifted the dead weight of Carey's body onto the quayside, Ronnie Kray gazed down at a scene reminiscent of a human abattoir and said:

### *"Cor, gone vampire 'ave you Kim."*

The Krays left Tangier shortly after this episode and most of the Beirutis had been locked up, the threat was over, except Kim had lost his skipper and his chum.

Shortly after this episode, Kim's MTB was shot at by the Gibraltar Coast Guard on the return run back to Tangier, he sensed the whole operation was on borrowed time. He was both bored with his bohemian lifestyle and worried, he yearned for all his Chelsea friends and hated the lack of sophistication in Morocco. He'd become very tired of the Moroccan and Spanish hookers.

He had now achieved international notoriety; the French robbery had been written about on both sides of the Atlantic. He was branded a criminal by the establishment. The Kray twins had expanded and moved on to other ventures and Kim didn't want to really be involved, he thought he could wind up dead.

Kim sometimes saw the Woolworth's heiress Barbara Hutton who he had met at El Morocco in New York a few years earlier, she was with her sixth husband Baron Gottfried Alexander Maximilian Walter Kurt von Cramm. Hutton's mosaic palace in Tangier was magnificent and her sexy parties were always sensational. Kim always happily accepted an invitation.

Kim and McKew paid off the original loans from Sara Skinner, but she would end up helping Kim again during the following year.

It was late 1958 and Kim decided to take a gamble and return to London for a short visit despite knowing he could face arrest. He wanted to legitimise his cash at his London bank and see his chums. He left McKew to look after Dandy Kim's bar and the ski school and flew home.

Kim often talked to me about Carey's tragic death. I never asked what they did with his body. I just listened and presumed Raoul and McKew must have helped with its disposal. It plagued his mind until his own demise.

**Billy Hill          Ronnie Kray with 'friends'**

**Kim at the ski school, Barbara Hutton and a World War II Motor Torpedo Boat similar to the one used by Kim in Tangier.**

158

The Kray Twins, Ronnie & Reggie

Lord Boothby with Ronnie Kray & East End burglar
Leslie Holt who was intimate with them both

# CHAPTER SIXTEEN

## SAMANTHA SARA & SOLITARY
### (1959 – 1961)

In late 1958, Kim flew back to London and booked into the Dorchester hotel. His brother, Johnny, threw him a welcome home party which was attended by the usual 'Chemmy' crowd as well as Lucien Freud, Stephen Ward, Robert Pilkington, various aristocrats, villains and some very beautiful new talent.

Kim hadn't seen much of Johnny over the past few years but they had remained very close. Johnny had climbed the social ladder and made a small fortune out of illegal 'Chemmy' games with John Burke, who was a genius with a pack of cards.

Kim noticed a change in his brother, he looked pale and gaunt and he had lost part of his vibrant personality. He just shrugged it off and thought he was either tired or run down.

Kim couldn't help noticing the budding actress, Samantha Eggar, at the party. He was supposed to be dating Sara Skinner but this young girl really stood out from the crowd and sparkled, she really made an immediate impression on Kim. He performed his usual charms and asked her out for lunch the following day and she willingly accepted. The next few days was a frenzy of restaurants and clubs before retiring back to the Dorchester Hotel.

The following week the front page of the Daily Mirror read:

**"Dandy Kim's secret girl, the aspiring actress Samantha Eggar, has been seen around London on the arm of Michael Caborn-Waterfield, known as 'Dandy Kim', a conman convicted for robbery on the**

*French Riviera, a dashing playboy and amateur jockey."*

Kim adored Samantha and they began a whirlwind romance. Kim encouraged and paid for her to take acting lessons at the Webber Douglas Dramatic School in London. Together they explored London's kooky and kinky venues. They shared a love for fast cars, dogs, horses and the countryside. Lovingly, Samantha wore Kim's signet ring on her finger. Kim organised a wonderful Christmas in London with Samantha and then celebrated his twenty ninth birthday at Les Ambassadeurs club with his new nineteen-year-old lover. Kim hadn't felt like this for a long time, it reminded him of his relationship with Dors ten years before. He spent a few more blissful days with Samantha and made several large cash deposits at his bank in London. Fearing arrest, he knew he couldn't hang around London for long, but before returning to Tangier, he found time to see Dors prior to her departure to America.

After her disastrous marriage to Dennis Hamilton, she now had a new boyfriend Tommy Yeardye, who was a stuntman in the movies.

The next few months were not easy, Billy Hill was pressurising Kim and McKew to make more frequent night time dashes across the Straights of Gibraltar, with the MTB laden with cigarettes and whisky. The Customs were becoming more and more determined to wipe out smuggling forever.

One morning during March 1959 the telephone rang, it was Yvonne, Kim's mother. Kim instinctively knew something was very wrong, firstly, he very rarely heard from her, secondly, her voice was trembling. Slowly she informed Kim that his twenty-seven-year-old brother, Johnny, had passed away the day before after a short fight with cancer. Kim just froze, not believing what he was hearing. The tone of Yvonne's voice reminded Kim of when he heard the news of his father's strange death, fifteen years earlier.

Kim assured his mother that he would return home immediately without telling her of the risks involved. He took a massive gamble and flew back to England, heartbroken, it would have been terrible insult to his mother and relatives if he had been arrested at his own brother's funeral.

This chapter of Kim's life is vague because although Kim confided in me, he would always prefer not to discuss Johnny. About twenty years ago I first asked Kim various details concerning Johnny's death, his eyes welled up and he just simply and quietly said that he didn't want to discuss it. I never mentioned Johnny again.

While Kim was in the London to attend his brother's funeral, he obviously saw Samantha Eggar but their relationship was waning due to the fact that Kim was away most of the time in Tangier. She was also aware of his predicament regarding the French authorities and the possibility of arrest in England. There was the added problem that Samantha had also become romantically linked to the actor Terence Stamp.

*(Later, Samantha Eggar starred with Stamp in the cult movie 'The Collector'. The film was nominated at the 38th Academy Awards for best Actress in a leading role, best director and best written screenplay. She won the best actress award at the Cannes film festival and also won a Golden Globe award for best performance by an actress in a motion picture drama.)*

Samantha moved to Beverly Hills in California but kept in contact with Kim in London for the rest of his life.

Following Dors' divorce from Hamilton, Dors discovered that her company, Diana Dors Ltd., was seriously in debt. Hamilton had steered the company toward the dual purpose of publicising his wife and helping himself. He had under paid tax bills to establish

his own financial stability. Dors had been forced by
Dennis Hamilton to sign over all of her assets on their
separation and she needed to pay her divorce lawyers and
accountants. She therefore agreed to the suggestion of
agent Joseph Collins, who was Joan Collins' father, to
undertake a theatre-based cabaret tour entitled, 'The Diana
Dors Show'. Yeardye and Dors hired the comedian,
Dickie Dawson, who worked in New York, to script the
show and write most of the material but Dors started a
relationship with Dawson and ended the relationship with
Yeardye.

Diana Dors returned to England from America in
April 1959. She had married Dawson after a whirlwind
romance in New York the previous week. Tommy
Yeardye, had subsequently looted her cash deposit box at
Harrods of £15,000 and then sold his story to the press.

Dors was totally broke and bankruptcy was looming.
She had to accept an offer from the News of the World
newspaper for an expose on her life. They wanted it to be
saucy and revealing. Dors, being her open and honest self,
gave it all. It was a twelve-week serialisation, and sadly for
Dors, it ended up looking cheap and tacky. The journalist
sensationalised her ex-husband Hamilton's addiction to
sex, and Dors was disappointed that her stories were
embellished to sell more Sunday morning papers. She had
a number of telephone conversations with Kim during this
time and agreed to exclude him out of her revelations, Kim
was relieved.

The resulting backlash was phenomenal. Dors came
under some of the worst attacks she had ever experienced
and the Archbishop of Canterbury denounced her as a
wayward hussy.

Campaigners for decency stated the best thing she
could do for her unborn child was to have it adopted at
birth. The British public, although lapping up the scandal
and sensation, condemned Dors for allowing such stories
to be printed.

Kim spoke to Dors whenever possible. They would discuss their individual problems for hours. They had become real soulmates and totally confided in each other. Dors turned to Kim for help in recovering the £15,000 that Yeardye had stolen. Kim contacted Billy Hill, and was referred to the Kray twins, who he had already met in Tangier. He duly telephoned Reggie Kray who loved to be associated with anything to do with show business. After Reggie had listened to Diana Dors' dilemma, he invited Kim for Sunday lunch. Reggie suggested they meet at his mother, Vi's, home in London's East End, it was an eventful lunch.

Ronnie Kray was also there. He was in a difficult mood and was becoming very agitated by the sound of continual dog barking coming from their neighbours' front garden. He rose from his chair and stormed out to the adjoining house. He found the small dog and hacked its head off with a knife right beside the neighbour's front door. The door was now open and one hell of a commotion had started. Ron then threw the dog's head into their hallway past the open door. He returned a few moments later smothered in the animal's blood. The neighbours amazingly did not call the police, presumably through fear of Violet Kray's twins. The lunch was conducted in hushed whispers and the atmosphere was bleak, but Reggie assured Kim that they would have a 'word' with one of their many bent police officers and make sure Dors would see her cash again.

Kim left the small house feeling a nervous wreck. It was the last time he ever ate a meal with the Krays.

Amazingly, Yeardye was forced to return the cash in the presence of police officers, while the actress counted out every last penny dressed in a champagne-coloured sheath dress with a golden belt and wearing heavy golden earrings.

**"He has never looked after my business affairs; we are completely finished,"** she said.

But Yeardye was not so easily shaken off, a few weeks later he was reported to have enquired at a Zurich bank about one of the actress's accounts.

*"Why does Yeardye do this to me? I have made him what he is today. Everything he owns I bought for him. Last week, I gave him £1,000 to go and get lost. Why doesn't he?"* she demanded tearfully.

If only Yeardye had realised the police were working for the Kray twins.

This brought negative publicity to her new show, but the audience numbers remained high, which allowed Dors extra time to explain her affairs to the subsequent H.M. Revenue investigation of her cash holdings.

Kim returned to the ski school only to receive another blow by telephone, it was Dors again, this time to inform him that Dennis Hamilton had died from tertiary syphilis. Nobody was very upset, but Dors did attend his funeral.

As Dors' friend, the singer, Dorothy Squires, once said: *"He treated Diana like something you'd scrape off the bottom of your shoe, yet she had nothing but praise for him after he died. It really was a case of good riddance to bad rubbish."*

She was facing enormous debts left by Hamilton, although amazingly, one of Hamilton's business partners did very well by his death, he took ownership of Hamilton's yacht, moored in the south of France.

By October, there was a warrant out for Kim's arrest in both France and the United Kingdom. The French authorities were closing in on Kim and McKew and after a local 'tip off' on November 18th Kim rapidly fled to Ceuta, crossing the border to Spanish Morocco. McKew stayed at the ski school thinking that Kim had overreacted, but on November 20th he was arrested and thrown in to the Kasbah prison. After a few days McKew was moved to another foul jail in Rabat. He was then flown to Toulouse on November 22nd and driven to Aix-en-Provence where eighteen months previously, an appeal court had added two years to his three-year sentence.

He was sent to Les Baumettes prison which had the reputation of being the toughest prison in Europe. It was built like Colditz and still had a guillotine.

Kim roamed around North Africa for five weeks and finally on January 1st 1960, still mourning his brother's death and having a very lonely thirtieth birthday, made an arrangement with Scotland Yard to surrender and return to the United Kingdom the next day.

On January 2nd 1960, Kim was arrested with a French police warrant at London Airport upon his arrival. He was remanded into custody to await extradition to France at Brixton Prison.

He appealed the extradition order and appeared at Bow Street Magistrates Court on the 13th January 1960 charged with robbery and theft.

Barbara Warner's statement read:

*"He asked me if I knew where the key to my Father's safe was and said that if I did not help him he would tell my Father about events that had happened the previous year."*

She went on to describe how Kim had helped himself to bundles of cash.

*"He then took out a handkerchief and carefully wiped the walls and the safe to wipe out the fingerprints."*

She added the handkerchief detail cementing his reputation as 'Gentleman Thief, a modern-day Raffles.

The court described Kim as:

*"Michael Caborn-Waterfield, known as 'Dandy Kim', is thirty-year-old company director. He is seductive, witty, courteous, unscrupulous and the possessor of a criminal record."*

(Kim's criminal record was established when he had his fight with Dors's husband, Dennis Hamilton, in the Embassy club and was 'bound over'.)

The case was adjourned until February 17th 1960 and Kim was released upon a £12,000 bail. The bail was put up by twenty-three-year-old Sara Skinner, the heiress, who had always adored Kim and would have willingly married him and supported him forever.

The same day Kim heard that Dors had just given birth to her first child.

Despite Kim's lawyer's pleas to the Home Secretary, Rab Butler, to intervene, Kim was found guilty on all charges on March 9th 1960 and was sentenced to four years' imprisonment and a court order to repay the sum of £25,000 plus interest, being the entire amount stolen from Jack L. Warner's safe in the south of France. He was also ordered to serve his term in a French jail and immediately extradited to France.

Kim boarded the aircraft bound for Paris under police escort; the aircraft was full of British journalists. He then learnt that he could actually serve up to five years' imprisonment under French law. He even told the Daily Mirror's journalist Hugh Saker who was on the flight:

**"There's absolutely nothing I can do about it, though I shall try to fight it in any way possible. I just don't know what's going to happen to me."**

Kim was now 30 years old, broke with no credibility left, but he still owned half of the ski school in Tangier.

Upon his arrival in Paris, he was transferred to Fresnes Prison, which was the second largest prison in France, located in the town of Fresnes, Val de Marne, south of Paris. It was a large men's prison with about 1200 cells. Kim became Prisoner No 6544.

Worse was to follow. The senior prison governor immediately took a particular dislike to this very unlikely prisoner and set him up as an example giving him two hundred days' solitary confinement in cell number 140.

During this hopeless loneliness Kim was convinced that he should somehow make contact with the French advocate, Michel Koenig and use the Elsa Maxwell dossier as leverage with Warner and the French authorities for his freedom.

One morning Kim was watched by a Daily Mirror reporter being let out for his morning exercises, it comprised of a ten-minute shuffle around the prison yard. The journalist wrote:

**'Dandy Kim was clomping around the prison yard in his hob nail boots, surrounded by murderers and tommy gun bandits, more bad publicity for England.'**

The publicity surrounding the 'L'Affaire Warner' convinced the French authorities that Kim represented a danger to the system and swiftly moved him to the infamous La Maison De Poissy high security prison for a couple of months.

Back in London, Sara Skinner had been constantly hounded by press, she seemed to enjoy the publicity and pledged her love for Kim at any opportunity and even gave an interview stating:

**"I love Kim, we are engaged and I will marry him in prison if necessary."**

Her highly-respected father was livid and Kim was bewildered.

In the summer of 1960, McKew was transferred from Les Baumettes prison to Fresnes prison, where Kim had recently been returned to, they hadn't seen each other for over a year. They both agreed that the Elsa Maxwell dossier was all they had to bargain with.

From her London base, Sara Skinner was always thinking about Kim and wondering how she could win his affection and loyalty on a permanent basis. She desperately wanted to be with Kim and have him back in London. She therefore employed the services of the French barrister Pierre Pasqini and the legal intricacies began.

The situation reached a climax a few weeks later when Kim was summoned to the prison governor's office and duly introduced to Maitre Suzanne Blum, acting for Jack L. Warner and Pasqini. They were sitting with the prison governor and a guard.

Maitre Suzanne Blum was not a woman to be trifled with, she was ugly and authoritative. Blum is an unusual name and Kim remembered how charming Lilo Blum was at the stables many years before, this woman was the complete opposite.

He reflected and later said:

*"That Blum woman was bloody terrifying. I realised while sitting in the governor's austere office what a fuck up I had made of my life, I was only thirty years of age, what were the next few decades going to bring? If only I had known."*

Everyone in the office spoke fluent English and Maitre Blum methodically explained that she had been advised by Jack Warner of delicate matters that he had been unaware of when he made his accusations of theft.

She then announced that she had in her possession a document that could ensure Kim and McKew's immediate freedom. She certainly had Kim's attention. The document was basically an agreement to return Elsa Maxwell's dossier immediately, repay the sum of £25000, swear a forty year 'Oath of Silence' and sign a non-disclosure agreement.

Kim pondered, firstly he had never taken the entire sum of money from Warner's safe, merely the money that Barbara had owed him, he always had presumed that Barbara had pocketed the rest of the money and lied to her overpowering father.

Warner once said:

*"If I'm right fifty-one per cent of the time, I'm ahead of the game."*

Well, this time he was wrong. He was worried stiff that if Kim and McKew remained in prison, they could 'spill the beans' which could have caused both terrible social and political repercussions.

Kim agreed to return the file and sign the 'forty-year non-disclosure agreement' provided the legal claim for £25,000 was rescinded by Warner. An agreement was reached, Kim, and McKew, were released after serving only fourteen months in prison.

Maitre Blum had the reputation of being one of France's toughest lawyers. She was born in 1898 and began to practice in 1922. During her career, she had represented Warner Brothers against the composer Igor Stravinsky, converting his damages from $1,000,000 to $1. She also represented Twentieth Century Fox, MGM, Charlie Chaplin, Walt Disney and Rita Hayworth during her divorce from Aly Khan. The most important client during Maitre Blum's career was the Duke and Duchess of Windsor.

The pieces of the jigsaw puzzle were now coming together. Elsa Maxwell had obviously confessed the contents of the dossier to Warner, and the Windsors had also found out that Maxwell was in possession of highly sensitive information, the two parties had joined forces and used the mighty forces of France's most prolific lawyer to negotiate the dossier's return.

Having paid out massive legal fees Sara Skinner travelled to Paris to bring the love of her life back to London.

Pierre Pasqini later said:

**_"She tells me that she loves this chap."_**

Kim later said:

**_"I was happy to give that pledge and keep silent; I was thirty years old with a life to live and God I wanted to live it."_**

Some years later, Sara Skinner eventually moved to Marbella and became romantically involved with her prodigy Alejandro Valeja-Nagera, a Spanish ex barman from the newly opened Marbella club. He was known as 'The Gypsy'. Kim was finally 'off her hook'.

Later in the 1960's, Tommy Yeardye met the trendy hairdresser Vidal Sassoon and went into partnership with him to market his hair care products. He remained Sassoon's partner until 1981, helping to make the Sassoon product line a global brand and himself a multi-millionaire. He went on to buy the Jimmy Choo shoe business for his daughter and he remained chairman until his death in 2004.

Maitre Suzanne Blum's services were retained by the Duchess of Windsor. As the Duchess became older, Blum took over the Duchess's house, reinterpreted her wishes, quaffed her champagne, ate from her china, and spoke on her behalf. There is a staggering inventory of all the Windsors' missing objects, paintings and jewels, including twenty-five bespoke Van Cleef & Arpels pieces, which should rightfully have come back to Britain. Instead, they slipped into the evil hands of Maitre Blum.

Blum even prevented the Duchess from leaving her room and barred her friends from visiting, lest it be noticed that the royal treasures were disappearing. Some of these Blum pocketed, others she gave away. Most she sold for preposterously low prices.

The manuscripts and dossiers Wallis wanted destroyed such as 'Elsa Maxwell's dossier' and the 'love letters' between herself and the Duke, Blum kept for future publication and insurance.

The Duke of Windsor died in 1972, the Duchess died in 1986 and Blum finally died in 1994. None of the objects or private files have ever been recovered.

Kim was never quite the same after serving time in jail. He was paranoid about ever returning to America. He was convinced that Warner had used his influence in the States with J. Edgar Hoover to create both a C.I.A. and an F.B.I. file on him, Kim never returned to the U.S.A. or France again.

Kim knew that he had his security locked away if he ever needed it.

171

Kim appearing at Bow Street Magistrates Court with
Sara Skinner.  Kim's extradition to France.

Diana Dors & Tommy Yeardye, Maitre Suzanne
Blum & Fresnes Prison near Paris

# CHAPTER SEVENTEEN

## DEATH AT THE DORCHESTER
## (1961)

Kim was only thirty-one years of age. He returned to London with Sara Skinner and Bobby McKew, they were free men.

They couldn't believe their luck, when they were picked up at London Airport by a chauffeur driven Bentley S1 Continental and taken to the Dorchester Hotel on London's Park Lane. All Kim's old chums had clubbed together and reserved the Oliver Messel suite at the hotel for his arrival. He had become the ultimate hero and rascal amongst the 'Chelsea Set'.

Sara Skinner was disappointed because a welcome home party was planned that evening and she wanted to be alone with him at her home. After a row, Sara was very upset and left the hotel.

All the usual crowd started arriving, including Stephen Ward, Robert Pilkington, Lucien Freud, John Burke and John Aspinall. They had all excelled themselves and brought a menagerie of London's most beautiful and sexy girls with them for Kim's appraisal.

It was a wonderful homecoming and as the evening drifted into the early hours, Kim was left with three of the best-looking girls. He was in heaven and didn't emerge from the suite for three days.

As Kim later said:

***"That was a serious party, plenty of hoof with a proper desert. Three girls, for three days… perfect."***

It was even rumoured that Peter Collinson used this scenario in 1969 when he directed Michael Caine leaving prison at the beginning of the original movie, 'The Italian Job', except he filmed the scene at the Royal Lancaster Hotel instead.

Paradoxically, Johnny's death was a life line for Kim. He inherited the bulk of Johnny's estate and McKew sold Kim's half share of the ski school in Tangier back to Billy Hill. For once, Kim was not in financial trouble and he actually had real money in the bank.

Bobby McKew linked up on a more formal basis with Billy Hill. Hill had continued to run gambling dens, but now McKew began to host his own gambling evenings. He operated in his wife Aggie's club in Gerrard Street called Le Cabinet and had one 'high rollers' game in Eaton Square.

During the next few weeks, Kim returned to Paddon Brothers in Cheval Place and treated himself to a second-hand Bentley Continental, it was almost identical to the car that he was picked up from London Airport a few weeks before; he was swayed into buying the car because it was finished in dark blue, Kim's favourite colour.

One night, he took a two-minute stroll down Park Lane to dine at Les Ambassadeurs club and then to taste the delights of the Milroy nightclub upstairs. The lights were low and the tone was set by his old friend, the lecherous band leader Paul Adam, who always ensured that Kim had his favourite alcove table.

Les 'A' was the favourite dining spot for film producers and directors, which, in turn, made it extremely popular with film stars, starlets and the beautiful models of the moment. Most of the latter were stunning and after dinner conspired to dump their older escorts and make their way to the Milroy.

Errol Flynn was a member of the club and always said:

**"The wildest, most beautiful girls in the World were to be found in London and most of them practically lived at the Milroy."**

One of the sexiest and randiest girls who frequented the club was the beautiful, but married, Mariella Novotny.

174

She was nineteen years old and supposedly born in Czechoslovakia. Kim had previously met her through his old friend Stephen Ward, the osteopath and party organiser. According to Christine Keeler, Wards latest prodigy, her real name was Stella Capes. She had changed it to Mariella Novotny because it 'had a more whiplash ring to it'. She also claimed that she was the niece of the former President of Czechoslovakia.

Mariella had married Horace Dibben, a very wealthy antique and 'official secrets' dealer known as 'Hod' the year before. They had a lavish ceremony at Caxton Hall and one hundred guests drank champagne at Dibben's West End club, the Black Sheep afterwards. Dibben announced that he had given Mariella a twenty room, sixteenth century mansion in Sussex and a luxury flat in Eaton Place for a wedding present. Her engagement ring was a two-hundred-year-old diamond. Hod owned nightclubs in London's Shepherd Market and Mayfair. Visitors to his nightclubs included Princess Margaret's husband Anthony Armstrong-Jones, the Duke of Kent, Christine Keeler's friend Lord Astor, Stephen Ward and the Kray twins who supplied young boys to wealthy men.

Hod and Mariella had an open marriage and organised many parties with Stephen Ward that were nothing more than outright orgies involving diplomats, politicians and young girls. Mariella was suspected of being a Communist from Czechoslovakia and of being a tool of the British security services.

She may have been used by some shadowy elite that involved agents of Mossad, the KGB, the CIA and MI6. Mariella had just returned from America where she had been at a party held by singer Vic Damone and shown into a bedroom where she had sex with the President elect John F. Kennedy.

It was rumoured that she had played a sex game called 'nurse and patient' while sleeping with Kennedy in Washington. Damone's Asian girlfriend had made an unsuccessful suicide attempt at the party and had been found in the bathroom with her wrists slashed. The apartment quickly emptied. Kennedy disappeared with his bodyguard and his associates. The incident was hushed up, but Novotny was arrested on March 3rd 1961 by the FBI and charged with soliciting. The FBI case against Novotny was eventually dropped.

On May 31st 1961, Novotny boarded the Cunard liner Queen Mary using the false name of Mrs R. Tyson. By the time the ship reached Southampton, the British immigration authorities had received word from the FBI that Tyson was really Mariella Novotny and that she was wanted in the United States in a 'sex for sale' case which involved politicians in 'high elective offices and the United States government'. Novotny had returned to running sex parties in London. So many senior politicians attended that she began referring to herself as the 'government's Chief Whip'. As well as British politicians, such as John Profumo and Ernest Marples, foreign leaders such as Willy Brandt and Ayab Khan attended these parties.

Kim left the club, somewhat inebriated and tired, in the early hours of the morning, he nearly fell over her.

*"Getting a little air?"* Mariella murmured in a soft sensual voice.

She seized Kim's hand and they weaved their way up Park Lane on foot back to the Dorchester. After great difficulty in negotiating the lift, Kim poured a nightcap back in the suite. He decided to take a quick cold shower was the only way to bring himself back to life. Glowing from a brisk towelling, he walked naked back to the bedroom to find Mariella, equally nude, had passed out on the bed.

After ten minutes of cajoling, shouting, slapping and pinching her, he came to the terrible realisation that she must be dead. He couldn't find a pulse or detect a heartbeat and rushed for his shaving mirror and held it to her mouth. Nothing; not a whisper of a breath. He tried again, the same, absolutely nothing. Now he really believed that she was dead. He grabbed the bedside telephone and called the switchboard. No response, he tried again, the same. God knows what number he was dialling; he was absolutely pissed. The enormity of the problem suddenly hit him. A naked girl who might be a spy was in his bed! Artificial respiration? Kim leapt back onto the bed and straddling her back, he began to massage her like fury, until he remembered that she should be on her back. He then struggled to turn the dead weight of a lifeless body and gave another five minutes of mouth-to-mouth resuscitation. After a furious amount of breast massage, Kim was exhausted, and Mariella was dead!

Kim grabbed a brandy glass and tilted it between her bluish lips, no effect, the alcohol just dribbled down her chin. He finished the rest of the brandy and poured another. He tried the switchboard once more, it was useless. Kim was shitting himself, just having been released from jail and now a dead girl in his bed. He conjured thoughts of being sentenced for attempted rape and murder, at least Jack Warner would have been thrilled to hear the news.

Kim panicked, he seized Mariella's discarded clothes from the floor and flung them onto the bed and began a desperate hour of trying to dress the lifeless body. A nightmare of uncooperative limbs and baffling female attire, he laddered her stockings and the mysterious mechanics of suspenders to hold them up! Panties, before or after? The impossibility of keeping her bottom up as he awkwardly attempted to pull them on, and then the brassiere over the astonishingly erect nipples was yet another problem in higher mathematics. Kim needed another drink before he attempted the north face of the unassailable mountain that the obscenely beautiful dead body of Mariella presented. Kim wondered how the hell he was going to get her back into her evening dress. Two more cognacs later, he managed to stagger the corpse from

177

the bed and bend it over the back of an arm chair in the sitting room. He only dropped her twice and he questioned whether or not dead bodies bruise.

It was impossible. Her slumped body resisted all attempts to pull the dress over the head. Resolution by crisis! He ripped the Norman Hartnell creation right down the back and after a brief rehearsal, managed to drag the damned thing over her body. A few minutes later, he'd pinned the tent back together, only to recoil in shock to find blood on his hands. Kim had pricked himself with the safety pin! He put on a dressing gown and cautiously opened the door, only to see highly polished shoes outside the other suites, it was all clear.

Some minutes later, he leant exhausted against the lift doors draped with a dead Mariella Novotny. As the lift went down, Kim even thought about an inquest, a coroner's inquest! As the doors opened, his shameful prayers were dashed, but there was an improvement. Mariella lay curled up as if she had decided to take a quick nap in the lift on the second floor and Kim lived on the third! For a delirious moment, Kim thought that his drunken strategy could actually work, but he sensed that something was missing, her handbag. He dashed back upstairs to his suite and recovered Mariella's elbow length white evening gloves and Hermes handbag. He tore back to the lift, but the doors were closed, Christ! Was she going down improperly dressed? Kim pressed the buzzer frantically and miraculously the doors opened.

Unbelievably. she was still there. He dashed in and kneeling beside her, he placed the bag and gloves in the corpse's hand. As he turned to flee, he was stricken with a wave of conscience. He lifted the poor darling's head and kissed her lifeless lips.

A sultry tired voice murmured in his ear:
**_"Hell of a… long time getting a drink, Kim."_**
Kim was so relieved. They crashed out on the bed and slept. They woke at lunchtime. Kim was convinced

that Mariella had been on amphetamines or 'purple hearts' as they were known. Never one to miss a moment, Kim spent the rest of the day with the exotic young beauty making love in ways that even he didn't know about!

Kim later said:

*"Never ever in my life had I come across a mover like Mariella. She was only nineteen and I was thirty-one. I was definitely her pupil. I don't know how Hod dealt with her, he was sixty years old! What a lay!"*

Christine Keeler later claimed:

*"She was a siren, a sexual athlete of Olympian proportions. She could do it all, I saw her in action. She knew all the strange pleasures that were wanted and she could deliver them."*

Kim moved out of the Dorchester a couple of weeks later and rented a flat in Chapel Street in Belgravia. Sara Skinner phoned Kim every day and always brought the conversation around to love and marriage, Kim only wanted sex and freedom, it was an unlikely recipe for success. He knew he had to end the relationship.

Kim had only been back in London a few months. He had settled in his new flat and finished with a very tearful and bitter Sara Skinner after an 'on-off' two-year relationship.

He regularly saw McKew who was always trying to coax Kim into bringing his wealthy friends to gaming evenings. Gaming had changed and just been legalised. Billy Hill was expanding.

One afternoon, Stephen Ward passed Kim in the King's Road. He was sitting in his new Ford Thunderbird convertible with two pretty hairdressing girls that he had been on a date with. Stephen stopped his Jaguar XK 150 and walked over to the Thunderbird.

*"Looks like you're having fun old boy,"* said Stephen.

*"I had a good time, just a brief moment of*

179

*depression when I finished with one and started on the next one,"* replied Kim.

*"Aren't they a little young, even for you?"* asked Stephen.

*"Young girls' mothers have a radar that tells them the moment I meet them that I'm no good,"* replied Kim.

Kim invited Stephen and Robert Pilkington with a few girls over for a small party at his new flat in Chapel Street that evening. The verbal invitation suggested clothing was to be jeans, but what jeans! Those worn at Kim's party all, as far as Stephen could judge, had been run up by expensive tailors to be the last word in tightness, and the casual shirts were the best that can be bought, with their owner's initials embroidered on them. Kim wore his roll neck shirt, cavalry twill trousers and his signature suede Chelsea boots.

Kim told Stephen how once a friend stole a woman whom he was fond of from him. Kim took the man's car, unfixed the panels on the inside of the doors and filled them with fish, then fixed them back and returned the car. For a few days, the motor smelled more or less as it always had. About a week later however, a most terrible smell became increasingly potent throughout the car. He took it to four garages. None of them could explain the smell. All that they could suggest was that it might be fish oil in the gearbox. Nobody could cure the smell and he finally had to sell it at a fraction of its value.

Kim told Stephen about his remarkable experience with Mariella Novotny in the Dorchester Hotel, Stephen was fascinated and wanted to know every last detail. Kim explained to Stephen that he has only been truly in love once in his life, it was with Diana Dors, who was no longer available. When Stephen pointed out to Kim that he only appeared to go out with wealthy women, he replied:

*"Fifty per cent of my girlfriends may be wealthy, but the other fifty per cent have equally great talents."*

Three starlets were dancing together in the centre of the room. One came up to Kim and said:

*"Bunny asked me to sleep with her tonight, do you think I should?"*

Kim replied:

*"Well, I'll tell you one thing honey, I don't honestly give a bloody toss. I don't want her."*

Kim called all women either 'Honey' or 'Luscious'.

*"But Kim, she's so wonderful, her skin is so smooth and all brown, she's just come back from Africa and her face is pert and lustrous,"* the starlet said.

The two girls quietly went upstairs leaving one girl standing awkwardly clustered in a corner with mascara caked eyes and her plump bosoms bouncing out of her dress.

*"Stephen this is Jackie Lane, a lovely starlet,"* said Kim.

She was standing sultrily and sexily in her tight skirt, her legs flared apart, peering sideways at herself into one of the mirrors on the walls of the room.

Kim shared a few more jokes with Stephen and Robert but he always remembered when Dors said she had found him sinister eleven years earlier.

After a while, Kim and Jackie Lane ascended the narrow open plan staircase together. Half an hour later they come down, arm in arm, as if to take a bow. Kim looked smugly proud, happy and bright eyed. He escorted her out through the front door which went straight out into the street. It was two in the morning and time to call it a day.

**Mariella Novotny**

# CHAPTER EIGHTEEN

## THE CLERMONT CON & THE FEAST OF PEACOCKS
## (1961 – 1962)

The 'Chelsea Set' had expanded and Kim was recruiting new members, who included Christopher and Valentine Thynne, both the sons of the Marquis of Bath, Suna Portman, Lord Portman's niece, Anthony Blond, the bisexual publisher and Michael Alexander who had taken a lease on 'The Gasworks', off the New King's Road. The honoury members including Robert Pilkington and Suna Portman met most days, usually in the King's Road Chelsea. Their parties and general carryings on had won them the attention of all the society columnists. The scene was very similar to the current television series 'Made in Chelsea', it was just set fifty-five years earlier.

Michael Alexander's restaurant was a curious establishment which looked more like an antiques shop than a restaurant. It attracted the bohemian inhabitants of Chelsea. The staff included London's first transsexual, April Ashley. Alexander was highly eccentric and aggressive; fights often broke out after he had told a punter to 'fuck off'. Alexander specialised in being as objectionable as possible to create publicity and gain notoriety.

The 'Swinging Sixties' was in its infancy and sweeping changes throughout the fashion world were generating new ideas and images. Whereas fashion had previously been aimed at a wealthy, mature elite, the tastes and preferences of young people had now become important. The shape of clothes was soon transformed by the new ideas emerging from London's 'Chelsea Set'. Men's suits had become sleeker and were often accessorised with bright, bold shirts and high heeled boots.

The flamboyant look was in and Kim really believed that he was responsible for influencing the trend of modern fashion.

Mary Quant once said:

**"The Chelsea Set revolutionised the way women and men shopped. Both Duchesses and typists were soon jostling all the way along the King's Road."**

Kim was in an unusual social situation. He was often mentioned in the gossip columns and had become someone that many social climbers aspired to be seen with. He was the perfect conduit between many members of the old establishment who were looking for young girls, sexual encounters and general shenanigans. On the other hand, the young, and often 'chinless wonders' from Chelsea, yearned to mix with both aristocrats and politicians.

Bobby McKew was assisting Billy Hill, John Burke and John Aspinall on their new gambling venture. McKew recognised Kim's potential value as a social networker for the new club that was about to open in Berkeley Square.

One June evening, Kim met up with Stephen Ward. Ward introduced Kim to Peter Rachman, a well-known property tycoon who owned Esmeralda's Barn in Knightsbridge, now the site of the Berkeley Hotel.

Rachman was being hounded by the Kray twins who wanted protection money from him. He had his own army of heavyweight intimidating thugs, rent collectors and enforcers. Rachman tested the Krays by bouncing a cheque on them and he held out, but not for long. He gave the Kray's his interest in Esmeralda's Barn upon the agreement to leave the rest of his business' interests alone. What worried Peter Rachman the most, was that the Kray twins would demand more in the future.

A special police unit had been set up to investigate Rachman and it had uncovered a network of thirty-three companies controlling his property empire. They also discovered Rachman was involved in prostitution. He was prosecuted twice for brothel keeping.

Rachman had married his long-standing girlfriend Audrey O'Donnell in 1960 but remained a compulsive womaniser, maintaining Mandy Rice-Davies as his mistress at Bryanston Mews West, London W1, where he had previously briefly installed Christine Keeler.

Both Stephen Ward and Kim were well known in certain circles for hosting exciting parties, but there was a major difference in their parties. Kim's parties were 'naughty but nice', very beautiful girls from heiresses to hairdressers would be present, but there was no sexual expectation and drugs were prohibited, the parties were just frivolous, flirtatious fun. Ward's parties, by contrast, were an excuse for the guests to indulge in their very complicated sexual perversions, loaded with drink and drugs while being watched over by Ward.

Kim had learnt many of Ward's preferences from Mariella Novotny and had often found Ward's sexuality questionable ever since he had met him with Dors on a film set over a decade before. By this time, Kim also questioned a few other aspects of Ward's complex personality, he wondered how Ward had become so friendly with Lord Astor to the point that Astor had let him have the riverside house on his estate and why did many senior politicians socialise so frequently with him? Was he merely an artistic osteopath? There were other questions too, was he using the girls he knew such as Christine Keeler and Mandy Rice-Davies, who were only hostesses around the London clubs as prostitutes for the social gentry? Or worse still, was he a spy? Kim never asked Stephen Ward intimate questions, it was a friendship based upon mutual social advantage and a fascination of discussing women.

Ward invited Kim and Rachman to a Sunday party at his country home the following week. He suggested that they bought swimming trunks with them because Ward had the use of Lord Astor's pool at Cliveden. Thankfully both of them were already busy and therefore declined. The party went ahead on the weekend of July 8th & 9th 1961 at Cliveden, the country home of Lord Astor. Christine Keeler was among several guests of Ward at the Cliveden riverside cottage. That same weekend, at the main house, Lord Astor was hosting a party in honour of Ayub Khan, the President of Pakistan. John and Valerie Profumo were among the large gathering of guests from both the worlds of politics and the arts. On the Saturday evening, Ward's and Astor's separate parties mingled by the Cliveden swimming pool. Keeler, who had been swimming naked, was introduced to Profumo while trying to cover herself with a skimpy towel.

She was, Profumo said:

*"A very pretty girl, and very sweet."*

Keeler did not know initially who, Profumo the Secretary of State of War was, she was impressed that he was the husband of a famous film star and she was prepared to have a bit of fun with him. The next afternoon the two parties reconvened at the pool, joined by Yevgeny Ivanov, who had arrived that morning. Ivanov was naval attaché at the Soviet Embassy in London and was also engaged in espionage. He became friendly with Ward after being introduced to him by the managing editor of the Daily Telegraph during a lunch at the Garrick Club. MI5 saw Ivanov as a potential defector and persuaded Ward to try and convince him to shift his allegiance to Great Britain.

There followed what Lord Denning later described as:

*"A light-hearted and frolicsome bathing party, where everyone was greatly attracted to Keeler, and promised to be in touch with her."*

Ward asked Ivanov to accompany Keeler back to London where, according to Keeler, they had sex. Keeler was generally outspoken about her conquests yet said nothing about sex with Ivanov until she informed a newspaper eighteen months later.

On July 12th 1961, Ward reported the weekend's events to MI5. He told them that Ivanov and Profumo had met and that the latter had shown considerable interest in Keeler. Ward also stated that he had been asked by Ivanov for information about the future arming of West Germany with atomic weapons. Profumo's interest in Keeler was an unwelcome complication in their plans to use her in a honey trap operation against Ivanov, to help secure his defection. The issue was referred MI5's director general, Sir Roger Hollis.

Kim had no knowledge of what was going on at this at that time.

A few days after the Cliveden weekend, Profumo contacted Keeler and they began regularly meeting at Keeler's house in Wimpole Mews, which was coincidentally rented from Peter Rachman, who was noted for renting his properties to prostitutes because they achieved higher rental income. In November, Keeler left Wimpole Mews and moved to a flat in Dolphin Square, overlooking the Thames, this was where she entertained her friends and perhaps clients.

John Profumo's affair with Keeler lasted until December 1961 which was the same month Ward asked Kim if he would like to attend another party, this time being held by Mariella Novotny, and her husband Horace Dibben.

Kim reminisced the amazing sexual session he had in the Dorchester hotel earlier in the year, and although he understood that they had an open marriage, he didn't want to tempt fate, so he duly declined.

It was the party that became known as the 'Feast of Peacocks'. There was a lavish dinner which included roast peacock, served by a man wearing only a black mask with slits for eyes, laces up his back and a tiny apron similar to those worn by waitresses in 1950's tearooms. He pleaded to be whipped if people were not happy with his services.

In her autobiography, Mandy Rice-Davies described

what happened when she arrived at Novotny's party in Bayswater:

*"The door was opened by Stephen, naked except for his socks. All the men were completely naked; the women were naked except for wisps of clothing like suspender belts and stockings. I recognised our host and hostess, Mariella Novotny and her husband Horace Dibbins. Unfortunately, I also recognised a number of other faces belonging to people so famous you could not fail to recognise them. A Harley Street gynaecologist, several politicians, including a cabinet minister of the day, now dead, who, Stephen told us with great glee, had served dinner of roast peacock wearing nothing but a mask and a bow tie instead of a fig leaf. After dinner, he went under the dining table, I could not put into words what he did then, to both male and female guests. This man was on extremely friendly terms with our Queen and members of her immediate family!"*

Novotny refused to comment on her activities and the man in the mask remained unidentified.

After many delays, John Aspinall finally opened his opulent new club in 1962 and named it 'The Clermont', after Lord Clermont, a well-known gambler who had previously owned the building at forty-four Berkeley Square. It was the first London casino opened by John Aspinall, also known as 'Aspers', after he received a gaming licence under Britain's new gambling laws. The original membership list included five dukes', five marquises', almost twenty earls and two cabinet ministers. Society figures included Peter Sellers, Ian Fleming, Lucien Freud, Lord Lucan, Lord Derby, Lord Boothby, the Duke of Devonshire, Stephen Ward and of course, Kim.

Businessman members included James Goldsmith, Gianni Agnelli, Jim Slater and Kerry Packer. To curb the influx of players, the membership in the club had been

188

deliberately limited to six hundred people. It couldn't have looked more respectable. A smart address in an 18th century mansion in London's Berkeley Square, well-spoken young toffs in dinner jackets, champagne and pheasant pie, beautiful women straight out of Debrett's, and a clientele which comprised of the rich, aristocratic and famous.

But all wasn't as it appeared. Bobby McKew had informed Billy Hill that Aspinall was desperate for money to open the new club. Hill met Aspinall and outlined his proposal for what became known as 'The Big Edge'.

Aspinall found the idea irresistible and the stage was set for one of the most outrageous cons of the century. The gigantic con was being played on hundreds of unsuspecting gamblers, a scam devised by the Marseilles mafia, but which led to millions of pounds being shared by the unlikely and secret partnership of the ultra-snobbish Aspinall and London's biggest underworld boss Billy Hill. Bobby McKew was in charge of keeping an eye on Aspinall and making sure that his boss, Hill, received his half share of the profits.

McKew always encouraged Kim to bring well known people and stunning girls into the casino to boost its social status, this always insured Kim a magnificent dinner, a bottle of champagne and a few complimentary gambling chips.

Everyone knew that gambling was a dodgy business and that the bookie always won, yet for years London's smartest society would gather trustingly and succumb at John Aspinall's discreet gaming tables.

John Burke, the Clermont's financial director once said:

**"Despite Aspinall's genteel airs, charm and smart accent, he was a successful thief and clever conman."**

The Clermont con, known as the 'Big Edge', was brilliant. Marked cards in Chemin de Fer, the fashionable game of the time, would have been too easy to spot. The scam was simple in its execution and depended on doctored packs of cards. A mangle like machine was constructed that would bend the Clermont's cards a fraction, one way or the other, to denote their value. The cards were then put back into their cellophane wrappers, sealed as new and delivered to the club for the night's gaming. A trained 'reader' would then sit in at the game for the house. Since he alone could distinguish the approximate value of his own and other players' cards, he could deduce which hand was more likely to win and make his bets accordingly. The readers were often out of work actors and were well-paid for their work.

As well as playing and reading the cards, they had to maintain a false identity front. Because the bends in the cards were so tiny, they practiced for hours and hours with the cards coming out of the shoe. The con gave them the ability to know if a card was high or low. That was enough to tip the odds and it gave them, and the House roughly a 60-40% edge. As the months went by, that edge turned into millions of pounds in net profit which was divided between Aspinall and Hill. On the first night of the operation alone, the tax-free winnings for the house were about £14,000 (£280,000 in today's money), even by Aspinall's standards that was big money. The members were rich and respectable. It was a masterstroke of psychology. Aspinall knew that they had the money to squander, thus, one-night landowner Lord Derby, who Aspinall seemed to have considered his private piggy bank for the raiding, lost over £20,000 at Chemin de Fer.

They were all there. The 'thick as two planks' drone Lord Lucan, who would later murder his children's nanny mistaking her for his wife. James Bond creator, Ian Fleming, Claus von Bulow and Aspinall's friend Jimmy Goldsmith, who later became a billionaire. Then there was Lord Boothby, who had an affair with Dorothy Macmillan, the wife of the Prime Minister, as well as a homosexual relationship with the villain, Ronnie Kray. There was also the tragic Dominic Elwes who would later commit suicide when he was dropped by Aspinall and all his other society pals.

What's so intriguing, was how so many episodes, involving the rich, the dodgy and the outright criminal, fitted so neatly together to make up this 'Hogarthian Tableau' of a generation gone by.

The Big Edge continued undetected for over two years and was only stopped by Aspinall when his partner, John Burke, fearing an enquiry, decided to take early retirement. He then cut his links with Hill, giving the reason that the scam was getting too difficult to conceal. Amazingly, Hill agreed and bowed out gracefully. It took over fifty years for the whole truth to become public knowledge.

As Kim later said:

**"Jack Warner always wanted my blood, but if I had blown the whistle on this scam, quite simply, I would have ended up dead in a car boot."**

The Clermont Club Berkeley Square Mayfair, John Aspinall, John Burke, Bobby McKew and Aspinall's mother, Lady Osborne.

# CHAPTER NINETEEN

## THE DEATH OF RACHMAN & WARD
## (1962 – 1963)


Kim had a couple of business meetings with Peter Rachman with a view of buying several of his dilapidated properties and refurbishing them for resale. Rachman was an intelligent man with a genial personality. Though not blessed with conventional good looks, being short, balding and dumpy, he had the power to charm women and mixed with all classes of society from prostitutes to the aristocracy. He was flamboyant in the way he displayed his wealth, driving a Rolls Royce, chewing on a cigar and sporting dark sunglasses. Rachman was denied British citizenship on the basis of his racketeering reputation and therefore, he was technically stateless.

Rachman felt it was time to liquidate a part of his massive property portfolio for two reasons. Firstly, the police were continually making enquiries into his business affairs and after a severe heart attack, his health was failing.

Through Stephen Ward and Rachman, Kim also met Dr Emil Savundra who had just formed the Fire, Auto and Marine Insurance Company (FAM). The company took advantage of the thriving motor insurance industry when car ownership in the United Kingdom was increasing and road networks were being developed. FAM offered low insurance rates, with crude, but revolutionary at the time, computerisation in collaboration with IBM.

Dr Emil Savundra led a lavish, high-profile lifestyle, he threw many spectacular parties at his mansion in Bishop's Avenue, Hampstead.

Savundra's activities had included powerboat racing in the Daily Express Cowes to Torquay powerboat race, where many photographs still exist of Savundra mingling with rich and powerful figures. In his first race, he had crashed and fractured his spine, he had been referred by a colleague to osteopath Stephen Ward. Dr Savundra had also become intimately involved with Christine Keeler, and Mandy Rice-Davies.

Kim was on great form because Dors was back in the United Kingdom, filming 'West 11', a crime movie, set in London's Notting Hill directed by Michael Winner. They had a great deal of news to catch up on. Kim was fascinated by Dors' recent infatuation with a New York playboy simply called 'Frankie'. Kim always hoped that she would return permanently.

Kim's negotiations with Rachman were well under way during the late autumn of 1962, when suddenly Kim received a phone call on November 30th from Stephen Ward to inform him that Rachman had died the previous evening in Edgeware hospital after suffering a further heart attack. He was only forty-three years old.

To make matters worse for Stephen Ward, on December 14th 1962, an ex-lover of Keeler turned up at Ward's house in Wimpole Mews, where she was temporarily seeking refuge, and fired five shots at the building. His arrest and subsequent trial brought Keeler to public attention and provided the impetus from which the scandal known as 'The Profumo Affair' developed. Reporters soon learned of her affairs with both Profumo and Ivanov. Suddenly, all hell broke loose.

Desperately, Stephen Ward telephoned Kim and explained that:

### *"The shit is going to hit the bloody fan."*

Needing cash for legal costs, Ward had arranged an exhibition of his paintings and sketches at the Museum Street Galleries for the following summer. The estimated value of these pictures was £19,000, the sketches of the Royal Family, which included Prince Philip, Lord Mountbatten and Princess Margaret were to be priced at £500 each. The others which included Ivanov and several of Christine Keeler were priced at £150 each. The

194

problem was that these etchings were only being lent to the gallery on a sale or return basis and therefore would not generate immediate income for Ward.

Ward offered Kim to sell him some of his artworks at a discounted price in return for an instant cash payment. Kim met Ward and purchased a portrait of his old flame, Vicki Martin, along with portraits of Christine Keeler and Mandy Rice-Davies. He also purchased a pornographic drawing of an unknown woman being sexually violated with a double ended mechanical dildo, signed by Ward! Kim kept the etchings for nearly fifty years.

Paris Match magazine intended to publish a full account of Keeler's relationship with John Profumo, the Secretary of State in the government and the national newspapers reported that Keeler had not appeared in court as the main prosecution witness because it was believed that she had fled to Spain.

The following day Profumo made a statement attacking the Labour Party MP's for making allegations about him under the protection of Parliamentary privilege, and after admitting that he knew Keeler he stated:

**"I have no connection with her disappearance. I have no idea where she is."**

He added that there was:

**"No impropriety in their relationship."**

He also said that he would not hesitate to issue writs if anything to the contrary was written in the newspapers. As a result of this statement, the newspapers decided not to print anything about Profumo and Keeler for fear of being sued for libel. However, the MP's refused to let the matter drop and on May 25th 1963, they once again raised the issue of Keeler, saying this was not an attack on Profumo's private life but a matter of national security. On June 5th 1962, Profumo resigned as War Minister. His statement said that he had lied to the House of Commons about his relationship with Keeler.

The next day the Daily Mirror said:

*"What the hell is going on in this country? All power corrupts and the Tories have been in power for nearly twelve years."*

Some newspapers called for Harold MacMillan to resign as Prime Minister. This he refused to do, but he did ask Lord Denning to investigate the security aspects of the Profumo affair.

Some of the prostitutes who worked for Stephen Ward began to sell their stories to the national press. Mandy Rice-Davies told the Daily Sketch that Christine Keeler had enjoyed sexual relationships with Profumo and Ivanov, the Naval Attaché at the Soviet embassy.

On June 7th 1963, Keeler told the Daily Express of her secret 'dates' with Profumo. She also admitted that she had been seeing Ivanov at the same time, sometimes on the same day, as Profumo.

In a television interview, Stephen Ward told Desmond Wilcox that he had warned the security services about Keeler's relationship with Profumo.

The following day Ward was arrested and charged with living off immoral earnings between 1961 and 1963. He was refused bail because it was feared that he might try to influence witnesses. Another concern was that he might provide information about the case to the media.

In June 1963, the American FBI boss, J. Edgar Hoover wrote an internal memorandum on Profumo Scandal as follows:

*"For information: John Profumo was British Minister of War until his recent resignation following disclosure of his relations with Christine Keeler. Stephen Ward, London osteopath, has been arrested in London charged with living on the earnings of both Christine Keeler and Mandy Rice-Davies who are prostitutes. Ward's operations reportedly are part of a large vice ring involving many people including many prominent people in the US and England including other Ministers of British Cabinet... Other individuals*

*involved include, Yevgeny Ivanov, aka Eugene
Ivanov, former Soviet Naval Attaché, London, who
patronised Keeler and who reportedly requested
Keeler to obtain information from Profumo. Horace
Dibben, British citizen, in whose residence sex orgies
were held is husband of Maria Novotny; Maria
Novotny is prostitute who operated in NYC and was
victim in white slave case involving her procurer, Alan
Towers. She fled to England and has participated in
orgies at the Ward residence. Alan Towers is
reportedly now permanently residing behind Iron
Curtain. Novotny alleges Towers was a Soviet agent
and that Soviets wanted information for purposes of
compromise of prominent individuals; Lord Astor of
England on whose Cliveden Estate sex orgies
reportedly occurred: It was here that Profumo first
met Keeler; Douglas Fairbanks, Jnr, movie actor; Earl
Felton, American screen writer; and many others also
involved."*

On June 14th 1963, the London solicitor, Michael
Eddowes, claimed that Keeler told him that Ivanov had
asked her to obtain information from Profumo about the
nuclear weapons that were being sent to West Germany.
Soon afterwards Christine Keeler told the News of the
World newspaper that:

**"I'm no spy. I just couldn't ask John for
secrets."**

Ward's committal proceedings began on June 28th
1963, at Marylebone magistrates' court, where the Crown's
evidence was fully reported in the press. Ward was
committed for trial at the Old Bailey but was released on
bail pending trial. In his account of the trial, which began
on July 22nd 1963, Richard Davenport-Hines described it
as an act of political revenge:

**"The exorcism of scandal in high places
required the facade of Ward's conviction on vice
charges."**

197

While living with Ward, Keeler and her fellow model, Mandy Rice-Davies, had made small contributions to household expenses, and had repaid money lent to them by Ward. The thrust of the prosecution's case, in which Keeler and Rice-Davies were their principal witnesses, was that these payments indicated that Ward was living off their immoral earnings. Ward's approximate income at the time, from his practice and from his portraiture, had been around £5,500 a year, a substantial sum at that time.

The prosecution's case looked weak. Ward's perceived image had been heavily tarnished in the committal proceedings. None of his well-known influential friends offered to speak on his behalf, and MI5 did not reveal the uses they had made of Ward as a channel of communication to the Russians.

The prosecuting counsel, Mervyn Griffith-Jones, portrayed Ward as representing 'the very depths of lechery and depravity', while the judge, Sir Archie Marshall, adopted a similarly hostile attitude. Ward testified that he had informed MI5 about Keeler's affairs with Profumo and Ivanov. This was denied by MI5.

Towards the end of the trial, information relating to another case, in which Keeler had been a leading witness, was revealed by the Court of Appeal. This indicated that Keeler's evidence in that earlier case had been false. Marshall did not reveal the salient fact to the Ward trial jury that the reliability of the prosecution's chief witness had been compromised, and effectively invited the jury to disregard the appeal court's decision.

Dr Emil Savundra was referred to at Ward's trial as 'the Indian doctor', although he was neither an Indian nor a doctor. Because the scandal centred around the Minister of War, the Russian defence attaché, a well-known actress, call girls and a senior member of the House of Lords, Doctor Savundra did not receive much attention, much to his relief

On July 30th 1963, Marshall began his summing up,

in a speech that was so damning that Ward despaired. That evening, after writing numerous letters to friends and to the authorities, Ward took an overdose of sleeping tablets and was rushed to hospital.

On the following day, Marshall completed his summing up. The jury reached their verdict and found Ward guilty 'In Absentia' (absent from Court) on the charges of living off the immoral earnings of Keeler and Rice-Davies, while acquitting him of several other counts.

Sentence was postponed until Ward was fit enough to appear, but on August 3rd 1963, Stephen Ward died without ever regaining consciousness.

Many people, including Kim, considered the guilty verdict to be a gross miscarriage of justice.

The journalist, Philip Knightley argued:

*"Witnesses were pressured by the police into giving false evidence. Those who had anything favourable to say were silenced. And when it looked as though Ward might still survive, the Lord Chief Justice shocked the legal profession with an unprecedented intervention to ensure Ward would be found guilty."*

At the end of the Ward trial, newspapers began reporting on the sex parties attended by Christine Keeler and Mandy Rice-Davies. The News of the World immediately identified the hostess at the dinner party as being Mariella Novotny.

Various rumours began to circulate about the name of the man who wore the mask and apron. This included John Profumo and another member of the government, Ernest Marples, a British Conservative politician who served as both Postmaster General and the Minister of Transport. Another minister, Lord Hailsham, the leader of the House of Lords at the time, issued a statement saying it was not him. However, Time magazine speculated that it was film director, Anthony Asquith, the son of former Prime Minister, Herbert Asquith.

199

On August 9th 1963, a coroner's jury ruled Ward's death a suicide by barbiturate poisoning.

According to reports, Ward left several notes, one of which read:

**"I'm sorry to disappoint the vultures. I feel the day is lost. The ritual sacrifice is demanded and I cannot face it."**

On the day of the inquest, after a private memorial service in the chapel at St Stephen's Hospital, Ward's remains were cremated at Mortlake Crematorium. In their accounts of the security aspects of the Profumo affair, Anthony Summers and Stephen Dorril provide extra information concerning Ward's last hours, his movements and his visitors. They also quote from an interview with 'a former MI6 operative', who asserted that Ward had been murdered by an agent working on behalf of MI6. The main motive for the killing was Ward's continuing ability to embarrass the government and the Royal family. The method, apparently, was to encourage Ward to continue to take barbiturates until a fatal dose had been ingested. The reporter Tom Mangold, one of the last to see Ward alive, dismissed the murder theory, while allowing that there are unexplained circumstances relating to Ward's death. Novotny refused to comment on her activities and the man in the mask remained unidentified.

Kim said later:

**"Stephen was a strange friend. Dors never liked him. He was cold, distant and a total snob. The poor man was not a pimp; he was just naïve. He was desperate for acceptance by the establishment and believed that surrounding himself with beautiful young creatures would buy him an entrance ticket. The game was up, he had become a 'loose cannon'. He knew too much and he had become an embarrassment to the British establishment, the KGB and the CIA. He stood no chance, he had to go. The girls were for other people's enjoyment, not his, he**

*was merely a voyeur trying to gain popularity by providing willing sexual participants to a very powerful but, kinky crowd."*

Strangely and coincidentally, Stephen Ward's artworks were on display at the Museum Street Galleries during his trial and the publicity surrounding the court case had created a huge amount of interest in the portraits.

Immediately after the guilty verdict was issued, all the pictures in the gallery depicting any member of the Royal Family were purchased by Sir Anthony Blunt, who had been given the distinguished position of 'Surveyor of the Queen's pictures. Blunt's contribution was vital in the expansion of the Queen's Gallery at Buckingham Palace, which had opened in 1962. He organised the cataloguing of the entire collection. It later turned out that in fact Blunt also worked with MI5 and had been a double agent. He had been a member of the Cambridge Five, a group of spies working for the Soviet Union from some time in the 1930's to at least the early 1950's. It was a closely guarded secret for many years, until his status was revealed publicly by the Prime Minister, Margaret Thatcher in November 1979. He was stripped of his knighthood by H.M. Queen Elizabeth II immediately thereafter.

Needless to say, the Ward portraits depicting any member of the Royal Family have never been seen again. One can only presume that the Royal Family did not want any embarrassment that might have been caused by their association with Ward.

As Kim later said:

*"You can't fight the establishment. The Royals wanted those portraits out of circulation. That traitor Blunt was sent to buy them all at any price."*

Kim still often thought about Dors, who was busy touring Australia, where had she begun an affair with a singer named Darryl Stewart. Afterwards, she installed him in the flat of her friend Pamela Mason, off Sunset Boulevard in Los Angeles. This finally led to divorce proceedings being issued by Dickie Dawson.

Kim stayed in touch with Christine Keeler and was in contact with her when he sold his Stephen Ward art collection in 2001.

**Christine Keeler, Mandy Rice-Davies, John Profumo, Dr Emil Savundra and Stephen Ward at court**

**Stephen Ward, Peter Rachman, Mandy Rice-Davies, John Profumo & Christine Keeler**

Stephen Ward, Captain Eugene Ivanov & the Daily
Mail headlines

# CHAPTER TWENTY

## HELICOPTERS HORSES GROOMS & PARTIES
## (1964 – 1967)

On January 17th 1964, Diana Dors counter filed for divorce from Dickie Dawson in America and claimed custody of their son, Gary. Kim was thrilled by the news and thought it might be the catalyst for Dors to finally return home. Dors had been in constant touch with Kim while she was away and was beginning to hate living in Hollywood. Kim was thrilled to hear that she had rented a house in Elyston Place, Chelsea, but a little disappointed to learn that she had fallen for the singer and musician, Troy Dante.

One evening, Dors arranged to have dinner with Kim. She brought along her old friend, Joan Collins, with her new husband, Kim's old chum, Anthony Newley. As usual, Kim enjoyed being the centre of attention and always had a tale for every occasion. He recited the story of their debauched trip to Paris fifteen years earlier, and how the unsophisticated, drunken Newley had urinated in a bidet at the Georges V Hotel. Needless to say, Miss Collins was not amused and the foursome never dined together again.

Kim was becoming bored. He was tired of being part of the wallpaper in the Clermont club, it was too frivolous, and he hated gambling anyway.

It was 1965 and time to move on. Kim knew that the late Peter Rachman had vast property interests across London, and he had previously met many of Rachman's associates. Kim actually went to work! He started buying some of Rachman's squalid Notting Hill apartments at discounted prices and then assembled a team of workers to refurbish the properties. He spent the year buying two or three at a time and actually made a handsome profit. Kim felt this business was slow and tedious and he yearned for more excitement and stimulus.

For years, Kim had dreamed of returning to the countryside and concentrating on his hobbies, flying, fornicating and horse riding. One morning in the Spring of 1966, he was reading the Country Life magazine and saw the most beautiful Jacobean estate near Shaftesbury in Dorset for sale. He telephoned the acting estate agents and agreed to view the property the following weekend. After a speedy drive down the A30 in his blue Bentley Continental, Kim drew up to the large imposing iron gates of Sedgehill Manor. He had mentally purchased the estate, before even knocking on the front door.

After an afternoon perusing the grounds and inspecting the magnificent house, Kim decided he would like to purchase the house and made an acceptable offer.

Kim had fulfilled his dream and thought of himself as a country squire. He just about had enough money from Johnny's estate and the Notting Hill profits to buy the house for around £50,000 (It would be worth about £2,500,000 today). Kim was thirty-four years old and Sedgehill Manor was the first house he had ever purchased for himself. He didn't believe in taking a mortgage out on the property because his view was either to own a property outright or just simply rent accommodation and retain his freedom. The only problem was the question of maintaining an imposing country house with no immediate income.

Although Kim remained in Chapel Street, he travelled down to Dorset at the slightest opportunity. He loved the drive and would ride with the South & West Wilts Hunt. He often reminisced his childhood while on horseback. Kim was reinventing himself and starring in his own show, but still living way above his means. The style he wanted to reflect was only possible for a privileged few.

Kim calculatedly developed a friendship with Dr

Emil Savundra, whose real name was originally Michael Marion Emil Anecletus Savundranayagam. Savundra was known to give the most glamorous parties in London at his mansion, called 'White Walls' in the Bishop's Avenue Hampstead. Savundra wasn't a popular figure; he was very pompous and conceited. Although he was married, he enjoyed extra marital relationships with much younger girls, albeit for a price. Kim was very useful to Savundra because he could always be relied upon to arrive with a bevy of beautiful models at his parties, and Savundra could show them off to his other guests, namely Bernie Cornfeld who also led an opulent lifestyle. Cornfeld was a well-known tycoon who ran a company called IOS. Over the years, IOS had raised in excess of $2.5 billion, bringing Bernie Cornfeld a personal fortune which had been estimated at more than $100 million. Cornfeld used to say:

**"Do you sincerely want to be rich?"**

The saying became a byword for success. Cornfeld became known for his flamboyance and lavish parties. Socially, he was generous and jovial, and generally surrounded by a collection of beautiful young women, including, Victoria Principal, who was later widely known as a star in the TV series 'Dallas'. He had romances with Audrey Hepburn, Alana Hamilton, the model and former wife of the actor George Hamilton, who subsequently married Rod Stewart.

Cornfeld owned a 12th century chateau in France, Empress Josephine's summer house on Lake Geneva, a townhouse at No1 West Halkin Street in Belgravia, London and the Grayhall mansion in Beverly Hills California. He also had his own fleet of private jets for travelling between his magnificent homes. Kim always wanted to purchase the West Halkin Street property from Cornfeld.

Cornfeld was quoted as saying:

**"I had mansions all over the world. I threw extravagant parties. And I lived with several girls at a**

*time."*

The Grayhall mansion was built in 1909 and at one time was the home of Douglas Fairbanks. Bernie Cornfeld's friends included Elizabeth Taylor, Warren Beatty, Laurence Harvey, Princess Ira von Fürstenberg, Richard Harris and Tony Curtis. The Grayhall mansion doubled as the home of rock star John Norman Howard (Kris Kristofferson) in the 1976 version of 'A Star Is Born' starring Barbra Streisand. Cornfeld often entertained the Playboy boss, Hugh Hefner, who would invite him back to the Playboy Mansion parties.

Hefner always described Cornfeld as:

**"The playboy, who could never get enough lovers."**

Kim had his own reasons for befriending Savundra. He envied the Doctor's opulent lifestyle. He wanted to learn the intricacies of running a highly successful insurance company and try to emulate what he thought was in Savundra's highly creative mind. He also wanted to become close to Cornfeld, as they had much in common and a mutual fascination for having multiple relationships with beautiful young women at the same time.

Kim also met Jim Slater, the chairman of Slater Walker Finance at one of the many parties, this contact would prove to be very useful to Kim, later in the year.

Kim also believed that by becoming friendly with these two colourful characters, he would earn some 'crumbs from under their tables'. Little did he know that neither of them could sustain their extravagant lifestyles, and both were to be sentenced to jail during the years ahead for fraud.

At this time, both Christine Keeler and Mandy Rice-Davies published their autobiographies mentioning 'Doctor' Savundra. It might have been their revelations that started Private Eye magazine delving into Savundra's business activities in London.

Savundra was a convicted swindler and fraudster,

born is Sri Lanka. He gave himself the title of 'Doctor', and perpetrated huge financial swindles in Costa Rica, Goa, Ghana and China before coming to Britain. He was best known for the crash of his Fire, Auto and Marine Insurance Company, which left 400,000 motorists without insurance cover in 1966. In an attempt to defend his actions, he made a television appearance on The David Frost Programme. He made a complete fool of himself during the interview by calling the swindled British public 'peasants'. He was promptly arrested and sentenced to eight years' imprisonment for fraud.

Over the next year, Kim started developing the stables at Sedgehill Manor. He built a horse barn for eight thoroughbred horses and ponies. He wanted to start breeding horses and ride steeplechasers. Steeplechase racing over fences is shrouded by the mists of history, but by all accounts, it began in Ireland in the eighteenth century. Its roots were in the fox hunting field, and occasionally horsemen would match up their horses for races over considerable distances. They would race to landmarks such as church steeples, and thus one of these races was a chase to the steeple, or a steeplechase. A steeplechase horse is a thoroughbred. In addition to speed, the steeplechase horse must possess the ability to jump fences at a fast pace. They are usually a little older than the horses that race on the flat, but most of them have experience on the flat.

Because steeplechase races are longer than those on the flat, the steeplechase horse also must have enough stamina to carry its speed over two miles or more. Although Kim was in his mid-thirties, he had maintained his slight figure and kept his weight low. He was still competitive on horseback.

Kim personally interviewed and chose the three young resident grooms. They had to be tall, slim, blonde, single and available. The successful applicants had plenty of duties to fulfil apart from maintaining the horses, they had to keep the main house and the grounds impeccably and know how to behave and demonstrate social graces at the house parties which Kim was beginning to host at the Manor in Dorset.

The mid-sixties were a constant party for Kim. He alternated between Cornfeld and Savundra's exotic parties in London and his own venues at Sedgehill Manor. His style was also starting to gain the attention of the 'Dorset Set', which consisted of Henry, the Marquis of Bath, his brother Valentine Thynne from Longleat, and the Portmans, who lived at Bryanston and owned a major slice of the Marylebone area, in London.

Kim was particularly very attracted by Lord Portman's niece, Suna Portman, who he had previously met in Chelsea. Suna had a Scandinavian mother, she was blonde and long legged, she was also a top model and had been debutante of the year. Suna was a great friend of Mary Quant and was often featured in the fashion magazines and gossip columns. Kim was also very fond of the Marquis's wife, Virginia Tennant, she was formerly married to David Tennant, founder of the Gargoyle Club. She was a tall and elegant beauty with a beautiful smile. The celebrated lions arrived at Longleat in 1966, amidst hilarious publicity in the face of much local opposition, but the takings soared from £135,000 in 1964 to £328,000 that same year. Kim remained very close to Virginia, Lady Bath, and often visited her at Job's Mill, a converted mill with a wonderful maze, situated four miles away from Longleat. Unfortunately, she passed away in 2003.

Kim finally registered his racing colours, sometimes referred to as 'silks'. No two sets of colours can be exactly the same and must be based on a choice of patterns and shades laid down by the British Horseracing Authority. All new colour registrations had a unique body and sleeve combination. Kim chose a midnight blue and cream combination and then proceeded to have matching uniforms tailored for all three grooms. Kim didn't need a girlfriend when he was at Sedgehill because all the now uniformed grooms were pleased to be available for him. He imagined himself as a poor version of Lord Alexander Bath with his famous 'wifelets' at Longleat.

The familiar problem was beginning to arise again. His lifestyle was costing him a fortune, but surprisingly, Robert Pilkington always helped him out when he was asked.

Kim discovered the local airfield at Compton Abbas and with the help of Slater Walker Finance promptly ordered a new Piper Twin Commanche from CSE Aviation in Oxford. Kim undertook a full twin rating certification examination to qualify for a license to fly the new aircraft himself.

Further adding to his overheads, he now had two more obsessions. One was to buy a new Brantly B2B helicopter as was used in the James Bond movie, 'You Only Live Twice'. In order to fly the Brantly helicopter, Kim had to take further training to obtain a helicopter license and be able to land on the rear lawn at Sedgehill Manor. He completed the training in record time at Fairoaks airfield. The second purchase was the latest Rolls Royce convertible, which he purchased from my father in Sloane Street, part exchanging his Bentley Continental. Again, these toys were 95% funded by Slater Walker. All three machines were painted in Kim's racing colours of midnight blue and cream.

Just to complete his image, he purchased the 'Lordship of Sedgehill', which dated back to the Domesday Book, which is a manuscript recording the 'Great Survey' of England and parts of Wales. It was completed in 1086 by order of King William the Conqueror. While Kim was busy buying all the trappings of serious success, he somehow neglected to furnish Sedgehill Manor. There are still people around today who remember the lavish parties, and they recollect the exquisite cleanliness of the house, the pool, and the stables. Once inside though, there were very few chairs, the bedrooms consisted of just very expensive mattresses laid out on the floor. When it came to food, all the guests had to contribute in the kitchen, or not be invited again. There was never a shortage of wine and spirits.

There was also a top-quality hi-fi system which normally blasted out Dionne Warwick or Burt Bacharach music at full volume. Weather permitting, most guests were treated to an aerial view of the estate in the helicopter, Kim would take off from the rear lawn, usually with a bottle of claret on hand! Kim was now spending about three days a week at Sedgehill, flying back to Battersea Heliport in London, once or twice a week, hoping to find the next deal.

Dors' divorce from Dawson had become finalised. She had moved back to Britain and rented a new house in Sunninghill, Royal Berkshire, known as 'The Pavilion'. Kim was so pleased, he invited her down to Sedgehill in the new Rolls Royce to see the Manor and flew her back to Ascot on the helicopter. He still adored her.

A party invitation arrived at the house one day in the Spring of 1967, Kim knew it would be attended by many of the local characters, he attended the Friday night soiree and met the owner of the Royal Chase Hotel in Shaftesbury, who informed him that he wished to sell the hotel due to his age.

The Royal Chase Hotel is one of the oldest and most historically interesting hotels in Dorset. It is situated in Thomas Hardy country, in the heart of the Blackmore Vale on the outskirts of Shaftesbury. The hotel is a former seventeenth century monastery and boasts a most intriguing history. The hotel additionally offers easy access to Salisbury, Bournemouth and Bath with internationally renowned attractions such as Longleat Safari Park, Stonehenge or Shaftesbury's' own Gold Hill. It has thirty-three spacious and well-appointed en suite bedrooms and a large heated indoor pool; all of this is set in the hotel's own beautiful tree surrounded grounds.

Kim was enchanted by the idea of owning the best hotel in the area and envisaged creating a great new restaurant and nightclub within the hotel. The only problem was yet again, he hadn't enough money to make the acquisition. After considering the situation, he approached Suna Portman, whose family were perhaps the most respected people in Dorset and the owners of the mighty Portman Estates empire. Suna loved the idea and agreed to commit the funds, subject to her family's approval. This worried Kim because he was still tainted with the 'Riviera Robber' reputation, but surprisingly they agreed provided that Kim invest some equity himself. Kim agreed to put up 15% of the purchase knowing that in reality, he was broke again. To make matters worse, he was two months in arrears on the Slater Walker Finance agreements relating to the plane, the helicopter and the Rolls Royce. He knew that if he couldn't complete the hotel deal with the Portmans and didn't pay Slater Walker by the end of the third month, Jim Slater would foreclose on all the agreements and repossess the goods. His reputation would be in tatters.

**Kim's home, Sedgehill Manor near Shaftesbury in**

Dorset

Kim's Brantly B2B helicopter

Emil Savundra's mansion, 'White Walls' in
Hampstead

Kim's Piper PA-30 Twin Cherokee G-AVEH

Kim's 1957 Bentley S1 H.J. Mulliner Continental
'Fastback'

**Bernie Cornfeld with 'friends' in London 1966**

# CHAPTER TWENTY-ONE

## HAYSTACKS, HOTELS & HENDRICKSON
### (1967 – 1969)

Kim had to come up with some ideas and fast. Robert Pilkington had agreed to lend Kim the money for the hotel deposit in order for him to honour his word and save face with Suna Portman. He wouldn't help Kim keep his toys. Slater Walker Finance had just foreclosed on the hire purchase agreements and instigated legal proceedings for the return of the aircraft, helicopter and the Rolls Royce. The final settlement figures were just under £37,000 (about £700,000 in today's money).

In a state of considerable stress, he volunteered to return the aircraft. There was no way that he could hide it. In a desperate attempt to keep hold of the helicopter and the car, he asked his grooms to perform the most ridiculous task. They were instructed to bury the helicopter and Rolls Royce under the large haystack at Sedgehill Manor! The grooms thought that he had lost his mind, but Kim, being the eternal optimist, believed his luck would change and he would still be able to pay off the loans in full. He was also aware that if he allowed the finance company to repossess the items, they would be sold off at rock bottom prices and that he would then be sued for the shortfall. It was a sad day; the Piper Twin Cherokee was picked up from Compton Abbas airfield by a qualified pilot acting on behalf of Slater Walker.

Kim spent hours on the telephone with Dors discussing their mutual problems. Dors had just received a High Court writ from the Inland Revenue for £40,208. This figure was based upon years of unpaid taxes, which Dors naively believed her first husband, Dennis Hamilton, had paid. Despite their spiralling debts, the two of them often met for a boozy day out, and both of them were still

216

throwing wild parties without appearing that they had a care in the world. Kim and Dors had more in common than ever before.

As Kim once said:

**"Perception is reality, the substance is irrelevant. Image is everything and image trumps truth."**

In a bid to cut his overheads, Kim gave notice on the flat in Chapel Street and stayed full-time at Sedgehill Manor.

For the next few months, Kim concentrated on the refurbishment of the Royal Chase Hotel with Suna Portman, who had just opened her new boutique in the King's Road, Chelsea. The two business partners really enjoyed each other, but the Portman family, being expert property specialists, were becoming exasperated with Kim's crazy expenditure on the hotel. Kim kept changing the building specifications with the workforce, always finding faults and claiming it was not luxurious enough. He was taking the newly appointed restaurant to ridiculous standards, even insisting that the future guests would only 'drink out of Waterford crystal glasses'. The final bill for the discotheque and sound system was quite ludicrous.

Suna once asked him:

**"Darling, are you expecting 10,000 people for a pop concert in the basement?"**

Finally, the hotel was finished, to Kim's exacting standards, and it opened with a wonderful launch party hosted by Kim and Suna. Lord Portman, Lord Bath and their families all attended, along with many of Kim and Suna's society friends from London. The new basement discotheque named 'Kim's' was a complete success and blared Dionne Warwick until the early hours.

Kim was hoping that Diana Dors would attend the party, but she called Kim in a dreadful state, to inform him that the Inland Revenue had taken out a Bankruptcy order against her and to make matters worse, she had committed to the purchase of her new home, Orchard Manor in Sunningdale. They both owned Manor houses, but they were both horribly in debt.

Kim knew that it would take some time to recover the refurbishment costs on the Royal Chase Hotel and bring it into profitability, but he had no time to play with, he needed immediate income. He met up with Robert Pilkington at his home in Pont Street Mews and suggested that they started an insurance company focusing on high-risk motor insurance for young drivers, Pilkington actually thought it would be a good idea, they had both learnt the intricacies of the business from Dr Savundra. The only reason that Savundra's FAM Company had collapsed was that the Indian 'Doctor' had misappropriated all the premiums into a bank in Liechtenstein for his own selfish expenditure, which had cost him an eight-year jail term.

The plan was to employ a number of representatives around the Country to approach as many insurance brokers as possible, offering them a higher rate of commission if they placed their business in the new company's direction. For old times' sake, Kim decided to call the new company 'The Conalghi Insurance Co.', after his late father. Kim registered the new holding company in Andorra to save paying British taxes. Dors' problems had taught him quite a lesson regarding tax, he always registered his holding companies offshore from now on.

Kim started trying to become sensible, and he voluntarily surrendered his helicopter and Rolls Royce back to Slater Walker as they were threatening criminal charges. Kim knew that his past 'capers' would come back and haunt him if he played games for much longer.

Unbelievably, with the help of Eric Lombard-Knight, the founder of Lombard Finance, he managed to buy a new Rolls Royce Silver Shadow as a flagship vehicle for the new venture, it was specially ordered in navy blue with cream leather trim, of course. The Rolls Royce was fitted with the latest Lear Jet stereo system and the earliest

Storno radio telephone, which had a five-foot-high aerial stuck on the rear wing of the car. The unit in the boot was the size of a suitcase and the call sign was 'heiress'. It was an alluring signal.

During the next few weeks, Kim travelled around the whole country in the chauffeur driven Rolls Royce and succeeded in interviewing and appointing a number of salesmen to represent Conalghi insurance on a commission only basis. Kim had a true flair for promotion and it seemed that the project might just work.

One evening, Kim met Pilkington for dinner at his old friend, Alvaro's, new restaurant in the King's Road. Alvaro had trained at the famous Mirabelle restaurant where he had met up with fellow Italian restaurant entrepreneurs, Mario and Franco. Mario, Franco and Alvaro were to food what Gianni Agnelli was to cars and Sophia Loren was to glamour. La Terrazza was an immediate success and the talk of the town. Everyone from Hollywood royalty, Gregory Peck, Sammy Davis Jr, Frank Sinatra, Elizabeth Taylor to showbiz royalty like Michael Caine, Terence Stamp and Albert Finney frequented the place.

By 1967, Alvaro was ready to go it alone and he relocated to the up-and-coming trendy, King's Road to open up his own place which he simply called 'Alvaro's'. The celebrity clientele followed and soon the name of Alvaro's was the most popular table in town. Less than a week after the opening, Lord Snowdon and Princess Margaret brought friends for dinner. Within a few months, the story spread that 'Alvaro's Trattoria' had become so exclusive that its telephone number was now ex-directory. There were only two hundred people in London who knew the number, naturally Kim not only had the number, but also his favourite table.

Alvaro placed books of matches on the tables embossed with a picture of him with a finger to his lips and the caption:

### *"Sshh! If you know who I am, don't say where I am!"*

It was Kim's favourite Italian restaurant in the King's Road, he particularly liked a young Italian waiter from Ischia called Mimmo, who later opened his own famous restaurant, Mimmo d'Ischia, in Elizabeth Street.

That evening, Kim managed to persuade Robert Pilkington, who was a heavy drinker, that he would have to take a salary out of the embryonic company in order to survive and be able to pay the grooms wages at Sedgehill Manor. Luckily, Pilkington accepted that none of his investments into either the insurance company or the hotel were going to pay short-term dividends. Very quickly, it became apparent that the Conalghi Insurance Company was vastly underfunded and the claims were beginning to mount up, on the surface it looked like Kim ran a wildly successful insurance company which took in premiums, but in reality, the claims were already outnumbering new policies, the writing was on the wall.

The Company was beginning to operate on the novel business model of never paying out on any claims under any circumstances. Inevitably this scheme went very wrong and the 'Board of Trade' were becoming interested in the company's activities. Eventually it all went terribly wrong and Kim was obliged to remove himself rapidly, when the company went into receivership. Unfortunately, what Kim had learnt from Savundra had taken him down the same avenue, the company was hopelessly insolvent. Kim was lucky not to have been jailed. The Rolls Royce was sold off and Kim had to justify the losses to Robert Pilkington.

Licking his wounds, Kim retreated back to Sedgehill Manor. Yet again, he needed to make some fast money. He possessed some real and diverse talents, but his taste was often for quick money, the scam, and the thrill of pulling it off. If only he had chosen to focus on them legitimately, he could have achieved great genuine success.

Kim knew that he had to make financial amends with Robert Pilkington, and over the next few weeks he concentrated on improving the profits of the Royal Chase hotel, his luck prevailed, he was approached by a customer, who wanted to buy the entire operation.

The sale price agreed repaid Pilkington, and Suna Portman was happy to take a profit on the business and concentrate on her new boutique in Chelsea. Although Kim was enjoying country life and his horses, he knew that he had to return to London and find a new project.

In October 1968, Dors met her future husband, actor Alan Lake, during a TV pilot rehearsal in London. On October 29th 1968, she and Lake made their engagement official with an amethyst and silver ring and after a whirlwind romance, they married in Caxton Hall on November 23rd 1968. Kim decided not to attend, thinking that Dors was being very rash and premature.

Interestingly, it was around this time that Kim was recommended to Nicholas of London's new hair salon at the Britannia Hotel in Grosvenor Square. Nicholas groomed Kim, and recommended that he try the new manicurist, her name was Annice Summers. Kim wasted no time with this attractive young girl and discreetly asked her out for dinner. She accepted. Kim had no idea where this date would take him the following year.

One evening, Suna Portman hosted a dinner party with Kim, for a number of guests in Chelsea including her uncle Lord Portman and his solicitor Lord Goodman.

Arnold Goodman was the greatest negotiator of the period. He was solicitor and advisor to the British Prime Minister, Harold Wilson. He was chairman of the Arts Council of Great Britain and British Lion Films, as well as being a director of the Royal Opera House and Sadler's Wells. He was also Governor of the Royal Shakespeare Theatre, a Senior Fellow of the Royal College of Art and an Honorary Fellow of the Royal College of Art.

Goodman, who never married, was one of the chief parties responsible for suppressing investigations by journalists which exposed how Lord Boothby and others were responsible for protecting the Krays from justice earlier in 1965. Official MI5 records declassified on October 22nd 2015, revealed that the association between the bisexual Boothby and the Kray twins had been the subject of a MI5 investigation in 1964. Had the truth emerged at the time, the Wilson's government would have been toppled and a repeat of the 'Profumo Affair' would have taken place. Arnold Goodman was created a life peer as Baron Goodman, of the City of Westminster in 1965.

Kim was fascinated by Goodman. The two men discussed the law and the Kray brothers for hours. Goodman was aware of Kim's history and success with the opposite sex and jokingly suggested that he wrote the first British sex manual. He advised Kim that publication could be difficult, due to censorship laws, but added that if it didn't contain photos of genitalia, he might be able to win the acceptance and approval of the British Arts Council. Kim was fascinated by the idea. Goodman was often portrayed by Private Eye as a sinister 'power' behind the throne' exerting a huge influence on the British establishment. Private Eye often referred to him as Lord 'Two Dinners' Goodman, a reference to his massive girth.

Kim became more and more interested in Lord Goodman's idea and started to investigate the laws surrounding sex and promiscuity. He learned that he could legally write a sex manual to explain in concise and lucid terms, an infinitely greater variety of coital positions than would have previously been within the knowledge and experience of the average man. With the aid of accompanying photographic illustrations, he could demonstrate the physical means whereby enjoyment of the act of sexual intercourse between couples could be both heightened, and prolonged.

Kim rented a basement studio in Glebe Place, Chelsea, a well-known area for artists and bohemians to congregate and practise their arts. He started to advertise for a young attractive couple who would be broad-minded enough to openly demonstrate multiple sexual positions for the proposed new book with a photographer present. The response was amazing, over two hundred couples answered the advertisement, all willing to be photographed in any position that Kim required. After a number of interviews, Kim finally found the perfect twenty-four-year-old couple, he employed them for an agreed fee of £500, upon completion of the photographic sessions. After considerable thought, Kim decided to write the new book under a pseudonym, not only would the gossip columns have a field day if he used his real name, but the whole 'Riviera Robber' caper would be written about yet again. He chose the name 'Terence Hendrickson'.

I asked Kim why he chose this name, and he replied:

*"It was the first bloody name that came to my head and it sounded quite intellectual at the time."*

The photographic sessions actually went very well. Kim had hired a professional photographer and all four of them interacted successfully for three very giggly weeks, during which time Kim had written all the accompanying narratives to blend with each applicable sexual position. He employed a photographic editor who was responsible for blurring any exposed genitalia. Kim named the new book 'Variations on a Sexual Theme' and started to look for a publisher. This was not an easy task. Most publishing companies were conservative and therefore were worried that the sexual subject matter would be controversial. Others were just simply disapproving.

After a few weeks, Kim registered the name 'The Julian Press' and self-published. He ran advertisements in the Sunday tabloids and men's magazines with the heading 'How to Improve your Sex Life by reading Variations on a Sexual Theme'. It was a massive overnight success.

The first edition was duly printed, with a total of fifty thousand copies at a unit price of around fifty pence each. Kim sold every book by mail order for £4.95 plus postage and packing. Kim would wait for the postman to arrive at Glebe Place in the mornings, before scurrying down to his bank with literally hundreds of cheques.

Kim really fancied the manicurist from the Britannia Hotel, Annice Summers. He offered her a job to be his secretary and to discreetly wrap and dispatch the books in the afternoons. They soon became lovers, although Kim had also been seeing Angela Sieff, an ex-model who had married Jonathan Sieff, the heir to Marks and Spencer fortune and a prominent racing driver in 1966.

Incredibly, this little project earned Kim in excess of £250,000 within six weeks after expenses.

Kim was flying high again, it was time for a holiday and a well-earned break, Kim decided to visit Thailand for Christmas and his thirty-eighth birthday.

**The Royal Chase Hotel, Shaftesbury & The Hon. Suna Portman**

Virginia, Lady Bath & Diana Dors

Kim's Rolls Royce Silver Cloud III Convertible before
being hidden in a haystack!

# VARIATIONS ON A SEXUAL THEME

## Terence Hendrickson

Variations on a Sexual Theme by Terence
Hendrickson. A.K.A. Kim

# CHAPTER TWENTY-TWO

## DEUTSCHLAND & DILDOS
## (1969 – 1970)

In December 1968, Kim gave notice on the Glebe Place studio and headed back to Sedgehill Manor to pay all the grooms wages prior to his departure to Thailand. The night before he left, he had dinner in London with Lord Goodman, who was full of enthusiasm following Kim's recent success with the sex manual. Goodman encouraged Kim take the sexual theme further and actually open the first sex supermarket in Britain.

Kim listened intently as Goodman recited the career of Beate Uhse and her sex shops in Germany to him.

The following day, Annice Summers drove Kim to London airport and he flew to Bangkok, first-class naturally. During the thirteen-hour flight, he pondered upon Goodman's words, the previous evening, and wondered whether Britain was broad minded enough for such a project. He checked in at the Mandarin Oriental hotel located on the banks of Bangkok's Chayo Phraya river, the view was wonderful. Kim couldn't wait to start exploring the city.

Kim found the Chatuchak weekend market, which is the ultimate shopping destination in Bangkok. Every Saturday and Sunday, tens of thousands of people come to hunt for bargains at one of the fifteen thousand stalls, or simply soak up the busy and exciting atmosphere.

Eventually, he found an English-speaking dealer who specialised in various oils and foams which were supposed to be aphrodisiacs. It was the start of an on-going commercial relationship; Kim gave the dealer an order for 2,500 cans of Love Foam and 5,000 Go-Go tablets to be shipped to London. He couldn't find a dildo wholesaler as they were illegal in Thailand at the time, which he found unbelievable, considering Bangkok was the sex capital of Asia and maybe of the world.

The city was famous for its go-go bars and massage parlours, the scale and extent of sex for sale in Bangkok was mind-boggling. The girls were not only confined to the red-light districts and most of the massage parlours gave 'happy endings'. Kim was in his heaven; the girls were young and gorgeous. He found a newly opened parlour near the Nano Plaza; it was one of the first to offer jacuzzi facilities in Bangkok. Nothing was out of bounds and Kim very quickly learnt about all the different types of sex operations offering a different range of specialist services from soapy massage to bars that offer oral sex to male customers or to use the vernacular term 'blowjobs'.

Kim carried on enjoying the pleasures of Bangkok for a month and having spent a fortune, returned to London determined to open his own sex supermarket. In February 1969, a somewhat bow-legged but refreshed Kim arrived back in Britain. Annice Summers was at the airport to meet him. Kim could not hide the grin on his face. He had enjoyed the holiday of a lifetime. His next stop was going to be Munich in Germany. He wanted to meet Beate Uhse who founded the world's first sex shop.

Beate Uhse was the only female stunt pilot during the 1930s. Her career as a fighter pilot ended after the war because former members of the Luftwaffe were not permitted to fly. The young widow therefore had to find some other way to earn money to feed her son. First, she made a living on the black market and then she sold products door to door and met many housewives and learned of their sexual problems. The men returning from the war were impregnating their wives, not caring that there was no apartment, no income and no future for the kids. Many women went to untrained abortionists.

Uhse remembered the lectures that her mother, who had died during the war, had given her on sexuality, sexual hygiene and contraception. She researched information on the Knaus-Ogino method of contraception using a rhythm method and put together a brochure, which explained how to identify a woman's fertile and infertile days. By 1947, Beate sold thirty-two thousand copies of her 'Pamphlet X' and began to expand her business to larger cities such as Hamburg and Bremen. Many people wrote her letters, asking for advice on sexuality and eroticism.

She later wrote in her autobiography:

***"These people were totally unaware of the facts of life."***

In 1951, with four employees, she started the Beate Uhse Mail Order Company, offering condoms and books on marital hygiene. Just two years later, the company had fourteen employees. During 1962, she opened her first speciality store for marital hygiene in Flensburg. It was the first sex store in the world. She offered, both in her store and her catalogue, more and more articles for sexual pleasure and marital hygiene. Soon the police began acting against the items in her store, which supposedly served to inflame and satisfy lustful desires in a manner contrary to decency and morality. By the end of the decade, she owned twenty-five shops, selling magazines, lingerie and other stimulatory products.

Kim wanted to gain access to Beate's warehouse in Munich and survey her range of merchandise to collect ideas for his future products. He could not tell her that he intended not only to replicate her brands but also open a sex store in London. He telephoned Beate's head office in Germany and asked to speak to the formidable lady herself. To his surprise, he was put through to her personal office. Kim introduced himself as Terence Hendrickson, the author of 'Variations on a Sexual Theme'. Kim then explained that he was a great fan of Uhse's work and would like to meet her in Germany and discuss the possibility of writing a book about her adventurous and interesting life story. Beate fell for the bait and told Kim that she would be delighted to show him the warehouse and discuss both her life and her products in a personal interview.

As Kim's ex-wife Penny Brahms later said:

**"He knew how to spot a good idea and make it his own."**

In March 1969, Kim flew to Munich and met up with the famous lady. Kim presented himself to Beate Uhse opulently tanned, white polo-necked and wearing his trademark caramel suede jacket. For the first time in his life, he was speechless as he inspected the lines of plastic and rubber dildos in many different shapes and sizes.

Uhse really liked Kim. They were both aviators and had much in common. She showed him all sorts of strange sexually orientated items, specifically designed to increase a woman's libido. Kim was absolutely fascinated, but he had to keep up his facade and pretend to be merely an author. As it happened, Uhse had bought a copy of 'Variations on a Sexual Theme' prior to Kim's arrival, which gave him great credibility. The following day, Kim returned to London with a suitcase full of prototypes, including sex toys and various sexual literature, albeit printed in German. He was very worried about being detained by H.M. Customs upon his arrival.

The Mandarin Oriental Hotel in Bangkok

Beate Uhse, Lord Goodman & Annice Summers

## CHAPTER TWENTY-THREE

## THE RISE & FALL OF ANN SUMMERS
## (1969 – 1971)

Kim rented a Victorian house in the Upper Richmond Road near Putney; this property was going to serve as the distribution centre. After weeks of research Kim found a reliable dildo manufacturer in Hong Kong, he sourced the massage oils and lotions in Bangkok and agreed to purchase various magazines from the Gold brothers, who were unheard of in those days.

Having finally decided on all the products, he started a massive advertising campaign in the tabloid press and a variety of women's magazines. Kim was selling dildos, sex toys, blow up dolls, erotic lingerie, and massage lotions as well as books and magazines of a sexual nature.

Kim was familiar with the mail order business after his success selling the sex manuals a few years previously.

Kim decided to call the new venture Ann Summers, a name, affectionately taken, from his secretary and lover, Annice Summers. Annice was born in South Africa in 1941, as Annice Goodwin, her father had died and her mother brought her to Britain when she was ten years old. Annice's mother married Harry Summers in London and Annice assumed her new stepfather's surname. She was educated at a convent and went on to take a secretarial course, followed by a beauty course. She started her job in the Brittania hotel as a manicurist at the Nicholas of London hair salon in Grosvenor Square.

Kim hoped the name would conjure up the image of an innocent 'English Rose', although he was aware that she was bisexual. He designed the Ann Summers logo as a red apple with a bite out of it, representing the bite that Adam took out of Eve's apple in the Bible.

The new stock duly arrived and within a few months, the new business was going very well, the takings sometimes topped £25,000 per month and £15,000 of that was pure profit. Annice was working flat out and Kim decided that they needed some more helping hands, Annice suggested that Kim employed her friend, Caroline Walker (who I later married) to help her wrap and post the discreet brown paper parcels and generally help with the daily running of the business.

Kim rarely had time to drive home to Sedgehill Manor, he often stayed at the rented house, but before long, he decided to rent an apartment from his old friend Clive Raphael, the property tycoon, at Montrose House which was situated at the northern end of Princes Gate.

His magnetism was flowering, he was back to his old tricks, spending a fortune and living a lavish lifestyle again with three or four permanent girlfriends competing for his attention. Annice was also playing around, Kim believed that she was his faithful lover, in fact she was conducting three affairs, including a relationship with my own father!

Kim celebrated his fortieth birthday on New Year's Eve 1969 and toasted the new decade in with a massive party in London for all his friends including Lord Goodman, who reminded Kim that the original business model used for the creation of Ann Summers, included the opening of the first sex store in Britain. Kim was happy enough with the profits that the mail order business was making, but at the same time, he liked to impress Lord Goodman, and be seen as a great success in the portly solicitor's eyes.

Over the next few months. Kim started looking for a suitable West End property in order to launch London's first sex shop. Eventually, Kim found an available shop unit at Marble Arch beside the Odeon cinema. The rent was ridiculously high, even in those days, but it was the perfect location and it would make an ideal flagship store. Kim signed the lease in the Spring of 1970 and immediately instructed a building company to refurbish the property. The image of the new store had to be a combination of naughty but nice, as well as respectable, so as not to alert various governmental authorities, who Kim always believed would frown upon such an enterprise.

Up until now, the business had been very discreet, but Kim was worried that the opening of the new sex shop would attract a lot of interest from the press and he did not want his dubious and colourful reputation from the past to hinder the business. He therefore created a separate company called Ann Summers (Sales) Ltd and appointed Annice as the company secretary and a couple of nominee directors to protect his own identity.

As Kim later said:

**"Annice was the perfect image for a company which traded on its insistence that it was natural to enjoy sex."**

Kim stayed away from the Marble Arch store and took a 'back seat' role and promoted Annice as the founder of the store, feeling that her image was far more suited to promoting women's sexual aides than that of his own.

Annice was very happy to oblige and being quite sharp and grasping, she negotiated an annual salary of £10,000 per annum and a 40% stake in the new sales company. Kim and Annice agreed to give 10% of the shares to Caroline Walker, who had become close to Kim by this stage.

After many delays caused by the builders, the shop was finally finished and Kim organised a 'grand opening' hosted by Annice herself, on September 9th 1970. As Kim predicted, the shop immediately attracted an enormous amount of publicity. There were literally crowds of people gathered outside the shop, gazing into the window, hoping to see the sex toys and a glimpse of Annice.

As Annice said:

*"What I want to do is make sex open, take it off the back streets and place it in an entirely acceptable and hygienic form on the high streets."*

The shop made a storming start, taking £5,000 in its first week. Dildos, Love Foam and Go-Go tablets were the greatest sellers, but already the store was catching the attention of the bureaucracy and the Department of Health. Undeterred, Kim's optimism and determination were very apparent when he announced the opening of a second store in Bristol at Christmas time.

Kim believed Lord Goodman would be capable of squashing any proceedings that might be brought against the new company by either the Department of Health or the Vice Squad.

Annice revelled in her newly-gained notoriety and she rented a country house in Kent, known as Egypt Farm. The house in Plaxtol village was a delight, but nobody knew that in fact three of her lovers, including Kim, were actually paying her rent at the same time, therefore earning Annice a great monthly profit on top of her salary from the business. She had to plan her evenings at the house carefully so that none of her suitors would ever find out about each other.

The relationship between Kim and Annice was starting to become fractious as she was becoming both more difficult and precious.

Kim later said:

*"Annice was a terrific looking girl, ideal for the role. But we weren't really full-time lovers. It was more an occasional thing."*

Unfortunately, Kim's enthusiasm and zest were always 'over the top' during the embryonic stages of a new scheme or adventure, he was never really interested or focused in what he considered merely, the 'petty details'. The company now needed professional management and accounting in order to survive. Whilst the mail order business based in the Upper Richmond Road carried few overheads, the shops were a different proposition.

During 1971, Ann Summers started to experience problems and the bills were mounting, as was Kim's lifestyle. Annice was becoming critical of the products that Kim was importing and she was further incensed when her monthly cheque bounced. The same week, David and Ralph Gold, property and soft porn tycoons, came to the shop. The company owed them money for a shipment of erotic magazines.

David Gold later said:

*"We were interested in the kind of customer the shop attracted. The thing we couldn't understand is why a shop taking £5,000 a week could not settle a £450 invoice for a shipment of magazines."*

Kim had been using the recent national postal strike as an excuse for non-payment of overdue accounts. The company overdraft had now risen to £78,000 and the bank was threatening foreclosure. The only way Kim could pay this money back was by mortgaging Sedgehill Manor, which he was loathed to do, or put the company into voluntary liquidation.

Annice had another boyfriend called David Jones, who was an accountant by profession, but he also had contacts in Fleet Street. Jones had been secretly negotiating a fee for Annice in return for an exposé by the News of the World newspaper. Over the following weeks, the newspapers increased its offer to £15,000 (about £250,000 in today's money) provided the article was both 'juicy and spicy'. Annice succumbed but kept the forthcoming newspaper article a secret from Kim. Two weeks later, the 'News of the World' ran a front-page spread, allegedly written by Annice, which stated:

*"I think it is correct to set the record straight, and state that I am only a figurehead for Ann Summers. It was really created by the well-known playboy and jockey 'Dandy' Kim Waterfield who I*

236

*have been involved with for the past two years. It was*
*his idea to start a sex shop and sell sex toys. I am*
*only a pawn in his game. The company is broke*
*despite the vast profit margins being made from the*
*imports from Hong Kong."*

The article went on to reveal the financial weakness
of the company and exaggerate Kim's already tarnished
reputation. This was the company's downfall.

The shop was then raided by the vice squad and the
bank foreclosed the following Monday morning. Kim
couldn't believe what Annice had done. He realised the
company was finished, but he didn't know that Annice had
already taken advice from an accountant called Bernard
Phillips, who shortly afterwards appointed himself as a
receiver during its subsequent liquidation.

At the time, Kim said:

*"It was disastrous. Until then, it was perceived*
*as naughty but nice. Her revelations condemned the*
*Ann Summers shop to seediness. I trusted that*
*damned woman with everything. She just simply sold*
*me out."*

Ralph and David Gold were interested in acquiring
the business as a going concern from its ultimate liquidator
and intervened. With the agreement of the creditors, they
bought the shops, the stock, including 15,000 Go-Go
tablets, 3,000 cans of Love Foam and the Ann Summers'
name for £1 along with all the debts. A further discreet
payment of £10,000 was made to Kim in the hope that he
would disclose his suppliers and generally ease the
transition of ownership.

A more sobering encounter took place shortly after
the liquidation started, when a senior representative of the
Department of Health went to the shop and expressed his
concerns over the safety of some of the earlier lines carried
by the original company. He revealed that they were
considering commencing proceedings against the directors
of the original company who might be regarded as

responsible. Kim was unavailable and the only other officer, Annice, who gave her name to the company, said that she had no managerial responsibilities and refused to comment.

Kim and the Golds did not have a pleasant relationship. Kim, unfortunately, remained bitter about the whole saga for the rest of his life.

Kim would always refer to Annice as:

**"That bloody Judas woman."**

A third shop was soon opened by the Golds in West London in May 1972 of that year. They persuaded Annice to return and manage the new store, but she quit again a year later, after problems arose with the day-to-day running of the business. She later moved out of the country and married Murray Resnick, who was one of the world's largest handbag manufacturers. She lived in New York, Miami, Hong Kong and finally as a millionairess widow in a magnificent nineteenth century villa in Umbria, Italy. She had left the world of Ann Summers behind her forever and died of cancer in 2012.

Ann Summers, although still having the shops, ran mainly on the mail order business for the next nine years. It is now operated by David Gold's daughter, Jacqueline Gold.

Today, the company sells two million vibrators every year which amounts to 5,000 every day or seven sex toys every minute! Kim's was spending far too much money, but his concept wasn't wrong.

1970 Ann Summers catalogue, Annice Summers opens
the Marble Arch store & Ann Summers mail order
form

**In 1970, Annice Summers opens the Marble Arch store**

# CHAPTER TWENTY-FOUR

## FIVE PENCE & FOUR NUDE PHOTOGRAPHS
## (1971 – 1972)

After the Ann Summers venture, Kim was broke yet again. He retrenched himself in Montrose House, still smarting over Annice's betrayal and literally perceiving her actions as a matter of treason. He retained Caroline Walker as a part-time secretary whose main job was as a personal assistant to Alan Freeman. Freeman was the famous Radio One disc jockey, known as 'Fluff', who used to introduce the 'Pick of the Pops' show every week. Caroline spent the evenings with Kim cooking dinner for him while he studied legal and case history books. He was out for revenge and was determined to find a legal way of making Annice Summers and the Gold brothers pay for what had happened with his business.

Caroline had to pack an old estate car with food and booze on Friday afternoons for Kim's weekly pilgrimage to Sedgehill Manor, often accompanying him for the weekend. Kim hated the idea of mortgaging Sedgehill Manor and constantly looked to his old friend, Robert Pilkington for financial support. Pilkington always obliged because he had his eye on Caroline Walker with whom he had become romantically involved, naturally Kim encouraged the relationship.

Kim was now back in daily contact with Diana Dors, whose husband Alan Lake, had just been sentenced to twelve months' imprisonment for creating a violent drunken brawl in the local pub near their home in Sunninghill, Berkshire. Dors frequently arrived at Montrose House and Kim would have the task of consoling and calming her.

During this period, Kim would often visit Clive Raphael, who not only lived in the same building but also owned the entire freehold block. Raphael was an unusual character; he was only thirty-one years of age and was a self-made millionaire. He also had full control of Land & General Developments Ltd, a major property company which had two subsidiary companies. One was a printed greeting cards business, the other was an engineering company which was an umbrella to three further companies, one of which was the Sterling Armament Company which had recently supplied the Malaysian government with a large quantity of sub-machine guns.

Raphael had just bought himself a Beagle 206 twin engine aircraft from GKN out of the immense profits from the arms deal and converted his Private Pilot's Licence to incorporate a twin-engine rating. The two men had much in common; they both loved flying, women, property and had a mutual understanding of the arms business.

Raphael was sympathetic towards Kim's recent downfall due to the collapse of Ann Summers and did not press him for the outstanding rent he owed. Clive had been dating Britain's first transsexual, April Ashley. April was unimpressed when she first met the millionaire playboy, she put aside her misgivings aside to holiday with him in Beirut and Majorca but the relationship did not last. Raphael then dated and married a much younger model by the name of Penny Brahms, who was the Vogue model of the year in 1968. Penny Brahms was born in 1951 and had been in a few movies including, 2001: A Space Odyssey (1968), Lady Chatterley Versus Fanny Hill (1971), Games That Lovers Play (1971) with Joanna Lumley and Dracula A.D. 1972 (1972).

Old habits die hard. Kim was mesmerised by the twenty-year-old actress, who he nicknamed 'Jaime'. He often took the lift up to Clive's flat, really just hoping to see Jaime, before long Jaime realised what Kim's intentions were and the two of them started to secretly meet of a day. Penny Brahms was twenty years younger than Kim and

Raphael was aware of the situation. Surprisingly, everyone remained friendly and Raphael quickly used the situation as an excuse to serve divorce proceedings on Penny, claiming that she had committed adultery with nine different men.

The divorce was never finalised because on March 6th 1971, Raphael planned a flight with a new girlfriend and his parents to Toulouse in France. The Beagle 206 aircraft (G-AVAL) left Leavesden airfield at 08.45 am for Luton Airport where customs clearance was obtained. At 10.00 a.m. Raphael filed a flight plan and the aircraft duly took off at 10.50 a.m. The aircraft followed a route around London at an altitude of 1,500 feet, before climbing to 5,500 feet across the English Channel. The flight time was estimated to be 3½ hours, cruising at 180 knots and all the flight preparations were satisfactory.

Raphael had underestimated the meteorological conditions. At 11.55 a.m., Raphael changed radio frequency from London flight information to Paris flight information but the latter received no call from G-AVAL. There were serious communication problems with the plane's radio system from the start of the flight and the weather conditions had deteriorated during the trip. Raphael was not sufficiently qualified for instrument flying.

At about 13 45p.m, the plane had reached Poitiers. The cloud base had lowered to approximately five hundred feet and it was snowing heavily, therefore the visibility had dramatically diminished. Instead of climbing, Raphael ignorantly descended the aircraft to about 500 feet in order to try and gain some visibility, not realizing that the wings of the aircraft were icing up. The engines started to misfire and Raphael lost control. The aircraft crashed into a field leaving a half mile trail of wreckage before smashing into a tree and exploding, killing all four occupants.

The fatal crash attracted front page news and many rumours abounded that the crash was an act of sabotage due to Raphael's shady deals in the armoury business. In fact, the French Bureau Enquetes-Accidents, Inspection

Generale de l'Aviation Civile carried out an investigation and concluded in a fourteen-page report that a combination of bad weather conditions and pilot inexperience were the causes of the accident.

April Ashley later said:

*"I heard nothing more of Clive until 1971 when, while piloting his parents and a new girlfriend across France, the aeroplane exploded, killing all four of them. It was rumoured that the explosion was the result of a planted device and that he had caused offence while gun-running to the Middle East."*

Raphael's widow, Penny Brahms, took the news badly especially when she heard the terms of Raphael's last will and testament two days later. Raphael had apparently bequeathed his wife, a shilling and five nude photographs of herself and left the bulk of his fortune and his white Rolls Royce to his good friend, the talented, if devious, barrister Ronald Shulman. Penny Brahms was understandably aggrieved at Shulman's luck and sought comfort from Kim, who did not believe the contents of the will from the beginning on the basis that it was only signed two days prior to the fatal crash.

The press had already written many articles about the crash, but now they focused on Kim's relationship with Penny. They were both regularly featured in the Daily Express' William Hickey gossip column. Kim used the publicity to promote a case against Shulman and publicly accused Shulman of being a forger, not a barrister. Eventually, the police took notice of Kim's accusations and began investigating the case. Firstly, all Raphael's assets were frozen in order to stop Shulman gaining access to the funds, secondly, they began investigating two of Shulman's associates, a Mexican banker called Eric Alba-Teran, the Duc d'Antin and Shulman's twenty-two-year-old mistress, a teacher, named Shelagh Macintosh.

It turned out Alba-Teran used fake documentation to take possession of Raphael's white Rolls Royce which had prompted the first arrest. After interrogation, Alba-Teran admitted to conspiracy, Shulman and Macintosh were then also arrested but later released upon bail. The opportunist Shulman fled the country to Brazil before his committal, setting a precedent for Ronnie Biggs. All of Raphael's assets remained frozen until the case was tried at the Old Bailey the following year.

In the latter part of 1971, Penny finished making the movie 'Games That Lovers Play' with Joanna Lumley and Kim was spending more and more time with her. He enjoyed her company immensely and felt that Penny would be a perfect partner. He was also beginning to feel that it was time to walk away from his illustrious past and settle down in life, Kim had always quietly yearned for a family of his own, especially the idea of having a daughter.

After a quiet Christmas and forty first birthday at Sedgehill Manor, Kim finally proposed marriage to Penny, despite being totally broke. Penny accepted, and a small ceremony was arranged in the local church. Penny's mother, Gillian, was delighted at the new match, saying:

**"She has never been happier. I have met Michael and I liked him enormously."**

The feeling soon passed.

During January 1972, Britain faced a sharp change and teetered on the verge of a general strike for the first time in nearly fifty years. A wave of factory occupations and sit-ins had swept the country. The post-war upswing had healed the wounds of the crisis-ridden 1930's and had served to strengthen the working class. Nevertheless, the difficulties of British capitalism were rapidly mounting. Unemployment was close to a million, inflation was at 8% and growth was stagnant. By February, supplies of coal were so low that many industries were put on a three-day week. There were blackouts and a state of emergency was declared. The Prime Minister, Edward Heath, was terrified and set up a Court of Inquiry under Lord Wilberforce to settle the dispute.

The newly-wed couple were desperately short of money. Kim knew that Phillips Electronics had developed a home video cassette format that had just become available on the consumer market in 1972. Philips named this format 'Video Cassette Recording'. Kim was convinced that this new format was the future and decided to borrow some more money from Robert Pilkington in order to launch a new video appropriately named 'The Joy of Sex'. The purpose of this video was to show as many coital positions as possible and to teach both partners how to be a great lover and consistently enjoy great sex.

Its marketing slogan read:

***'Would you like reliable erections that don't wilt in the middle of lovemaking? Would you like superb ejaculatory control? Would you like your penis to be as large as it possibly can be? Do you want women to sing your sexual praises? All these sexual benefits can be yours when you watch 'The Joy of Sex' and take its message to heart.'***

Kim arranged a meeting with a director of W.H. Smith who agreed that the company would distribute the new video in the U.K. provided that it was endorsed by a governing body and could never be interpreted as pornography. Kim began interviewing appropriate young couples and found an ideal pair. Filming began at West London Film Studios which Kim had rented for the production. Kim won approval from the Arts Council, again using his influence with Lord Goodman. Naïvely, Kim did not sign a contract with W.H. Smith or anticipate the failing economy. One thousand copies of the video cassette were produced which were going to be marketed at £25 each, netting Kim £10' in profit per cassette.

Unfortunately, this was a time of great austerity and W.H. Smith were cutting back, anticipating a general fall in sales. They therefore walked away from Kim and the sex videos, making Kim and Penny's finances even worse. The boxes of unwanted videos were sent to Sedgehill

Manor and kept in the garage block. Kim thought he could repeat his previous success by directly marketing them by mail order; it turned out to be a total disaster. Penny accepted a small part in Dracula A.D. 1972 starring Christopher Lee, Peter Cushing and Stephanie Beacham in order to help ease the financial situation … but everything was about to change.

In the autumn of 1972, the forged will case opened at the Old Bailey. The national press was fascinated by this trial and carried a front-page story most days of the week. The Daily Express had shown specific interest in the case and their coverage levitated Kim and Penny into the 'A list' of celebrities. The case had become known as 'The Shilling Will Case' nationally.

There were various difficulties with the case in as much as if Penny Brahms won, she would inherit the Sterling Armament Company. The company would then surely lose its crucial permission to deal in prohibitive weapons especially since she had since married Kim who not only had a criminal record but was also a rumoured gun runner. The recently nominated chairman of the company Peter Edgington, realised the company needed to be divorced from Land & General Developments Ltd. He appointed John Skelsey of Boothe Anderson & Co as the new financial director to find a purchaser and oversee the transfer. The company was sold for £81,000 to James Edmiston.

By November, the jury had learned that Shulman had forged the will after learning of his friend's death. He had threatened to bash Shelagh Macintosh's head against the wall if she didn't type out a new will in favour of himself. His unfortunate former mistress had typed the will out with one finger.

Her counsel said:

**"She had sold her soul to the devil."**

She was told by the Common Sergeant, Mervyn Griffiths:

*"If you take my advice, you will see no more of this other man and forget this now. You are still young, go back to your family and start again."*

She was put on probation. Eric Alba-Teran, the Duc d'Antin, received a three-year sentence with another year tacked on for appropriating Raphael's white Rolls-Royce. He was also recommended for deportation.

The final verdict awarded the sum of £500,000 to Penny Brahms.

Over the years, there have been alleged Lucan-like sightings of Shulman and, in absentia, he was credited with the 'Shulman defence' to cocaine smuggling. At Lewes Crown Court, so many defendants from South America were claiming they thought the drugs they were found to be smuggling were in fact emeralds. It was deemed they must be receiving expert English legal advice.

With the jury's verdict, Penny Brahms found her one shilling (5p) bequest had grown to something in the region of £12million at today's money.

April Ashley later said:

*"Far more bizarre than Clive's death was his will. In it, he left £500,000, but not to Penny Brahms, his wife. He left her only one shilling and four nude photographs of herself. She challenged it in the courts where the will was discovered to have been a fraud cooked up by Clive's lawyer, a teacher and a Sardinian boar-hunting duke."*

Kim and Jaime were in the money again.

**Investigation Report. A Beagle 206 Series II aircraft.
Penny Brahms**

**Penny Brahms' movies: Games That Lovers Play
(1971) & 2001: A Space Odyssey (1968)**

# CHAPTER TWENTY-FIVE

## ADULT CHAT & ADULT BEHAVIOUR AT THE ADELPHI
## (1973)

After a fabulous Christmas and a terrific forty second birthday party at Sedgehill Manor, 1973 was set to be a great year for Kim. His new wife had settled into country life and there were no financial problems. Kim honestly believed that he had engineered and orchestrated Jaime's recently acquired fortune and took on the task of managing her money. He paid off all the debts, including a small fortune owing to Robert Pilkington, and spent a king's ransom finally furnishing Sedgehill Manor. Kim spent most of this time enjoying his horses and returned to the local hunt, Jaime had also become very interested in the stables and riding.

To help alleviate the age difference between the newly-wed couple, Kim felt it was time to change his image. No more Rolls Royce's. They were too stuffy and becoming common, mostly driven by celebrities and spivs. Many of his friends had Ferraris, so he wanted something completely different. He purchased a new Range Rover which suited his country image brilliantly, naturally it was dark blue. Kim's attire was beginning to change as well, his trademark 'dandy' suits were changed for a more casual look mainly in denim. He had a young wife and he was determined not to appear the 'old man'.

Although life was carefree, Kim was becoming increasingly bored without a new project or business scheme. He often made excuses to drive to Chelsea on business just to get back to the 'land of the living' and see his old Chelsea chums. His old friend, Mimmo, who worked at Alvaro's, had recently opened his new restaurant called Mimmo D'Ischia in Belgravia which became Kim's 'second home'. He loved the restaurant, which was frequented by many film stars and celebrities. Kim had his own table and would always be treated like royalty. He did not know that the new venue had been funded by his old nemesis, Michael Eland who now lived in Paris with his new supermodel wife, Jane.

Kim had become fascinated by a new concept of running phone-based competitions as a way to generate revenue and to pay for the 'prize'. He thought he could apply the same principle by creating adult chat lines. Premium-rate telephone lines were telephone numbers for which certain services are provided, and for which prices higher than normal were charged. Unlike a normal call, part of the call charge is paid to the service provider, thus enabling businesses to profit via the calls. The common misconception was that premium rate telephone numbers were reserved for sales lines and big companies, but this wasn't the case, anyone could set up a non-geographic telephone number.

Kim's plan was relatively simple, he applied his old philosophy. Sex was always one of the easiest services to sell and what better way to keep people talking on the telephone than to open an adult chat line service. The rent and labour rates were cheaper in the North of England so he rented a large office in the Royal Liver Building in Liverpool and booked a suite for himself at the famous Adelphi Hotel.

The first task was to set up a call centre. Kim negotiated with The General Post Office which was the national telephone provider in those days, a flat rate of commission of 3 pence per minute of used telephone time. He then registered the telephone number 0800 069 6969 and called the new company 0800-69'er Limited. Kim advertised for a number of girls or women, whose age and appearance were irrelevant. All they needed was a pleasing flirtatious manner, a sexy voice and be very open-minded. Kim received about fifty job applications and the diversity of the potential employees was enormous. They ranged from young Liverpudlian school leavers to old char ladies looking for an easier life. The interviews were hysterical, the girls would either blush, or start giggling and even Kim was sometimes out of his 'comfort zone'. He wrote a colourful script for the initial interviews which he personally conducted from his hotel suite. When the applicants arrived, Kim asked them to sit opposite him and recite the following:

*"Hello, 0800-69'er. My name is Tara. What is your pleasure this evening? What was that, I didn't quite hear you? Oh, this is your first time calling. Okay, I'll do my best to make sure you enjoy your first experience with me. So, why don't you go ahead and get undressed and comfortable for me. Are you ready? Good... now lay back, close your eyes and imagine me. I'm a blue-eyed, raven-haired 24-year-old woman. I'm petite, five-foot three, but voluptuous. My skin is creamy and pale and my breasts are pert. My nipples are a dark dusky pink, the same colour as my full pouty lips. Imagine that I'm walking towards you in a dark blue push up bra and matching panties. My breasts are gently swaying as I walk. I stop right in front of you. Reaching down, I undo the front catch of my bra and I slowly let it fall from my breasts. I move even closer to you and drop down to my knees between your parted thighs. I run my hands up the insides of your thighs, approaching your already hard and throbbing cock. I notice there is already some pre-cum moistening that luscious plump head. Mmmm... I lick my lips, wetting them in anticipation of the treat to come. I gently wrap my small hand around the base of your cock and lower my mouth to that purple head, licking my lips and gazing up at you as I lick around that juicy crown and across that slit, tasting you.*

Three days later, Kim had narrowed his choices down to ten girls ranging from twenty to sixty years of age. He asked them to return one by one and interact a further script with him.

As Kim later said:

**"I felt so embarrassed and such an arsehole sitting in that hotel suite reading that bloody ridiculous script."**

Kim selected the six finalists, he was particularly enthralled by a thirty-year-old red head called Kat. He loved her name and thought 'Kim and Kat' sounded wonderful. Despite being newly-wed, Kim couldn't resist asking her to join him in the Adelphi grill room that evening for dinner. She duly agreed to meet him in the bar at 7.30.p.m. After a boozy mouth-watering dinner of Sole Veronique washed down with Puligny Montrachet, Kim used his thirty years of experience to entice Kat upstairs back to his suite with him. He couldn't open the double door fast enough. The couple fell into the suite and collapsed upon each other. They both giggled hysterically as they jumped into the bed, pulling the covers up over their heads. After two hours of steamy passion, Kat suggested that she should leave, but Kim replied:

**"Darling, the very least you could do is to stay for breakfast in the morning."**

His short period of monogamy was over.

To quote Kim:

**"Kat was a true redhead... aflame, mop, collar and muffs."**

(This quotation has often wrongly been used in association with Kim's friendship with the ex-wife of Randolph Churchill, Pamela Harriman, the US ambassador to Paris. Kim always denied any sexual relationship with her and insisted that he had resisted her charms.)

Kim began the marketing campaign for 0800-69'er Limited, he placed multiple sexually explicit advertisements in his friend Paul Raymond's magazines, Men Only,

Mayfair and Club International magazines. Among the nude models featured in Raymond's magazines was Fiona Richmond, who was a friend of Kim's, before becoming Raymond's girlfriend. She drove a Jaguar E Type bearing the registration number FU 2. Fiona travelled the World picking up sexual partners of different nationalities and then wrote a monthly article in 'Men Only' describing the explicit details of her sexual encounters.

Raymond invested millions into buildings, especially in Soho, starting in the 1970s through his company Soho Estates. By 1977, he was buying one Soho freehold each week. He also acquired property in Chelsea, Kensington and Hampstead. Raymond was a frequent name on lists of the UK's wealthiest individuals, reportedly with an estimated £650 million fortune by the time of his death in 2008.

Kim's new business seemed to take off. The phones didn't stop ringing with sex starved men happy to spend 6 pence per minute talking filthily to one of the six girls, who were divided into pairs for three 8-hour shifts, enabling the office to function 24 hours a day. Kim visited the Liverpool office every week to pay the wages and go through the figures, but there was a massive problem. The General Post Office owed 0800-69'er Limited many thousands of pounds in commission, but they were not crediting the new company's bank account with the commissions due to it. They claimed that the business was in unchartered territory and questioned its morality and legality.

To make matters worse, there was a large movement in the UK aimed at the establishment to censor sex and violence. Mary Whitehouse had started campaigns against the permissive society in the early 1970's, along with Malcolm Muggeridge, Cliff Richard and the Labour Catholic peer, Lord Longford. Whitehouse was a leading figure in protesting against the commercial exploitation of sex and violence. She launched the Nationwide Petition for Public Decency in January 1972, which gained 1.35 million signatures by the time it was presented to the Prime Minister, Edward Heath in April 1973.

Kim wanted to take legal action, but he was aware that his reputation preceded him, and the G.P.O. would use his somewhat decadent past as a major part of their defence.

Kim could only envisage months and months of costly litigation. He knew that he would be fighting a national institution which would have taken years to bring to the High Court. Reluctantly, he closed the whole operation down, having lost a fortune.

Back at Sedgehill Manor, Jaime was becoming fed up with Kim. She always mistrusted his fidelity and she did not like the idea of Kim starting new businesses with what she considered her money. By the end of 1973, Kim knew his short marriage was in trouble, but the situation rapidly changed just before Christmas. Jaime announced that she was pregnant. Kim was overjoyed.

An 0800-69'er advertisement

The Adelphi Hotel & The Royal Liver Building

## CHAPTER TWENTY-SIX

## A DAUGHTER A DIVORCE & AN
## UNPUBLISHED NOVEL
## (1974 - 1977)


In early 1974, Kim was on great form. He was so excited by the thought of fatherhood that business, projects and schemes took a rear seat. Kim was secretly praying that the new baby would be a little girl, he had always yearned for a daughter, he had no interest whatsoever in having a son. Rumour had it that he'd already sired a son by a well-known London model who had subsequently married, the new husband had taken the baby boy on, thinking that the boy was his own creation and Kim had agreed to keep the secret forever. For obvious reasons, this couple cannot be named. Kim would never discuss this matter, he neither confirmed nor denied the rumour.

Kim had become seriously health conscious. His days were filled with riding the horses at Sedgehill Manor and making sure that Jaime lived a very nutritious lifestyle and suffered no stress whatsoever, although they both knew that their funds were beginning to dwindle.

Robert Pilkington introduced Kim to Mario Condivi who owned MTC Cars in Bayswater.

Pilkington had just bought his girlfriend, Caroline Walker, a new Fiat 500 from Mario. Condivi had been recently appointed as the UK sole importer for the new De Tomaso Pantera. The word 'Pantera' is Italian for 'Panther'. The Pantera had the qualities of both an Italian sports car and an American muscle car. It was beautiful, brutish and yet reliable. Kim was fascinated by the thought of owning one of the first of these exotic vehicles in the country. Naturally, he ordered one, and as per usual, specifically requested for it to be painted in his racing colours, midnight blue with soft cream leather interior. In its day, this car cost more than a new Rolls Royce or Bentley and Elvis Presley had recently purchased one of these special automobiles. Some months later, the new car arrived from Italy and was duly delivered to Sedgehill Manor. Kim and Jaime were thrilled with their new toy, and despite the fact Jaime was pregnant, she loved driving the new supercar.

Although their marriage was rocky, the couple would often drive to London together to see their old friends. Upon one of these occasions, Jaime had dropped Kim to a restaurant in Chelsea and driven the new Pantera alone to party in North West London. After a very boozy dinner, she attempted to drive the powerful new car back to Chelsea in order to collect Kim. Catastrophe was to follow, having exited the Westway in Bayswater, she entered Bishops Bridge Road. Jaime misjudged a corner by a parade of shops, lost control, and ended up driving through the shop window of a launderette!

The new car was literally smashed to pieces as it sat inside the shop, surrounded by broken glass. Luckily, there was a telephone box outside and it was still intact. In a state of semi shock, she telephoned Kim at the restaurant in which he was dining and tried to explain what had happened. Kim, chivalrous to the end, told her not to notify the police until he arrived at the scene. Amazingly, nobody had telephoned the police before he appeared. When Kim arrived by taxi at the crash scene, he was staggered by the extent of the damage, but obviously, his main concern, was that for his pregnant wife, Jaime. He immediately called the police and when they arrived shortly afterwards, he took full responsibility for the crash.

Fortunately, the police believed him to be the driver, but unfortunately, he was breathalysed, arrested and charged with both drinking and driving as well as reckless driving. He lost his licence for eighteen months and fined heavily. After lengthy arguments with the insurance company, the De Tomaso Pantera was eventually 'written off'.

Now, unable to drive, Kim began to feel trapped at Sedgehill Manor, trains and public transport did not really feature in Kim's world and they were not an option. Jaime was in her final weeks of pregnancy and was therefore unable to help Kim make his weekly pilgrimages to London. Their marriage was becoming impossible and divorce was being discussed.

August was a life-changing moment for Kim. Jaime gave birth to a baby girl at Sedgehill Manor. Kim was elated and named her 'Campbell'. He had never been so happy. Ironically, Dors had been pregnant at exactly the same time as Jaime, but sadly, on August 28th, Dors gave birth to a stillborn son in a Berkshire hospital with Alan Lake at her bedside, which upset Kim tremendously.

Realising that divorce were imminent; Kim began to think about the sale of his beloved Sedgehill Manor and make a return to Chelsea. These thoughts were further compounded when he heard that his old friend Bernie Cornfeld wanted to sell his beautiful Belgravia home, No1 West Halkin Street. It had always been Kim's favourite house in London.

Cornfeld had recently visited Geneva and the Swiss authorities had arrested him. They charged him with fraud and he served eleven months in a Swiss jail before being freed on a bail surety of $600,000. Cornfeld had always maintained his innocence, but he knew it was time to leave Europe and settle in California.

Some months later, divorce proceedings had commenced and Kim put Sedgehill Manor on the market. It was not a good time to sell, as Britain was suffering a recession and property slump due to the OPEC oil embargo the previous year. By the end of the embargo in March 1974, the price of oil had risen from $3 per barrel to nearly $12 globally. The embargo had caused an oil crisis, with many devastating effects on global politics and the global economy.

As mentioned before, Kim was a very private individual. He had not divulged to anybody that during the recession he had been secretly taking out a number of mortgages on Sedgehill Manor to help sustain his lavish lifestyle. As a result of this, there was not a great deal of equity left over by the eventual sale in early 1975. However, Kim was relatively lucky. The final divorce was amicable with both sides pleading poverty and custody of Campbell being awarded to both parents.

Penny Brahms said recently:

*"The marriage didn't last. He was a chauvinist. He thought women were very beautiful, but he didn't really rate them. He didn't think they had a brain. It would never have worked out between us."*

Kim's marriage was now over; but he was still determined to buy Cornfeld's house in Belgravia. The property was on a relatively short lease so the acquisition costs were not that prohibitive. A deal was finally struck between them and Kim moved back in London with a vengeance, determined to rebuild his life. He set about remodelling the house which had its own sauna and discotheque. It was the perfect base from which to launch new schemes.

Tania Leaver, a model, who met Kim through his on-off girlfriend, Angela Sieff, once said:

*"Kim's house in Belgravia was impeccable. It was dripping with crystal. The floral arrangements would have to be by either Constance Spry or Moyses Stevens, the royal florists. There was no shortage of beautiful objects or beautiful girls."*

But yet again, Kim was short of money and needed a new project.

There was another problem. Campbell began spending more and more time with Kim as her mother, Penny Brahms (Jaime), was busy trying to resume her acting and modelling career.

Kim needed help. He advertised for a 'Girl Friday' in The Lady magazine and he was inundated with applicants. One such applicant was a sixteen-year-old girl called Paula Yates, she had just arrived from her mother's home in Majorca she had been a pupil at Bellver International College. Kim was mesmerised by this enchanting young girl and felt she was too young to take on the job, but he couldn't resist asking her to join him for lunch that day. Needless to say, despite her age, her name was added to Kim's long list of romantic conquests. Paula went on to become most notorious for her 'on the bed' interviews on the show The Big Breakfast produced by her first husband, Bob Geldof. She later married Michael Hutchence, the Australian lead singer and lyricist of the rock band INXS until his death in 1997. Sadly, on September 17th 2000, she died at her home in London of an accidental heroin overdose at only forty-one years of age.

Having finally found a suitable housekeeper and nanny for Campbell, Kim concentrated on looking for new businesses and more importantly, new relationships. He started dating Marianne Broome who was born in England but spent much of her childhood in Malaysia. She had recently appeared in London as a 'Page Three' nude model. The relationship was short-lived and the following year Marianne took part in the Olympic Games in Montreal as a member of the national swimming team from Malaysia before settling in Canada during 1980. She is now a renown floral artist based in Schomberg, a village in Ontario, Canada.

During 1976, Kim became fanatical about his physical fitness and joined a local gymnasium in Chelsea. He also became obsessive about his daughter, Campbell's, diet and hated her breathing in the polluted London air.

Kim was running short of money. The only assets he had left were the lease on West Halkin Street and the ageing Range Rover. He knew that he couldn't maintain his lifestyle for much longer and something had to change, there were simply no fresh deals. He was further irritated to hear that his arch adversary, Michael Eland was back in London and living at the Ritz Hotel. Eland had returned from Paris to orchestrate a reverse public company takeover involving a security company called PPR based in Stevenage.

To make matters worse, Eland had employed Kim's number one enemy, Annice Summers, to become his secretary. It was only time before the two rivals bumped into each other. A few weeks later Kim was having dinner with Angela Sieff at Mimmo d'Ischia and Eland walked in to the restaurant with his new sixth wife, Jane, a supermodel from Paris. The two rivals couldn't help but to say hello to each other and surprisingly, minutes later, the four restaurant guests were sharing a table. They reminisced about the old days when they had the smuggling operation in Tangier which totally fascinated Eland's wife, Jane. Kim was surprised to hear that Eland had originally funded Mimmo's restaurant and secretly displeased that he had been supporting Mimmo and therefore been contributing to Eland's profits.

He was captivated by Jane, and duly invited the couple back to his home around the corner for a 'nightcap' with Angela. Eland loved the house and was very impressed that it had its own sauna and discotheque, he was fed up with living in the Ritz and it wasn't long before he asked Kim if he would like to sell the lease on the property. Reluctantly and with dented pride, Kim agreed to sell Eland the house for a substantial profit.

With no new schemes in sight and before the sale of the house to Eland was completed, Kim decided to move to Geneva to concentrate on writing a new novel. In his mind, it was the perfect location, he would be reasonably near to London by plane, it would be a great location for Campbell to begin her education and it would be a wonderful way to have her to himself without her mother's influences. Another incentive in moving to Geneva was that there would be no taxes payable if Kim earned any sizeable money.

After a few exploratory visits to Switzerland, Kim agreed to rent a chalet on the banks of Lake Geneva and moved out of West Halkin Street. He sold many of his possessions and with fresh money in his pocket; he packed up the Range Rover and drove to Geneva with Campbell.

For the next six months, Kim formed an incredible bond with Campbell. He taught her how to ski at a young age and treated her as his best friend rather than a baby girl. He sat on the terrace of the chalet of a day, taking in the fresh air and with an amazing amount of imagination, conjured up the plot of a fictional book called 'Il Papa'. The story of the book centred around a young orphaned boy who was adopted by the Italian mafia and groomed to become the youngest pope in Papal history, thereby gaining access to all the Vatican's assets and secrets and turning them over to the Casa Nostra.

When the book was finally finished, Kim returned to London with the manuscript and hoped that he would not only secure a successful publication, but also have a great plot with which to make a blockbuster movie.

Upon Kim's return to London with Campbell in 1977, there was no great interest in the new book and Kim did not want to return to Switzerland without a publishing contract under his belt… but things were about to change in a most astonishing way.

Kim & Penny (Jaime)

Kim's 1974 De Tomaso Pantera GTS

Kim & Marianne Broom

Kim's new home, No. 1 West Halkin Street, Belgravia,
London SW1

# CHAPTER TWENTY-SEVEN

## A LORD A BEAUTY QUEEN & A PRESIDENT'S WIFE
## (1977 – 1978)

Having returned from Switzerland with Campbell, Kim immediately contacted his old soulmate, Diana Dors. She was down on her luck. During the seventies, her life had become a mixture of personal appearances, occasional undistinguished films and bored domesticity, mainly because of her husband, Alan Lake's, drunken, antisocial and often violent behaviour. He and his wife were rarely invited anywhere socially. Like Kim, she was desperately short of funds and had even recently sold her Rolls Royce Corniche, claiming that they had become commonplace in Ascot and Sunningdale.

Kim explained that he was back in England hoping to publish his new book, 'Il Papa' and suggested that she should start thinking about writing her autobiography as a means of generating fresh income.

A few days later, Kim visited a new restaurant in Egerton Terrace called Mai-Tai. This fabulous restaurant was the brainchild of the Queen Elizabeth's cousin, Patrick Anson, the 5th Earl of Lichfield, otherwise known as, Lord Lichfield.

Mai-Tai was the most fashionable place to be seen in and the first restaurant in London to feature gourmet Pan Asian food on its menus.

Lord Lichfield was the son of Viscount Anson and Princess Anne of Denmark and inherited the Earldom of Lichfield in 1960 from his paternal grandfather. In his professional capacity, he was one of the UK's best-known photographers and was known simply as Patrick Lichfield. He had recently married the Duke of Westminster's sister, Leonora.

Lord Lichfield started out as a photographer's assistant on £3 a week. He made the most of his show business and aristocratic connections, snapping everybody from Mick and Bianca Jagger on their wedding day to the Duke and Duchess of Windsor in exile. Lichfield's memory of the latter encounter was of deliberately falling off his chair to force smiles out of his straight-faced subjects. The great result won him a contract with Vogue magazine. Lord Lichfield had made a name for himself photographing and often squiring the new wave of young debutantes' models and actresses, including Britt Ekland, who were beginning to appear in the tabloid press and glossy magazines.

Kim's reputation had preceded him, Lord Lichfield knew who he was, he had read many revelations about him over two decades in the gossip columns. Kim found that he had much in common with Lord Lichfield, they looked similar, were both very dapper and had many mutual interests including women and sex. They both had an enviable sexual history and the two lotharios struck up an immediate friendship.

One evening, Kim met up with Lord Lichfield at his restaurant and they were joined by Lichfield's friend, twenty-year-old Karen Pini, an Australian beauty queen. Karen had entered her first beauty pageant in Australia the previous year, winning her the title of 'Miss West Coast'. As a result, she had automatically qualified for the 'Miss Australasia Beach Girl' competition, which was held in Perth, her hometown. She won that title, qualifying her to enter the 'Quest of Quests Pageant', a competition to select the Australian entrants for both the 'Miss Universe' and 'Miss World' contests. She won and was duly selected as the 'Miss World' representative for Australia. In November 1976, she appeared at Eric and Julia Morley's 'Miss World' contest held at the Royal Albert Hall in London, where she chosen as first runner up to the winner, Cindy Breakspeare.

Her success in the pageant opened the door to modelling opportunities in the U.K. She appeared as a topless 'Page Three Girl' in the Sun Newspaper and was considered for the cover model in a US edition of Penthouse' magazine, photographed by Lord Lichfield himself. Unfortunately, the photos were not used because they were considered too tame and pretty for Bob Guccione's Penthouse magazine.

The whole evening was spent talking about sex, beauty pageants and photography. Kim was in his element. During the conversations, Karen Pini, being a very liberated girl, jokingly suggested that there should be a 'Miss Topless Universe'. The two amused gentlemen listened and spontaneously agreed that it would be a great scheme. Lord Lichfield immediately said that it could never work in either Europe or the United States as it would be deemed 'bad taste' but added that the idea would work wonders in both Australia and South East Asia, where the audiences were far more open-minded. Lord Lichfield added that his heavy working itinerary would never allow him the time to base himself in Australia and promote such a project. Kim, always desperate for a new scheme, immediately spotted the obvious advantages of having the titled Royal photographer as a commercial partner and volunteered to research the concept further.

At the same time, Mariela Novotny had started publishing monthly revelations in Paul Raymond's Club International magazine in which she described her affairs with numerous members of society and celebrities. Kim contacted her and urged her not to reveal the crazy night they had enjoyed together at the Dorchester Hotel fourteen years previously in the pornographic magazine. He didn't dare risk any association with a suspected spy under observation by MI5, if his new venture with Lord Lichfield was going to be successful. Luckily, Mariela never revealed their intimate story.

Over the following weeks, Kim had several meetings with Lord Lichfield and it was agreed that they would become equal partners and develop the 'Miss Topless Universe' project with Kim moving to Perth Australia, to head up the new business, seek sponsorship and negotiate the television rights. The rest of his time was divided between spending time with Karen Pini, trying to find a publisher for the new book and looking after his daughter, Campbell.

Kim and Lord Lichfield agreed that Karen, having been Miss Australia, would make an ideal ambassador for the new business. She already had a great relationship with Channel Nine in Perth Australia and knew its owner, media tycoon Kerry Packer. They gave a small percentage of the new business to Karen in return for her endorsement and general support.

Inevitably, Kim and Karen soon became lovers and he even took Karen to meet Dors at a dinner party at Dors' home, Orchard Court in Sunningdale.

A few days later, Karen left for Australia to fulfil her various modelling commitments and pave the way for Kim's arrival. Back in London, Kim had all sorts of problems before leaving the U.K. Firstly, the successful, Lord Lichfield, presumed that Kim was a wealthy playboy who would have no difficulty in raising half the money needed to fund their new business, which Kim had agreed to do. He did not realise that in fact, Kim was broke.

Secondly, Kim did not know how in hell's name; he was going to start a new life 'down under' with no capital behind him and a three-year-old daughter to support. Kim immediately flew back to Geneva to close down the rented chalet and drive the old Range Rover back to London with his belongings and Campbell's toys. Upon his return, he organised a series of meeting with his old Chelsea chums in a desperate attempt to raise enough money to honour his commitment to Lord Lichfield. He was partly successful, and although there was still not enough money in his coffers, he arranged to fly to Perth with Campbell to meet up with Karen Pini in Australia.

When Kim and Campbell landed in Perth, Karen was at the airport to meet them. She had arranged an apartment for them at Peppermint Grove, a beautiful part of Perth, hugging the picturesque Swan River. Karen helped Kim immensely and almost took on the role of surrogate mother to Campbell. She organised a meeting with Mrs Rita McGregor, the Headmistress of St Hilda's Anglican School and arranged for Campbell to attend the kindergarten class.

Rapidly, Kim became a major player in Perth society. Karen's celebrity status had given Kim the passport to socialise with the Australian tycoons Alan Bond and Kerry Packer, the only problem was that Kim was desperately short of cash and he couldn't really afford to be involved with their extravagant lifestyles.

Kim's first meeting was organised by Karen with Channel Nine which was an Australian commercial free-to-air television network owned by the media mogul, Kerry Packer. It was one of three main free-to-air commercial networks in Australia and one of the two highest-rating television networks in Australia. Channel Nine had historically been the highest-rating television network since television's inception in Australia during 1956.

The meeting went very well and the television company's directors were very impressed by the 'Miss Topless Universe' project, especially with the knowledge that it involved 'Miss Australia' and that Kim's partner was none other than the famous Royal photographer, Lord Lichfield.

They enthusiastically agreed to purchase all the television rights to the contest provided Kim could demonstrate that he had all the contestants in place and that other television companies across Asia were also prepared to sign a commitment to broadcast the show, therefore allowing Channel Nine to syndicate the rights and recover most of their investment back prior to the actual pageant taking place.

Kim was out of his depth, he needed to achieve the commitment from other television companies across Asia before he could receive any money from Channel Nine. With no experience in television marketing, he started making frantic telephone calls to the television stations all over the Far East including Hong Kong, Singapore, Thailand, Malaysia and Indonesia, to no avail. Finally, he found out that the television networks in the Philippines were run by the government, under the direct control of President Ferdinand Marcos and his wife, Imelda.

Nervously, he called the government offices in Manila and was referred to an attaché who explained that Imelda Marcos would be the person to approach regarding 'Miss Topless Universe'. Kim put the phone down, seriously thinking he was wasting his time, but amazingly he received a call from Mrs Marcos' secretary the following day requesting further information and an invitation to the Philippines to discuss the project in greater detail. Kim couldn't believe that he had actually been invited for an audience with the President's wife. After pleading for more money to be wired to him from his London chums, he duly made travel arrangements to fly to Manila.

When Kim arrived alone in Manila, he quite expected to have to make hotel arrangements for his three-day stay, but to his great surprise, there was a chauffeured limousine waiting for him at the airport. The driver spoke fluent English and explained that Imelda Marcos would like to extend an invitation to Kim to stay for the duration of his visit at her husband's sumptuous mansion at Cabuyao, in the province of Laguna which was about a two-hour drive from Manila. Having driven cross country for what seemed like hours, Kim arrived at a magnificent palace in the middle of nowhere.

Apprehensively, Kim climbed out of the limousine

and a uniformed butler showed him to an opulent suite in the mansion, he was told that the President's wife had been detained on business in Manila but would arrive later that evening. Kim showered and changed into an immaculate Prince of Wales check suit, expecting to be called upon any moment, but nothing happened. Three hours later, nothing. The butler knocked on the door around midnight and explained that Imelda Marcos had been delayed in the Capital and would not be arriving at the mansion for a further thirty-six hours. Kim was mortified, he was stuck, miles from anywhere and he would obviously miss his return flight to Perth. Having asked the butler to change his flight plans, Kim retired to bed wondering what the hell he was going to do the following day.

After the most boring day and restless night which reminded him of his days in solitary confinement in France many years before, Imelda Marcos finally arrived amid much fanfare at the mansion. She had a very powerful presence but was much shorter than Kim had expected. The meeting went spectacularly well, Imelda Marcos not only asked all the right questions, Kim equally gave her all the correct answers, she agreed to issue a letter of intent in favour of Channel Nine, but also indicated that she would be prepared to head up a new syndicate should Channel Nine not perform.

Two hours later, Kim left the mansion and was chauffeured back to Manila airport, as much as he was niggled at being kept waiting nearly two days, he felt that he was returning to Perth with positive news to report to both Lord Lichfield and Karen. Back in Perth, Karen had received a couple of calls from Lord Lichfield asking for updates on the situation. Lichfield was already becoming impatient and beginning to suspect that Kim had no real money and that he could not see this project through to fruition. Kim immediately called Lord Lichfield at Shugborough Hall, his country estate, and informed him of the successful meeting with Imelda Marcos in the Philippines.

Kim sensed that Lord Lichfield was not happy with his investment, Kim and Karen stayed up all night discussing their finances and what to do next, it was all fruitless because the following day brought horrendous news. Kim received a telex that simply read:

*"Dear Mr Waterfield. It is with my regret to inform you that having spoken to the President; we have decided not to proceed with negotiations concerning Miss Topless Universe. We wish you well with your project and send you our apologies for a wasted journey. Please send our best wishes to Lord Lichfield. With kind regards. Imelda Marcos."*

Kim was horrified. Firstly, he knew Channel Nine would not sign a contract with him unless he could prove further sales to other television companies, secondly, how was he going to tell Lord Lichfield that everything he had reported to him the night before was absolute rubbish?

Perth is eight hours ahead of London, so Kim duly telephoned Lichfield the following morning and relayed everything that had happened. When Kim put the phone down, he instinctively knew that the short-lived partnership was over, it was time to retrench and return to London with Campbell and Karen and face the music. Surprisingly, Karen never fell out with Lord Lichfield and he chose her to feature in his 1979 Unipart calendar.

Karen returned to Australia later in 1978 to celebrate her 21st birthday with her family. The timing coincided with the launch of the Australian edition of Playboy magazine. Kerry Packer's ACP Magazines had secured the Australian rights to Playboy magazine. Karen was the natural first choice as the inaugural Australian Playmate of the Month, appearing as the centrefold in the first Australian edition of Playboy magazine. It was issued in February 1979, selling nearly 200,000 copies.

On November 5th 1979, Karen made her first

television appearance on Channel Nine, hosting the weekly New South Wales Lotto draw with Mike Walsh, a role she held for the next twelve years. Between 1979 and 1982 she regularly appeared in the Australian soap opera 'The Young Doctors', in the role as Nurse Sherry Andrews. She also made several appearances on 'The Paul Hogan Show', a popular Australian comedy show that aired on Australian television between 1973 and 1984.

Karen Pini later said:

*"Living in London for two years gave me a chance to work with some of the best photographers in the world including one of my favourite people, Patrick Litchfield. Sadly, Patrick is no longer with us but his work lives on and the memories of lots of laughter and beautiful images will remain."*

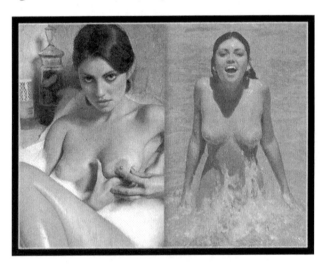

**Miss Australia, Karen Pini**

President Marcos' mansion in Cabuyao, Laguna,
Philippines

Kim & Campbell in Perth, Australia,
Imelda Marcos & Lord Patrick Lichfield

Shugborough Hall. Lord Patrick Lichfield's stately home

# CHAPTER TWENTY-EIGHT

## TV-AM & THE X-CEL DIET
### (1980 – 1983)

Kim arrived back in London accompanied by Campbell with his tail between his legs, he was quite simply washed up, his credibility was seriously tarnished after all of his recent schemes had been such a total disaster. He knew that his first priority was to look after Campbell who was still only four years old, but Karen Pini was no longer on hand to help him. He also knew that he couldn't rebuild his financial or personal life and be a full-time single father at the same time. There was only one option, despite her age, Campbell had to go to boarding school.

Education in central London was not an option so he decided to enrol her as a boarder at Knighton House School, near Blandford Forum in Dorset. The only problem, needless to say, was how he was going to pay the overwhelming school fees.

Kim was still having no luck in publishing his new book, 'Il Papa'. He had tried both Hodder & Stoughton and Harper Collins without success, he even considered self-publication again using his company, the Julian Press as promotors, the trouble was, that this was a fictional novel, and it really needed to be published by a recognised and established publisher. It certainly wasn't going to sell by mail order, which was Kim's forte.

It was Christmas time and Karen Pini had flown over from Australia to join Kim, while Campbell visited her mother for Xmas and the New Year holiday, it was a very lean time.

Kim was now in constant contact with Dors who had just hosted a wonderful New Year's fiftieth birthday party for him at Orchard Manor. The guest list was an impressive cocktail of well-known celebrities and many of the original members of the 'Chelsea Set', who Kim had mixed with all those decades before. The evening was a riot and the party was still in full alcoholic swing at dawn. Everyone went crazy, when Karen, who was quite used to removing her clothes, jumped naked into Dors' indoor swimming pool and enticed everyone to follow suit. Kim noticed that many of his old friends were ageing but nonetheless, it was an especially welcome treat for him at that time. Dors' life had become pretty dreadful as well, she was not being offered any work and her husband, Alan Lake's, drinking had become completely out of control.

As a result of being bored and staying at home cooking, her weight had soared to at least fourteen stone. Kim was disturbed by Dors' massive weight gain and being a keep fit fanatic, encouraged her to go on a strict diet.

One day in early 1980, Kim was casually walking down the Kings Road in Chelsea when he bumped into his old flame, Mariela Novotny who appeared high on drugs. She announced that she had started work on her autobiography which would include details of her work for MI5. She claimed that her book would include details of a plot to discredit the U.S. President John F. Kennedy.

She added:

*"I kept a diary of all my appointments in the United Nations building in New York. Believe me, it's dynamite. It's now in the hands of the CIA, heads will roll."*

Kim listened and thought she was a potential time bomb, about to explode. She was potentially dangerous and he decided to distance himself from her. It was the last time they ever met.

The book never appeared and Mariella Novotny was later found dead in her bed in London. It was claimed by the police that she had died of a drug overdose.

Christine Keeler later wrote:

*"The Westminster Coroner, Dr Paul Knapman,*

*called it misadventure. Along with people in
Moscow, I still think it was murder. A central figure
in the strangest days of my life always believed
Mariella would be killed by American or British
agents, most probably by the CIA. Shortly after her
death, her house was burgled and all her files and
large day to day diaries from the early sixties to the
seventies were stolen."*

It was also around this time that Kim had started
being mentioned not only in the gossip columns but also
in other authors autographical or biographical books. Any
reference to Kim always included the sorry story of his
demise over the Ann Summers business. He still often
reflected upon this chapter of his life and vowed to himself
that one day, he would teach the Gold brothers an
almighty lesson.

Karen Pini made a few more trips to London to see
Kim during 1980 but they were drifting apart, and on her
last trip, she informed him that she had found someone
else in Australia. On December 3rd 1980 Karen married
Stephen Fitzsimmons in Australia and sadly, Kim lost
touch with her.

While Kim had away been in Australia, Dors had
taken Kim's advice and written two autobiographies. The
first was 'For Adults Only' and the second was 'Behind
Closed Doors'. Both books had been successfully
published and she was working on a third, which was
going to be titled 'Dors By Diana'.

Age and illness were beginning to bury her famous
figure under more matronly proportions, but to the
public's surprise, the Dors lurking behind the image came
to the fore. She was revealed, to most people's surprise, as
far more endearing. She became a character actress of
considerable talent and a personality seen regularly on
television and heard on radio.

She was a popular chat show guest and she had a
recurring role in 'The Two Ronnies' during 1980, an entire

episode of 'At Home with Dors' was recorded with the presenter, Russell Harty, from her indoor swimming pool at Orchard Manor. Younger musical artists began to engage her persona, brought about after the success of Adam Ant's 1981 music video 'Prince Charming' where Dors played the fairy godmother opposite Adam Ant, who played a male Cinderella figure.

Kim was in touch with Dors on a daily basis, but his constant nagging about her ever-increasing weight was taking no effect, so he decided to take matters into his own hands.

He started designing a weekly diet for Dors based upon the nutritional content of many different foods. He thoroughly enjoyed doing this, and spent hours studying the calorific values of all sorts of foods. Suddenly, he had a brainwave. He thought about writing a new book which would be more like a calorie counter. The more he thought about this new project, the more it made sense, the country was becoming obsessed about weight, appearance and fitness. 'Weight Watchers' was at its peak and Kim decided to emulate it, but with a few twists.

Kim contacted his old chum, Robert Pilkington, who had since split up with Caroline Walker and subsequently both been married and divorced. Pilkington listened to his scheme, and willingly agreed to finance the new project as Kim had always eventually honoured his debts to him in the past.

The rusty old Range Rover really had seen better days, especially since it had lived outside all its life and been around the snowy mountains in Switzerland. Kim needed a new car urgently and I sold him a dark blue Mercedes Benz estate car as a replacement.

During 1981 and 1982, Kim wrote a book, titled the 'X-cel Diet', which he self-published (Julian Press ISBN 0901943-20-7). This marketing method worked wonders for him in the past with the book 'Variations on a Sexual Theme'. He supplied the book with a cassette, which verbally explained the nutritional value of various healthy foods, the cassette also suggested balanced meals and the relevant recipes. Kim also supplied a revolutionary new calculator which had been developed in China.

Its microchip had been modified and recalibrated to calculate calories as opposed to straightforward mathematics, enabling anybody to keep a running total as to how many calories they had consumed during one day. The screen would then flash if you had over indulged and exceeded the recommended calorific intake. The new product was especially loved by women and was years ahead of its time. It was delivered in a fine leather case, finished in burgundy with gold edges. The impressive package retailed for £29.95, showing a profit margin of over 100%.

Unfortunately, on June 24th 1982, Dors was rushed to hospital with severe stomach pains after opening a hotel. The surgeons operated and found an ovarian cyst which had ruptured, but there were complications during the surgery due to her weight. The cyst turned out to be malignant and she was diagnosed with cancer. She had to check in to the Charing Cross Hospital in London every week for two days and two nights to undergo chemotherapy. Her reaction to the treatment was severe and she could be sick up to five times an hour, but she never complained believing it would make her better.

Dors did get better. She possessed an unforgettable warmth and sincerity and nobody was surprised when she was voted 'Television Personality of the Year' in 1982. and then in October, she received the accolade of a second 'This Is Your Life' appearance, when Eamon Andrews surprised her at London's Royalty Theatre.

Kim toyed with the future development and expansion of his new venture and one day an exceptional notion came to him. He arranged to meet Diana Dors at Mimmo d'Ischia for lunch and after moaning about being mentioned in James Morton's new book 'Gangland: The

Lawyers'. He suggested that they rewrote the 'X-cel diet' together and rename it 'Diet with Diana'. The plan would then be to put Dors' on television and promote what the public would perceive as her own unique diet.

Dors had just been offered a job as an 'agony aunt' for the News of the World and had verbally agreed to a fee of £26000 per annum, but she had not signed the contract at this point. Kim advised her not to sign this contract until he had secured a regular TV slot for her. He thought that her potential new weekly column would have far greater value to the 'News of the World' if she publicly dieted on television. The public would become more aware of her humility, and then write to her in a more intimate manner, therefore attracting more interest in the new newspaper column.

Kim then played his master stroke which was more by luck than judgement!

Breakfast television was in its infancy and while the BBC's 'Breakfast Time' was successful, TV-AM's early ratings were disappointing. Its high-minded and somewhat starchy approach, sat uneasily at that time of day, compared to 'Breakfast Time's' accessible magazine style, which mixed heavy news and light-hearted features, famously moving cabinet ministers, after a serious interview, to help with a cookery demonstration. Some of the biggest names in television launched TV-AM's first national breakfast service on February 1st 1983, but it was beaten to air by its BBC rival by two weeks. It made daily broadcasts were between 6 a.m. and 9:25 a.m.

Within two weeks of the launch the ratings dropped sharply. The company's weekend show presented by Michael Parkinson initially became the only success for the station, largely because the BBC did not broadcast on weekend mornings. The Saturday editions drew 1.5 million viewers.

A boardroom coup ensued on March 18th 1983, when Peter Jay stepped aside allowing Jonathan Aitken to become chief executive of the station, after mounting pressure from investors who had demanded changes. On the same day, the newscasters Angela Rippon and Anna Ford came out publicly to support Peter Jay, unaware he had already left. A month later, both Rippon and Ford were sacked. A few weeks later, Anna Ford encountered Jonathan Aitken at a party attended by Kim in Chelsea. In a parting shot over the terms of her dismissal, Anna Ford threw her glass of wine in the face of Aitken, saying of her action:

**"It was the only form of self-defence left to a woman when she has been so monstrously treated."**

Kim seized the moment to have a brief private chat with the wine drenched Aitken and suggested putting Diana Dors on the new revamped show. Embarrassed by his appearance and what had just happened, he quickly exited the party after suggesting that Kim make contact with Greg Dyke, the new director of programmes for TV-AM. A couple of days later, both Rippon and Ford started procedures to sue TV-AM, but the case was dropped after an out of court settlement was reached.

Greg Dyke had just been brought into the ailing television company as director of programmes, to help overhaul the station's output. Kim contacted him; they shared a sense of humour and immediately developed an affinity for each other. After several meetings and negotiating Dors' fees, it was agreed that Dors would have a slot on the breakfast show.

Dyke had also agreed to give Roland Rat a new slot, the rat was devised by the TV-AM's children's editor to entertain younger viewers during the Easter holidays, which boosted the station's audience. On Friday April 1st 1983 (Good Friday and Fool's Day) Roland Rat made his first television appearance and in May 1983, Dors made her first appearance on TV-AM. Nick Owen, one of the show's newly appointed presenters, challenged her to shed weight in public with a weekly televised 'weigh in'. The goal was to lose 52 lbs. by her fifty second birthday on October 23rd 1983. Not wanting to let herself or her public down, Dors accepted the challenge and made a weekly 'Diet with Diana' appearance. She was weighed in front of the television cameras. The public loved her humility and the ratings soared.

She appeared on the first show wearing as much heavy jewellery as was possible in order to make the oversized scales give an inflated reading of her weight. She went to the toilet before the second week's appearance and removed all the jewellery in order to exaggerate her first week's weight loss result. She lost weight every week and the show went on to include a slot where she would cook healthy food in her own kitchen at Orchard Manor, in Sunningdale.

With Dors' recent success and fresh exposure, Kim approached the News of the World and renegotiated her 'agony aunt' contract from the initially agreed £26000 per annum to a staggering £56000 per annum. Dors signed the revised contract, ever grateful to her nearest and dearest friend.

As Kim later said:

*"Everybody wanted to lose weight and what better role model than Dors? Not only, had she become a national treasure, she needed money and she needed to shed her weight. The public now had great respect for her, she would, therefore be a wonderful endorsement and make a great wonderful public example. My next move was to engineer national publicity for her diet. Everyone was a winner with the TV-AM appearances, she lost weight and earned great fees. I sold thousands more of the 'Diet with Diana' diet packages, which were basically rebranded 'X-cel diet' packages and it all helped to save a flagging TV station. What could have been better? On TV-AM Diana was famous for openly shedding those extra stones. In the News of the*

*World agony aunt slot which followed, she answered readers' problems with a vision and depth that could only have come from living a life to the full. Above all, I knew she really cared. She possessed an unforgettable warmth and sincerity in her eyes and winning smile. Few knew these disguised the agony and trauma of a cancerous tumour which she was trying valiantly and courageously to overcome. I didn't realise how seriously ill she was."*

The publicity was wonderful for Kim. Dors had publicly announced that the 'Diet with Diana' weight loss programme was basically identical to the 'X-cel diet' and that Kim was the mastermind behind the scheme. Kim's mail order sales trebled during this period and on the strength of the profits, Kim purchased two Cadillacs from me, one Gucci limited edition model finished in cream with bright scarlet leather upholstery for Dors, and a bronze one for himself.

As Dors said:

*"I love the Cadillac; it matches my hair!"*

To quote Kim:

*"God, those bloody Cadillacs I bought from you were such poor taste. I used to feel like Liberace arriving."*

Dors did lose weight and it was a much shapelier Dors, who at the end of August, the same year, went back to her hometown and opened an airfield. Unfortunately, no one really appreciated that her dramatic weight-loss was far more due to her recurring cancer than eating more nutritional foods.

Diana Dors and Roland Rat were generally regarded as TV-AM's saviours. Roland Rat was later described as:

*"The only rat in history, to join a sinking ship."*

Roland Rat and Diana Dors helped take TV-AM's audience from 100,000 to over a million and made Kim and Dors a small fortune.

Diana Dors, the TV-AM 'X-cel Diet' & Diana Dors'
cream Cadillac Seville

The four autobiographical books by Diana Dors
1978  For Adults Only, 1979  Behind Closed Dors,
1981  Dors By Diana and 1984  Diana Dors' A-Z of Men

# CHAPTER TWENTY-NINE

## THE DEATH OF DIANA DORS & ALAN LAKE
## (1984)

In June 1983, Dors wrote an unusually melancholy note to Kim which read:

*"There has been much trauma and turbulence in both our lives. There have also been the times we disagreed quite fiercely, and no doubt we will again as we are strong and often volatile personalities. But I just wanted to say at this moment how much I respect you: your integrity, your business acumen and, above all, the real person, Michael, a boy I met so long ago, who, when all the 'Dandy Kim' scene is set aside, happens to be someone I am proud to count as one of my dearest friends - perhaps the only one?!"*

Kim was horribly aware that his lifetime soulmate was desperately ill. In September 1983, doctors had told Diana she needed a lifesaving operation, malignant cells had spread to the star's stomach and the cancer was back. Alan Lake kept the devastating news to himself when Diana welcomed the Press into her private room at the hospital, buoyant with optimism that they had operated successfully. After the New Year, Dors was busy working. She published her fourth autobiographical book entitled 'Diana Dors' A-Z of Men' and she wrote regular columns for newspapers. She appeared on her own programme 'Open Dors' and she also personally answered mountains of fan mail. Kim was annoyed yet again by two book referrals being 'Stardust Memories' by Ray Connolly and 'Great Disasters of the Stage' by William Donaldson.

In February 1984, Dors agreed to star in a film named 'Steaming' with Vanessa Redgrave and Sarah Miles which was to be the last film ever directed by Joseph Losey. It was later released in 1985, the year after his death. It was also to be the last of over seventy film and television programmes that Dors appeared in. The story centred on three women who meet regularly in a steam room and decide to fight against its closure. The film was featured later at the 1985 Cannes Film Festival.

It was during the filming of 'Steaming' that doctors changed her treatment and put her on a course of cancer killing tablets, she placed great store in these, and also prayed that her faith in God would cure her. She had started experiencing nasty side effects from the treatment and the crippling stomach pains. On April 28th 1984, she collapsed on the set of 'Steaming'. She was taken home and then taken by ambulance on a stretcher to the Princess Margaret Hospital in Windsor. On Monday 30th April, doctors operated on her to remove a blockage and discovered that the cancer had spread throughout her whole body, even to the marrow of her bones. The entire nation was praying for Diana Dors, but she deteriorated very quickly over the next few days and in the early hours of Friday 4thMay, a priest was called. Kim visited her an hour before she died. She simply held his hand. She was too ill to say anything.

Diana Dors died peacefully that evening. Her blonde hair beautifully brushed out wearing her own favourite shorty nightie in white cotton with green and red polka dots.

Her last words to Alan Lake were:

**"I love you and the boys. Look after them for me. I love you."**

Having converted to Catholicism in 1973, a funeral service was held on May 11th 1984 at the Church of the Sacred Heart, Sunningdale. The legendary glamour girl of the silver screen had been placed in a golden oak coffin clothed in her most sensational evening gown of gold lame with a matching full cape. Her thick platinum blonde hair was combed gently over her shoulders framed in a now tiny face. Around her neck she wore the unique gold D-

O-R-S necklace, that Lake had given her. Father Theodore Fontanari read one of the countless letters and postcards of tribute that had come flooding in. It said:

*"I am without faith. I know that something is missing in my life. Like millions, I loved our dear Diana, not as a sex goddess, film star, but as a genuine person who one could feel would befriend you. My heart is saddened. Without her lovely being, our world is much poorer. I will now search for what she had found."*

Diana was laid to rest just as she would have wanted. She was buried at the tiny Sunningdale Catholic Cemetery in the shade of a sycamore tree with a battery of photographers and film cameramen ready to record, in close up, the final emotional moments forever.

Thousands of flowers adorned the occasion. Kim attended the funeral, but was too emotionally distraught to attend the funeral wake afterwards at Orchard Manor, where many of the UK's top celebrities including Barbara Windsor, Lionel Blair, Danny La Rue and Lionel Jeffries were gathering.

It was a terrible time for Lake. He didn't cope at all well with the death of Dors. He was grieving inconsolably. He continued to live with their son, Jason, at Orchard Manor, which he had left in exactly the same way as it was on the day Dors had died. Bizarrely, Lake publicly burned all of Dors' remaining clothes after her funeral on the rear terrace, in front of all the mourners. Neither sleeping pills, nor his frequent visits to her grave could shake off the depression and loneliness.

On October 10th 1984, the exact day he and Dors had met for the first time sixteen years prior, Lake took a single barrelled shotgun up to his bedroom, put it in his mouth, pulled the trigger and blew his brains out one hour after speaking to the Daily Express columnist Jean Rook and to Kim on the telephone.

Dors had always joked that her Cadillac was the

same colour as her hair. When he telephoned Kim, he said:

*"I've torn my true love's hair. I'm going to exit, lovey."* What he really meant was that he had scraped the Cadillac on his garage wall and had endured enough of life.

Kim said:

*"It was the final straw for such a manic depressive."*

The housekeeper, Honor Webb, found him dead and called the police.

Although Kim was never very impressed by Lake's personality or behaviour, he was devastated by this further tragedy, he couldn't help but think about poor Jason, and what he must have been going through. Kim was actually the last person that Alan Lake ever spoke to.

Lake's death would not have made headlines in every daily newspaper were it not for the fact that the woman he mourned was Britain's greatest sex symbol, his wife, Diana Dors. He was buried a few days later next to her in the Sunningdale cemetery

The executers acting on behalf of Jason planned to sell the house quickly. It was put on the market for £360,000, but the executers accepted £280,000, although the house was still full of all their belongings. Sotheby's valued the contents at £100,000 which included everything as it stood. Lake's sister went into the house and tried to collect some personal belongings for the sake of Jason. The executers then loaded everything else deemed personal, such as the contents of drawers that contained bank statements, personal letters, and a box of photos that had been her fathers'. Precious memoirs, family photos and letters Diana sent to her parents as a child were all loaded into a number of suitcases and later auctioned off to help pay tax bills.

Jason had lost everything he held dear. His whole life had been packed up and sold by men in suits. After their work was done, the house sold and its contents gone forever, Diana's jewellery was then auctioned to the highest bidder at another Sotheby's auction. All the taxes and duties were paid, and finally there came the huge bill from the solicitors for their work.

Jason was left with virtually nothing but his memories. Not only had his mother and father died so tragically, but his whole life had been sold off on his behalf.

Rumours persisted that Diana Dors was much wealthier than she appeared. She had avoided the tax man like the plague and always asked to be paid in cash at every opportunity.

Dors had apparently hidden away what she claimed to be more than £2 million in banks across Europe.

After her second appearance on 'This Is Your Life' in 1982, Dors handed a sealed envelope to her son, Mark Dawson. Mark did not open the envelope until after his mother's death and then discovered that it was a code that would reveal the whereabouts of the money.

Alan Lake supposedly had the key that would crack the code, but as he had committed suicide, Mark was left with an apparently unsolvable code. He then sought out the computer forensic specialists, Inforenz, who recognised the encryption as the Vigenère Cipher. The Vigenère Cipher is a method of encrypting alphabetic text by using a series of different Caesar ciphers based on the letters of a keyword.

Inforenz then used their own cryptanalysis software to suggest a ten-letter decryption key, DMARYFLUCK (short for Diana Mary Fluck, Dors's real name). Although Inforenz was then able to decode the entire message and link it to a bank statement found in some of Lake's papers, the location of the money was not discovered and, if genuine, it is still unknown.

Contrary to claims by Mark Dawson, Kim was adamant that she left no hidden money, apart from £28,000 hidden in a suitcase in her attic.

Kim was left with his memories and in the Mail on Sunday dated April 25th 1999, he said:

*"Dors did not make enough of her talents. She never thought of herself as attractive. She didn't keep photographs of herself. Basically, she was not interested. She once said to me, "I just coast along." And that's what she did. She just coasted. In many ways, her talent was under-developed. Her real-life lines were funnier and saucier than most she was given to by scriptwriters. But she always valued my advice. We had known and loved each other for thirty-four years."*

When Diana Dors died, a part of Kim also died. She was the greatest friend he'd ever had.

To quote Kim:

*"If you can't get someone out of your head, maybe they are supposed to be there. I miss Dors, a little too much, a little too often and a little more every day."*

## Diana Dors dies of cancer

By David Nicholson-Lord

The actress Dianna Dors died at the Princess Margaret Hospital, Windsor, last night five days after undergoing major abdominal surgery for cancer. Miss Dors, who was 52, was admitted to hospital last Saturday after collapsing at home.

Her husband, the actor Alan Lake, was at her side when she died peacefully at 9pm. He said she had died peacefully, surrounded by cards and flowers from well-wishers.

"Her last words to me before she slipped away were: 'Oh my darling I love you. Take care of the boys and say farewell to everyone concerned.'

**Alan Lake, Diana Dors & a newspaper article about her passing**

# CHAPTER THIRTY

## THE SUMMERS SUCCESS & THE SOTOGRANDE FAILURE
## (1985)

Kim was in a sombre mood. He had lost his mojo and wasn't dealing with Dors's death at all well. After a very quiet Christmas and a non-existent fifty-fifth birthday he was further dismayed to hear of the death of Robert Pilkington, his old friend and financier. Pilkington was only in his early sixties, but the decades of alcohol abuse and excessive living had finally taken its toll. Kim still owed Pilkington, his sleeping partner, money from the 'Diet with Diana' and 'X-cel diet' programme, the sales of which had dramatically slumped as a result of Dors' well publicised recent demise. Pilkington's family never pursued him for these funds; he had died intestate and was the 'black sheep' of the famous glass empire. The family thought it best to 'let sleeping dogs die'.

Kim closed down the diet business; his days were becoming boring, drifting from one Chelsea wine bar to another in an alcoholic haze fuelled by inordinate bottles of Chablis.

One evening, Kim was having a drink in the newly re-opened Pheasantry on the Kings Road and met a rising international property developer, Martin Morris. Morris knew who Kim was and determinately engaged Kim into conversation. Martin was aware of Kim's previous acquaintance with Peter Rachman and was enthralled by Kim's tales of times gone by. After a few too many glasses, Martin's brother, Brian came to collect him in his new Bentley; Kim swapped telephone numbers with Martin and left the bar on foot.

Kim had lost his urge to pursue women and was fed up with hearing about the success of the Gold brothers, the porn and property tycoons. They had bought his ailing business, Ann Summers, from the receivers and twelve years later had turned it into a flourishing high-street chain worth many millions. The company was now being operated by David Gold's daughter, Jacqueline, who had started work there during May 1979, at the age of nineteen, after her father gave her summer work experience. Jacqueline was paid £45 a week which was less than the tea lady earned.

She started full-time with the company two years later and said:

**"It wasn't a very nice atmosphere to work in. It was all men; it was the sex industry as we all perceive it to be."**

But everything changed; she visited a Tupperware party held at an East London flat.

Jacqueline immediately saw the potential of selling sexy lingerie and sex toys to women in the privacy of their own homes. Jacqueline Gold launched the Ann Summers Party Plan. The Ann Summers parties were exclusively women-only and provided women with a forum to meet and talk about sex in a safe, female friendly environment. The parties included the presentation and potential sales of sex toys and lingerie in the informal atmosphere of someone's home; usually the home of one of the attendees. It had become so popular that such parties were now regarded as part of British popular culture. This format also provided the company with a safe and convenient way of circumventing legal restrictions about displaying sex toys for sale. Although in May 1985, Scotland Yard's Obscene Publications Squad used three articulated lorries to seize 250,000 magazines worth more than £1 million from the Gold brothers' 25,000 sq. ft. warehouse at Whyteleafe in South Croydon and their main distribution centre at Eagle Wharf Road in London.

Kim was delighted to hear their bad news and began taking an unhealthy personal interest in the Gold brothers

293

and David Gold's daughter, Jacqueline Gold. He had always resented this family which he indirectly blamed for the loss of his Ann Summers company. He considered them to be both crooked and uncouth.

Kim had also started talking to another 'Jackie'. His old flame, the ex-model, Jackie Lane called him from Marbella to say how sorry she was to hear of Dors' death. Kim was surprised to hear from her, they had lost touch after she left England to live in California where she co-starred with Elvis Presley in 'Tickle Me' and later appeared in several Hollywood films, before marrying Prince Alphonso of Hohenlohe-Langenburg who owned the famed Marbella Club.

The Prince's hotel guests regularly included Ava Gardner, Audrey Hepburn, Cary Grant and Laurence Olivier. The hotel is located on the southern Spanish Costa Del Sol on the 'Golden Mile' near Marbella 'Old Town' and Puerto Banus. During the conversation, Jackie explained that her twelve-year marriage to the prince was more or less over and that Kim would be a most welcome guest in Marbella and that they could both do with some comforting. It was time for a holiday.

As Kim's plane was landing at Gibraltar, he looked out of his window seat, down onto the Straights of Gibraltar and grinned, reminiscing the adventurous times he had experienced crossing that stretch of water on the motor torpedo boat loaded with cigarettes and whisky nearly thirty years earlier.

The 1980's saw a remarkable growth along the Costa del Sol and the Marbella Club reacted to the seismic social change by becoming simultaneously more overtly glamorous. The hotel had been admitted to the association of Leading Hotels of the World and also became a member of the Relais & Chateaux collection. Less than thirty years before, the Marbella Club had been little more than a clubhouse, its chief attraction a telephone, but now it was taking its place alongside the

Plaza Athénée in Paris, Claridge's, the Savoy and the Connaught in London.

Southern Spain had always held an attraction for raffish characters, among them was Don Jaime de Mora Y Aragon, a charming aristocrat, whose sister happened to be the Queen Fabiola of Belgium. During the eighties, he was the most elegant man in Marbella, he walked with a cane, wore a monocle, and sported the sort of beard that had been favoured by Napoleon 3rd of France. He had, of course, been to school with Prince Alfonso himself and was present at every Marbella Club party. Kim was thrilled to see Jackie again and adored the hotel. Late one evening, Kim, Don Jaime de Mora Y Aragon and Jackie Lane were having a drink at Regine's nightclub, the favourite haunt of Marbella's jet set. Jackie was bitching about her husband's recent behaviour and the two men were becoming bored. Don Jaime started telling Kim about a project to re-vitalise the Sotogrande estate.

Sotogrande was originally designed with three different districts: Coast by the sea, Bajo on the hills and Alto, in the mountainous forest, where one can enjoy incredible views over Andalusia.

Sotogrande was the largest privately owned residential development in Andalusia. Originally, a gated community, it composed of a twenty square kilometer stretch from the Mediterranean Sea, twenty-five kilometers east of Gibraltar, back into the foothills of Sierra Almenara, providing beautiful contrasting views of sea, hills and forests. Both the Rock of Gibraltar and Morocco were also in sight.

In order to re-vitalise Sotogrande, a new Marina and hotel had been planned with surrounding apartments intended to open up a different real estate market. However, the Guadiaro area which comprised of twenty-seven hectares of marshland on the west bank of the mouth of the Guadiaro River was a naturally protected area and stood in the way of the development. Land on the east side of the Guadiaro River would have to be acquired in order to facilitate the proposed development.

Don Jaime had an interest in this planned development, he knew the existing Filipino owners of the estate and also knew his way around the Spanish planning authorities, based in Malaga. He was eager to introduce partners to the deal and earn some commission; he was also impressed with Kim's manner and wandered if he might have the right contacts back in London to finance the acquisition and subsequent development of the land. Kim listened to Don Jaime intently, his first thought was to propose this project to Martin Morris, who he had met a few weeks earlier in London. He asked Don Jaime if he could supply a detailed business plan, exhibiting all the funding requirements and a site plan before his departure back to London. Don Jaime duly obliged, and after a fond farewell to Jackie, Kim returned to London and set up a meeting with Morris.

Morris was really turned on by this glamourous deal and after several weeks of due diligence, announced to Kim that he had a City pension fund lined up to finance the acquisition of the land in Sotogrande upon the condition that the fund were also a part of the subsequent construction and eventual profits.

Over the next few weeks Kim and Morris travelled weekly to Spain, holding meetings and negotiating with the owners of the estate and the planning authorities, aided by Don Jaime. Kim, Martin Morris and Don Jaime had agreed a profit of £3 million for themselves to be split three ways upon completion. Kim seriously thought that the deal would go ahead and he would earn a straight million pounds.

At the last minute, catastrophe struck. Sotogrande's owners were approached by a German bank who were happy to put the money up and finance the deal on an interest only agreement, without taking a percentage of the profit or paying Kim and his partners vast fees. The deal instantly fell apart and both Kim and Morris lost a small fortune in overheads and travel expenses.

Kim did, however, come out of this with two benefits. Firstly, he had lent Martin Morris a manuscript of his unpublished book 'Il Papa' to read. Morris was so impressed with the story that he purchased a half share in the book's rights and future film rights for £10,000.

Secondly, on his last trip back from Spain, Kim noticed a beautiful young girl in distress at Gibraltar Airport. Never a person to miss an opportunity, Kim naturally offered a helping hand. It turned out that the tearful young girl called 'Jo' was on her first modelling assignment abroad. She was only just sixteen years of age and nearly six feet tall. She had flowing blonde hair down to her waist and a perfect figure to add to her exotic aura. Kim learned that she was due to model at a bikini photo shoot in Puerto Banus that day and receive her pay directly from the photographer, once the photo session had been completed. But the photographer had never turned up, and she couldn't locate him. As a result, she had no money whatsoever, just her return ticket to Gatwick Airport and no means to return to her parents' home in North London.

Kim gave her some money and arranged that she sit next to him on the evening flight back home. During the two-and-a-half-hour flight, Kim became fascinated by Jo. She was young, refreshing and had a rebellious charm that Kim found absolutely charming. Just before touchdown, they swapped telephone numbers and Jo promised Kim that she would call him over the next few days to arrange repayment of the loan, which Kim had considered a gift. Jo was a genuine girl and did call Kim in order to repay him, but he insisted that instead of paying him back that she have lunch with him at Mimmo d'Ischia the following day.

As Kim waited for Jo in the restaurant, he suddenly noticed all heads turn. Jo had arrived, wearing the shortest white mini-skirt imaginable. Kim thought how sexy it looked against her tanned legs, but as she was shown to his table, he also noticed that everyone had a shocked look on their faces as if to say he was a 'dirty old man'. He put these thoughts aside, and the two of them got along like 'a house on fire' despite their obvious vast age difference. Kim invited her for a further drink after lunch, followed by coffee at his flat in the Kings Road. Of course, the inevitable happened, the problem was, how was Jo going to tell her parents that she had been out with a man older than themselves and how was Kim going to tell his daughter, Campbell, that he was courting a girl only three years older than herself. Somehow both of them self-justified their reasons and a few weeks later they really had become 'an item'.

Kim decided to move back to Eaton Terrace. He rented a two-bedroomed apartment and promptly moved in with Jo, shocking everybody.

The Sotogrande marina complex was eventually constructed that same year and inaugurated in 1988 with the official name Puerto Deportivo Sotogrande. The Real Club Maritimo hotel was constructed, as well as beachfront apartments and the Octágono beach club.

Nowadays, some of the richest and most powerful families of Spain have summer homes in Sotogrande. Inhabitants of Sotogrande now include ex-British Prime Minister Tony Blair. It has evolved into a sailing destination with iconic status, and the establishment of the Real Club de Maritimo de Sotogrande, has been endorsed by King Juan Carlos. Today the R.C.M.S. has over five hundred members and hosts many major international sailing events.

Kim just wished he could have been part of it all. Money was becoming a problem again and Kim needed to find a new senior school for Campbell to finish her education. He was finishing Jo's education himself personally in London!

Jacqueline Gold outside one of her many
Ann Summers retail shops

Prince Alphonso's Marbella Club & Sotogrande in
Southern Spain

# CHAPTER THIRTY-ONE

## BENTLEYS & BRINKS-MAT BANDITS
### (1986)

Most weekends Kim would drive down to Dorset in the Mercedes estate car to see Campbell at Knighton House School, near Blandford Forum. He often made the journey alone because if he took Jo with him, the two young girls, who were of a similar age, would simply twitter to each other about 'girlie' subjects, making Kim feel most uncomfortable, like a boring old man. When he travelled alone, he would always take the opportunity of popping in for a drink, with either his old girlfriend and confidante, Angela Sieff, in Hampshire, or Virginia, Lady Bath, at the Dower House near the Longleat estate. Both the ladies' homes were near Campbell's school.

He was bored with the Mercedes but couldn't afford a Bentley at this time, as I was about to find out. It was at this time I became closer to Kim; he knew that I was operating my classic car business in Elvaston Mews. Out of the blue, one Spring morning Kim arrived unannounced into my showroom. He was immaculately dressed in his signature Prince of Wales check suit, lemon woven tie in a Windsor knot and the usual beige suede 'Chelsea' boots.

***"Hi Nigel, I drove past last night and saw this Bentley Continental, beautiful car, shame it's such a turdish colour, how much is it?"***

I explained that I had only just bought this Bentley in an auction at Alexandra Palace and that I would probably export the car to Los Angeles, as the coach-built cars were highly fashionable in California at that time, and that was where I sold most of my classic Rolls Royces and Bentleys. Secretly, I suspected that he couldn't afford the car, but I told him the price was £14,950 anyway. To my surprise, Kim asked:

300

*"Can we go for a test drive, old boy?"*

Knowing that he had great experience with these cars, I replied:

*"Of course, Kim, you drive."*

We both climbed into the turd brown Bentley and Kim proceeded southwards down Queensgate towards Chelsea and ended up in the Kings Road. Suddenly, he pulled over and said:

*"I want you to meet a new friend of mine, Count Liechtenstein. He owns 'Le Casserole' restaurant just over there. He's running an old tub of a Bentley and wants a newer one in better condition. Put the price of this one up to £15,950 and cover me for a grand, old boy. I'll do my best to convince the 'c\*nt' to buy it, but you might have to take the old bucket in part exchange."*

Jokingly, I replied:

*"Kim, you've become a bloody car dealer."*

*"No bloody way, not my game,"* he replied.

We arrived at the restaurant and Kim introduced me to the Count. He was as camp as it gets, dandier than 'Dandy Kim', but quickly I realised that he was a serious buyer and he had a great knowledge of old Bentley Continentals. The gay Count invited me to join them for lunch in his restaurant and then took me to see his old car around the corner in the Vale. As we drove up the Vale, I could see this old silver Bentley covered in dust and dirt parked up on the kerb, smothered with parking tickets. Instinctively, I knew this had to be his car, sure enough, I was right and I politely explained that it would need a fortune spending upon it to bring it up to a saleable standard.

To make matters worse, the Count had purchased this Bentley from the disgraced actor Peter Wyngarde, who actually used the car in the television series 'Jason King'. The ITV television series was axed due to Wyngarde being caught in the Gloucester bus station public toilets with

Richard Whalley (a truck driver). He was arrested and fined £75 for gross indecency.

After much haggling with the Count, he finally bought the brown Bentley for £15950 and I gave him £4950 for his old wreck. As I left with the balance of £11000, he explained that he was leaving for Liechtenstein that evening and told me that Kim would collect the car the following morning from my showroom.

I was quite convinced that the homosexual Count was not from the famous European dynasty and that Kim had not only engineered a way to get his hands on a Bentley Continental to drive around the town again, but he'd also earned some money. I remember thinking 'Good luck to him.' As promised, the next morning, I drew £1000 in cash from Coutt's bank around the corner, expecting an eager Kim to be waiting at my front door for the 'readies', but, strangely, nothing… later in the afternoon he telephoned me and said:

*"My poor darling girlfriend is most unwell. Could you please deliver the Bentley Continental to my home in Eaton Terrace instead?"*

Accordingly, I drove the Bentley around to Eaton Terrace. Kim answered the door and invited me indoors for a glass of wine. We started talking, Kim always had such interesting stories to tell. I thought he was alone but there were strange noises and movements coming from upstairs.

Suddenly, I noticed a pair of thigh length suede boots start wafting down the staircase revealing the top of one of the best pairs of legs that I had ever seen. As this gorgeous girl came into sight, Kim announced:

*"Nigel, this is Jo. My poor baby darling has had a terrible day with growing pains and we're due to meet some of her friends for dinner this evening."*

I nearly blew a raspberry. She was over six foot in those boots. How much more was she going to grow? She looked young enough to be his granddaughter, but my

God she was beautiful, an absolute vision. I discreetly handed him a brown envelope and the keys for the Bentley and left. I shall never forget it.

Our friendship began.

The next morning Kim telephoned. I immediately thought that there must be a problem with the car, but I was wrong. Kim explained that the previous evening Jo's two girlfriends had arrived at Eaton Terrace, they were both teenage models, and in typical Kim language, he described them as a 'pair of absolute delights'. He was so impressed with the girls and knowing he had plenty of cash on him, he offered to take all three to Mimmo d'Ischia for dinner.

Having been duly welcomed by Mimmo personally, the four of them were shown to a round table next to a pair of cheaply pin-striped businessmen drinking champagne whose loud voices and showy mannerisms made them as inconspicuous as a fully dressed cardinal in a whorehouse.

With egos, the size of a football field, they made it impossible for anyone to remain within hearing distance. Having not failed to hear their conversations which centred around a court case, Kim had the insight to realise that the larger man was most likely a villain and the smaller chap was probably his lawyer or barrister. As the evening progressed and the two men became more and more intoxicated, their conversation began to turn towards Kim. In a very loud voice, Kim heard the larger man say:

**"Oy, what's an old poofter like that doing with those three tarts?"**

**"He must be paying dearly for that,"** replied the smaller man.

The insulting statements persisted and the other dinner guests were beginning to take offence by these two abrasively drunken fellow diners. Mimmo discreetly went over to their table and politely asked them if they could be a little quieter, but with no result.

**"But that bloke looks like a poof in that stupid jacket, he's a dickhead. Get us another bottle of shampoo,"** said the larger man.

That was it. Kim handed Jo the keys to the Count's Bentley parked outside in Elizabeth Street and asked her to take her friends to the car. Kim paid the bill and pretended to use the toilet situated at the rear of the restaurant. He returned through the centre of the restaurant and walked past the offending table. The two men were by now tucking into a large bowl of pasta. He lifted the larger man's bowl of Penne Arrabiata up and promptly dropped it again… straight into his lap. A huge fracas began, the sweet trolley was right by their table and as the larger man rose up threatening to kill Kim. The trolley dramatically overturned, showering all the surrounding tables and the dinner guests in Tiramisu, Italian Torrone Parfait and Venetian Sgroppino. One of London's most fashionable restaurants had just become a bombsite! The larger man was out for blood and chased Kim out of the restaurant, but luckily Jo was bright, she had started the Bentley ready for Kim's speedy exit.

After listening to all this, I wondered why Kim had telephoned me. He knew I was acquainted with Mimmo. His restaurant had been one of my favourites since he'd opened it when I was a very young man. He then asked me if I'd join him at lunchtime to revisit the restaurant in order to offer to pay for all the damage that had been created. I willingly agreed and as we walked into the restaurant Mimmo was there, with the biggest smile on his face, he looked at Kim and asked:

**"Kim, did you realise who you were taking on last night. That was the Brinks-Mat robber Kenneth Noye. He's been on the front pages for weeks. He's an animal and he's just got off a murder charge at the Bailey."** Kim was horrified and humbly asked Mimmo how much the damage was. Mimmo replied:

### *"There's no damage, Kim, now what are you both having for lunch?"*

Kenneth Noye had been a police informer for many years. He had begun a connection with corrupt officers by the time he was arrested for receiving stolen goods back in 1977. Active as a fence, Noye was among those involved in laundering a huge quantity of stolen gold bullion taken during the infamous Brink's-Mat robbery which occurred early on 26th November 1983 when six robbers broke into the Brink's-Mat warehouse, Unit 7 of the Heathrow International Trading Estate near Heathrow Airport in west London. At the time, it was described as 'the crime of the century'. When the gang had gained entry to the warehouse, they poured petrol over the staff and then threatened them with a lit match if they did not reveal the combination numbers of the vault. The robbers thought they were going to steal £3.2 million in cash, but they found three tonnes of gold bullion and stole £26 million (approximately £200 million in 2017) worth of gold, diamonds and cash.

While he was being investigated for his involvement in the crime, Noye stabbed to death Detective Constable John Fordham who was involved in the police surveillance of Noye in the grounds of his home. He had been acquitted of murder on the grounds of self-defence in December 1985, but he was later found guilty in July 1986 of handling some of the stolen gold.

Mick McAvoy, one of the quickly-arrested thieves, had asked Brian Perry to conceal the gold he had received, and it was Perry who brought in Noye and John Palmer, subsequently nicknamed 'Goldfinger'; Palmer was acquitted in 1987 of knowingly handling gold from the Brink's-Mat robbery.

Noye had smelted much of the Brink's-Mat gold he had received and mixed it with copper coins in an attempt to disguise its origins, although eleven gold bars from the robbery were still found hidden at his home. Sentenced to fourteen years and fined £500,000 with £200,000 in cost, he was released from prison in 1994, having served eight years. The loss adjusters of Brink's-Mat insurers bought a civil action against Noye while he was incarcerated and £3 million was eventually recovered from him.

Mimmo was the perfect gentleman, Kim certainly had no idea who he was up against. It was surprising that he was still here. Kim was relieved to hear that Noye was finally sent to jail in July 1986. Both Kim and Jo dined out on the story for months.

In the summer of 1986, Campbell left Knighton House School. She passed her entrance exam to Cranbourne Chase School, which was an independent boarding school for 130 girls situated at New Wardour Castle near Tisbury in Wiltshire. The magnificent castle later fell into a severe state of disrepair. It was later bought in 2010 for a knock-down price by multi-millionaire fashion designer Jasper Conran. The house, with its magnificent galleried staircase, was the setting for the Royal Ballet School in the hit movie Billy Elliot. The school was magnificent, but as usual, Kim was worried about the sharp rise in school fees he was about to face.

**Cranbourne Chase, Campbell's new school & Count Liechtenstein's Bentley Continentals**

Kim & Campbell

A selection of published books in which Kim is
featured

# CHAPTER THIRTY-TWO

## GOADING THE GOLDS
### (1987 – 1993)


Early in 1987, Kim was most surprised to receive a telephone call from Ron Coleman who was the managing director of Ann Summers and worked directly with Kim's arch enemies, David and Ralph Gold. Kim wondered what on earth he could want. Although the conversation was somewhat guarded, Coleman suggested that they should have a meeting, to which Kim willingly agreed. They duly met for lunch in London and Kim was staggered at what Coleman had to say.

He basically inferred that he was in fear of his life and the Gold brothers wanted him out of Ann Summers to make way for David Gold's daughter, Jacqueline, to take over the helm.

He further stated that during his many years of loyal service to the Golds that he had amassed a pile of records of their sales network and evidence linking them to the 'wanking booths' and 'peep shows' based in Soho throughout the 1960's, followed by organised 'f***erware' sex parties in London during the 1970's. Coleman explained that the Golds now saw him as a threat to their flourishing cleaned up operation. Basically, he had been around too long and he knew too much of their past shenanigans. Knowing how Kim felt about the Golds, Coleman thought that Kim was the natural custodian of the incriminating evidence. He knew that Kim would act upon it if necessary and he was effectively creating his own life insurance policy.

Coleman also explained that he had a serious heart condition. He then insisted that Kim swear to him that the sensitive documents and accounts would not be released to anybody or used in any future publication until after his own death. Kim was speechless, but even more fascinated when he started carefully reading the documents which showed the extent to which those involved went to in order to escape both the Inland Revenue and the British decency laws.

Coleman underestimated just how far he was fuelling Kim's fire. Kim had been yearning to have a stab at the Gold brothers for years and he thought that this might just be the first serious opportunity. Some months later in 1987, Kim found out that Jacqueline Gold had been appointed CEO of Ann Summers and that Coleman had been ousted. Kim instinctively knew that Coleman had been telling him the truth about his perilous position.

In the back of Kim's mind, the usual problem continued to persist. He was desperately short of cash and he was forced to give notice on the property in Eaton Terrace and therefore, rented a smaller property in Caroline Terrace with Jo.

In the autumn, Kim called me to say that the faithful old Mercedes Benz was on its 'last legs' and needed replacing as a matter of urgency, I popped around to see him and he sheepishly explained what he wanted me to organise:

*"Nigel, it's like this. I am somewhat short of cash. Would you please buy the old Merc for cash so I can pay Campbell's bloody school fees and then find me a good second-hand Range Rover which you can sell me on a finance agreement. By the way... you'll have to lose the deposit on the finance agreement."*

I knew exactly what he wanted me to do, but I had my reservations as to whether a 'bona fide' finance company would even accept him. Amazingly, I proposed him to a particular finance company and they accepted his references. I found a suitable Range Rover for him and inflated the sale price to therefore alleviate him the need of paying out any deposit monies whatsoever. Kim was thrilled. Little did I know that he wasn't going to be able to keep the he monthly payments!

During this period, I often met Kim for dinner after closing my showroom, usually at Montpeliano, just off Knightsbridge. We had many things in common. We both loved women, classic cars and restaurants. We were both single fathers. My first wife had recently left me and I was bringing up my children with the help of nannies.

I met many of his vast array of colourful friends and contacts, many of whom became my clients. It was on one of these occasions that we had dinner with Omar Sharif, the Egyptian actor the Egyptian actor best known for playing Sherif Ali in Lawrence of Arabia and the title role in Dr Zhivago. Aside from acting, Omar Sharif had almost another complete life. He was a world class bridge player and he was a columnist on the subject for the Chicago Tribune.

However, he was also an inveterate gambler which cost him considerable sums of money, hence his relatively modest net worth at the time of his death. In later life, he described himself self-deprecatingly as 'a useless person who plays cards', but his easy charm and good humour never faltered. Sharif was a household name and women worshipped him, but I couldn't believe how much smaller he appeared in reality and the garlic on his breath was rancid!

After Sharif left the restaurant, Kim emotionally told me that he had split up with Jo. Apparently, they had not been getting along for a while, mainly because of their forty-year age difference had begun to surface and the breakdown was further fuelled by Kim's lack of funds. She had found a younger man and finally went on to live in the Canary Isles. They remained good friends and Kim always said:

**"They all go back to their roots eventually. What was I thinking? Forty years my junior, I must be raving mad, but she was an enthralling creature!"**

The year 1988 was a non-eventful one for Kim. Business in London was booming but he just wasn't part of it. He was now single again and commuting to Dorset each week visiting Campbell at her new school and staying with his old flame, Angela Sieff, at her enchanting house in Hampshire. Kim always used to call Angela 'Boots'. They both used to cause quite a stir at the very conservative, thatched pub in Angela's tiny village. 'Boots' would turn up wearing a full-length Ocelot coat with glossy white high heeled boots, thick bright red lipstick and sporting fingernails which were like talons. Kim would wear his denim suit, immaculately pressed, with his cream suede Chelsea boots. All the locals knew Angela and smiled when she used to walk up to the old wooden bar surrounded by farmers and ask for her usual bottle of champagne. One thing was for sure, you couldn't miss this flamboyant couple!

Soon Kim found that even the flat in Caroline Terrace was becoming too expensive, it was also too small, especially when Campbell was home from school. They moved to a cheaper three-bedroomed house in Morgan's Walk Battersea. He finally bought a word processor and focused his concentration on writing a book about Ann Summers and the Gold brothers. He began typing, and while respecting his promise to Ron Coleman, he discreetly used some of Coleman's information, thinly disguised within some of the proposed chapters

Kim couldn't make up his mind whether to call the book 'Ann Summers and The Porn Barons Gold' or 'Ann Summers and The F***erware Plan'. Either way, Kim was determined that the title would incorporate an insulting poke at the Gold brothers.

It was around this time that Coleman suffered his first major heart attack.

For the first time in his life, Kim now wanted as much publicity as possible, he wanted the Golds to be aware that he was writing a sensational and revealing book about them. He quietly wished that they would approach him before publication and offer him a substantial sum not to publish the new book.

During 1989, Campbell left Cranbourne Chase after taking her O-levels. Although Kim wanted her to continue her education to A-level, he breathed a sigh of relief that the crippling school fees were finally over. She returned to London to live with her father in Battersea and against Kim's wishes started working for the Select Model Agency, one of the longest running agencies London. Select Model Management was responsible for turning the modelling world on its head, pioneering 'scouting' by getting out on the streets to find natural, individual and unique looks to be groomed into major names in the fashion industry.

Kim was thrilled to have her home once again. They were more like brother and sister. The house was kept immaculately and Campbell would often cook Kim a spectacular dinner if they were staying in. Campbell was extremely attractive and inevitably the issue of her boyfriends began. She only had to walk across Battersea Bridge to be in heart of Chelsea where all the eligible young studs hung out. Although Kim had every father's natural reservations regarding his sixteen-year-old daughter, he did draw the line at her driving off in his Range Rover and cruising, the Kings Road. She was both underage and uninsured.

Some months later, the book was still not finished, but Kim received a call from Ralph Gold himself. It was a fishing exercise to try and coax Kim to reveal some of the contents of the up-and-coming book. Kim told him very little, but dropped enough questions about Ron Coleman to alert Gold that they must have made contact with each other. Kim knew the Golds' vanity would not be flattered by such a book. In fact, the Golds always kept a well-cultivated low profile and despite numerous requests for interviews, they nearly always declined.

The saga continued for a further year, Kim was drinking reasonably heavily and he had been beaten up twice and lost his driving licence. I had the unenviable job of returning the Range Rover to the finance company. The finance agreement was horribly in arrears and Kim didn't want the repossession team to come to his home, especially with Campbell living in the house.

Kim could not make headway with the book. Quite simply, his heart was not in the project, but he knew of no other way to try and generate money, other than rattle the Gold brothers' cage.

The phone calls started again. This time it was David Gold who said:

*"Oh Kim, I've been looking through Ralph's notes on his conversation with you and it seems to me that he got the chemistry wrong with you. I'd like to see you myself."*

*"Where do you want me to come?"* asked Kim.

*"Don't worry, we'll come up to see you,"* replied Gold.

Kim felt that was extraordinary. Ralph was usually pretty relaxed, but David was a workaholic who never left his office.

David Gold arrived at the restaurant in Battersea with his daughter, Jacqueline. It was an edgy lunch, the only subject that came under discussion was what the Golds' referred to as 'that book'. The Golds continually used the word 'injunction', and matters became tenser, as Kim asked David Gold if he had been responsible for two recent attacks on him. Gold was furious at the back-handed accusation but was still intent on trying to sort out some sort of arrangement with Kim to stop the book's publication. Gold suggested that he sent a chapter to their solicitor, Peter Carter-Ruck at Carter Ruck and Partners, the eminent libel specialists. Kim quietly chuckled as he knew that not only was the book incomplete, the title was still undecided upon.

313

The non-conclusive lunch was followed by a further two meetings at the Ann Summers headquarters in south Croydon and the Golds actually sent a car for Kim upon each occasion, as he had lost his licence. They still feared that Kim might have had something far greater to throw at them than he actually had. Kim did send a chapter to the Golds' solicitors and explained:

*"It merely tells their story."*

But the lawyers replied:

*"It's open to misinterpretation."*

It was deadlock. In order to provoke a reaction, Kim gave a long interview to Andrew Lycett, threatening to publish the book by Christmas. The article appeared on October 17th 1993 in 'Night & Day'.

The Golds were past masters with the legal system and had fought some heavy court battles over their many years in business. In the end, they basically called Kim's bluff and walked away, suspecting that Kim was down on his luck and just wanted to wheedle some money out of them. Although they were concerned that Kim's proposed book might tarnish the clean image of Ann Summers, they were also worried that if the book became a best-seller, it might frighten off the thousands of lascivious housewives who set up giggly all-girl parties at which giant dildos, chocolate willies and G-strings are punted around to the general amusement of all, which provided the core income for the Gold brothers' spaghetti of businesses and networks.

Unfortunately, Kim received no money and it wasn't going to be his last fight with the Gold family. Kim went on to fall out with the Gold brothers but he had a robust admiration of their' business acumen. He always said:

*"They're careful to the point of meanness."*

During 1993, The Gold Group reported a turnover of £62 million in the year to June 1992. Out of this, the brothers had paid themselves salaries of over £1 million each. In fact, the total turnover of the Gold companies had been estimated at well over double that figure, and the Golds' own remuneration was also significantly higher.

Eventually, Jacqueline Gold transformed Ann Summers into a multi-million-pound business, with a sales force today comprising more than 7,500 women party organisers and 136 high street stores throughout the UK, Ireland, and the Channel Islands, coordinated from their Head Office in Surrey. There were around 4,000 Ann Summers Parties every week throughout Britain, Ireland, Holland, Denmark and Germany.

Kim was yet to receive a further major blow. Campbell had been spending less and less time at Morgan's Walk. One morning, she announced to Kim that she was moving in with her new boyfriend and that she was pregnant. Kim knew that the days of living with Campbell were over and his glamourous life in London had come to an end. Most of the original 'Chelsea Set' had died at a young age from one excess or another, leaving Kim to feel very lonely and very short of funds. It was time for a change.

I married Kim's ex-secretary Caroline Walker in 1993 and although we tried to invite him to several functions, including our wedding reception at the Savoy, he was always unavailable. In hindsight, I am sure he just wanted to be alone. We lost touch with Kim and were told by mutual acquaintances that he thought he had gone to live in Southern Ireland. I never believed that, and it would be eight years before our paths crossed again.

A Business Doing *Pleasure* Ann Summers

**Dandy Kim and the girlie mag millionaires**

High-born chancer Kim Caborn-Waterfield founded Ann Summers. A year later, he sold up to porn barons David and Ralph Gold. Now he's keen to publish his story. Unfortunately, the Golds don't want him to

An Ann Summers logo, Jacqueline and David Gold, Night & Day article

October 17th 1993, David Gold with his Hawker Siddeley HS 125 jet

316

## CHAPTER THIRTY-THREE

## DANDY DISAPPEARS TO DORSET
## (1994 – 2001)

From 1994 until 2000, Kim was missing as far as the World knew. All the rumours indicated that he was still in Ireland, but that was not true. Just before Campbell gave birth to a son and made Kim a grandfather, he had moved back to his beloved Dorset. He had become involved with a delightful lady, Boo, who was an ex-Olympian equestrian champion. They had a mutual interest in horses and lived very quietly in a cottage on a magnificent country estate near Tarrant Gunville.

Kim had received his driving licence back and was given a little Peugeot motor car in which he used to make his daily pilgrimage to the Langton Arms in Tarrant Monkton at the heart of the 'chocolate box' village for a couple of glasses or bottles of their wonderful Drostdy-Hof Merlot red wine. It was a far cry from the hustle and bustle of modern life in London and surprisingly, Kim seemed happy and basically content. He still saw 'Boots' regularly, and renewed his friendship with Virginia, Marchioness of Bath, attending many boozy functions at Job's Mill with its famous maze near the famous Longleat estate.

Determined to finally finish the Ann Summers book and write his own memoirs, he bought a new computer equipped with a very early voice activation programme which, to his frustration, never worked properly. He felt it would assist him in his attempts at becoming an author, he even registered two internet websites to market his books. In 1995, Kim was mentioned in a new book titled, Family Life: Birth, Death and the Whole Damn Thing by Elisabeth Luard. This made him even more determined to succeed with his own autobiography. Campbell would

317

sometimes visit her father. She knew the area well from her school days and in 1997, she gave birth to a baby girl, making Kim a grandfather for a second time. Interestingly, both her children use the surname Caborn-Waterfield to this day.

Kim was still in contact with Andrew Lycett who had interviewed him a few years previously regarding the Golds and he learned that ITV were producing a two-part mini-series called 'The Blonde Bombshell' based on the life and death of actress Diana Dors. It was produced by London Weekend Television for ITV and was first shown on the 26th and 27th of April 1999. Keeley Hawes played Dors during her early career (1945–1960) and Amanda Redman during her later years (1965–1984).

Diana Dors' son, Mark, later claimed that the series had portrayed the story incorrectly and Eddie Gibb of the Sunday Herald wrote:

### *"This is a sad story badly told."*

Kim was totally offended for not either being included or consulted about the mini-series. Although he had never married her, he always believed that he was the closest person in Dors' life and always referred to her as his greatest friend, lover and soulmate. Andrew Lycett interviewed Kim in 1999 and a long article describing their life story and friendship was published in the Mail on Sunday Review on April 25th 1999.

An ITV spokesman said that:

### *"Their dramatization simply didn't have 'space' for the most important man in Diana Dors's life."*

Kim had a super 70th birthday and saw the Millennium in with his old friends the Hardings at their idyllic farmhouse just outside Bournemouth. Many of Kim's old Dorset friends attended, including 'Boo' and 'Boots'. It was also a very poignant evening for him because it was the date that freed him from his 'Oath of Non-Disclosure' to Jack Warner forty years previously after securing his freedom from prison for the infamous robbery of Warner's villa on the Cote d'Azur.

In 2000, the Daily Mail reported that they had discovered Kim living in Ireland. The paper stated:

*"At first, he denied he was 'Dandy Kim'. He changed his mind when it was pointed out few 70-year-olds would sport shoulder-length white hair, tight jeans, denim shirt, suede boots and a cut-glass accent."*

The article was nonsense.

It was also around this time when the 'Diary of a Teddy Boy, A Memoir of the Long Sixties' by Mim Scala was published. The new book made many references to Kim's hedonistic lifestyle and relationship with Diana Dors. I believe Kim became friendly with Mim Scala who now lives in Ireland.

Coincidently in early 2000, Michael Eland, Kim's old nemesis, was on a short trip to London from Paris. He was now eighty years old, in perfect health and still up to mischief. I had known him for most of my life as had my wife, Caroline. Eland threw a surprise dinner party at Mosimann's restaurant in West Halkin Street and invited some guests, including Caroline, from his illustrious past, one of whom was Kim's old colleague and partner, Bobby Mckew. Caroline was seated next to McKew and she asked him if he knew the whereabouts of Kim. He replied that he did know where Kim was, but that he was on firm instructions not to divulge Kim's telephone number or address to anyone. Caroline politely suggested that she should give him her home number to pass on to Kim, therefore giving Kim the choice of coming out of the woodwork or remaining reclusive.

The rest of evening was a wonderful success and the food was incredible. Anton Mosimann has cooked for five British Prime Ministers at No. 10 Downing Street for visiting heads of state. He has cooked for four Presidents of the United States and four generations of the British Royal Family. In 2011, he was chosen to cook for the 300 guests at the evening reception of the wedding of Prince William, Duke of Cambridge, and Catherine Middleton in Buckingham Palace.

Two days later, I was at my desk at home and the telephone rung.

*"Is that you, Nigel?"* Kim didn't need to introduce himself. I recognised his distinguished voice immediately. After a long conversation catching up, I happened to say that if he was ever in London that he would be more than welcome to stay at our penthouse by Chelsea Bridge. Well, to my amazement the video intercom in the apartment rung three days later and there was Kim on the screen, suitcase in hand. I presumed that he was staying for a few days but a week later, it was easier to give him the spare keys to the flat. Having said that, he was an absolute pleasure to entertain, provided the fridge was filled with cold beers and at least half a case of a good French white burgundy.

Over the following weeks, we developed a great friendship. Kim would sit, glass in hand, watching the various boats sail down the Thames and recite, invariably late at night, many of his life's stories, most of which were quite fascinating and gave me the detailed information I needed to write this book. He received a message while he was with me that Ron Coleman had died. He explained to me that his passing meant that he had the freedom to use Coleman's explosive files at his own discretion and therefore make the Ann Summers book far more sensational.

Kim stayed for about a fortnight and then announced that he was returning to Boo in Dorset to try and finish his books.

In May, the following year Caroline and myself moved from London, although we had a flat in the south of France, the children were still at school until the end of July, we therefore needed to stay in the U.K. and rented an apartment in Bournemouth by the sea. It didn't take Kim long to realise we were only fifteen miles down the road from his home in Tarrant Gunville. Suddenly, I had a 'ready-made' social life. I used to meet up with him at the Langton Arms in Tarrant Monkton which sits opposite the beautiful 15th century All Saints Parish Church. After quaffing copious amounts of roast beef, he would climb into my Rolls Royce determined to introduce me to as many people as possible and show me all the local sights. Through Kim, Caroline and I were invited to numerous dinner parties at the Harding's farmhouse where we met many people including the actor, Michael Medwin. He was educated at Canford School in Dorset, and the Institute Fischer, Montreux, Switzerland. He first appeared on stage in 1940 and has been quoted many times as saying:

*"I knew at a young age I was going to be an actor. Acting has always been in my bones."*

He has also said that Charles Laughton and Edward G. Robinson were the two biggest influences in his life of acting, and that being awarded the O.B.E. (Order of the British Empire) in the 2005 Queens Birthday Honour's List for Services to Drama was the single greatest thing that had ever happened to him.

I finally met Kim's partner, Boo, a thoroughly delightful lady, and often visited Angela Sieff, known as 'Boots' at her cosy home, where there was always a chilled bottle of champagne waiting for us. Apart from developing a taste for Drostdy-Hof, Kim's favourite red wine, I also developed a taste for drinking champagne during the day. Kim would often like to drive back to Sedgehill Manor just to take a look and then stop off at the Benett Arms at Semley for a refresher before motoring on to Longleat to see Virginia, Marchioness of Bath, at Job's Mill.

Kim's relationship with Virginia, Marchioness of Bath, was extraordinary. They would speak to each other like kids. The Marchioness would always like to tease him about his antics and to ridicule his reputation with the opposite sex. I was staggered when one afternoon over a bottle of cold Bollinger in her sitting room, she suddenly looked at Kim and asked:

*"Kim, darling, when were you last laid?"*
*"A few days ago, thank you."* Kim replied smiling.
*"Um, I think more like a few decades ago, if you ask me,"* she replied.

She became Lady Bath when she married Lord Henry Bath in 1953. It was some time before they had a child. The poetess, Iris Tree, was responsible for suggesting that if Virginia wanted to get pregnant, Cerne Abbas was the place. The poetess directed her niece and her husband to 'pay their respects' to the Cerne Giant, a chalk figure with a phallus carved out of the hillside. Their ensuing daughter, born in 1958, was appropriately christened Silvy Cerne.

Her years as Marchioness of Bath coincided with her husband's development of Longleat as a major tourist attraction to rival the Duke of Bedford's antics at Woburn, and Lord Montagu's vintage cars at Beaulieu. The celebrated lions had arrived in 1966, amidst hilarious publicity and in the teeth of much po-faced local opposition. The takings soared from £135,000 in 1964 to £328,000 that same year.

In 1958, Lord Bath had handed over some of the estate to his eccentric son, Lord Weymouth, the present Lord Bath, while he and Lady Bath semi-retired to Job's Mill, a converted mill, four miles away from Longleat, allowing Virginia to concentrate on her painting. She was a talented painter of floral miniatures which she occasionally exhibited. She had an adorable personality and sadly passed away later in 2003.

Later in 2001, I was back in England and was invited to an art gallery opening just off Regent Street where I met a beautiful blonde girl who worked for the Proud Galleries in Pimlico. She started talking to me about art and I casually mentioned that I had a few original Stephen Ward drawings which I had purchased from a dealer in Windsor, the subjects being Mandy Rice-Davies and Vicki Martin. The girl asked me if I would be interested in exhibiting them or possibly selling them, I explained that I hadn't thought about it, but told her that I had a great friend of mine that had a further four Ward drawings which included a particularly sexually explicit sketch of an unknown female.

A few days later, I was telling Kim about the meeting and he suggested we should think about auctioning our joint collections and hold a private viewing at the Proud Galleries in return for which, we would give them a percentage of the sale proceeds. Kim not only had a drawing of Christine Keeler but had stayed in touch with Keeler over the years. Having agreed terms with the gallery he even asked Keeler for her support and to be present for the two private viewings, unfortunately she declined. The two evenings were a great success and an American art collector, who also owned a military museum in Texas purchased the offensive drawing for £4000 and said:

**"Gee, this must be ultimate vibrator."**

I was most amused when Kim replied:

**"It is a visible insight into the warped mind of Stephen Ward. I think its Ann Summers'."**

We celebrated our sales on the final evening with a splendid dinner around the corner at Mimmo d'Ischia."

323

**Why Diana Dors wasn't really sexy at all – by the only man she ever truly loved**

'Dandy Kim' Waterfield kept his silence for 50 years ... now he explodes a myth

By Andrew Lycett

Andrew Lycett's article:  The Mail on Sunday Review
April 25th 1999

# CHAPTER THIRTY-FOUR

## KIM BECOMES KAVANAGH Q.C.
## (2002 - 2013)


I was now living back in Kent and Kim became very much part of our furniture when he wasn't with Boo in Dorset. He had always been terrific with children and was especially fond of my son and daughter. I was, therefore, very surprised and somewhat shocked when he arrived one evening with a present for my youngsters, it was a VHS copy of the video that he had marketed years before, entitled, 'The Joy of Sex', nevertheless, my kids were enthralled! Kim also couldn't wait to also tell us that he had been referred to in Hugh Massingber's new book, Daydream Believer, Confessions of a Hero-Worshipper.

In 2002, Kim received a call from Jeremy Scott, his ex-wife, Penny Brahms' new husband. He had just finished writing 'Fast and Louche: Confessions of a Sinner'. Scott wanted to discuss the new book with Kim and judge his reaction to the references made by him of Kim in the book prior to its publication. The last thing he wanted was an injunction issued after publication.

In the new book, Jeremy Scott described Kim as:

*"An amusing, good-looking man, who seemed to take nothing entirely seriously, including himself. But he shared with Lord Byron, a reputation of being dangerous to know."*

Jeremy Scott said:

*"Dandy Kim.... Over thirty years ago he was my closest friend. Schism came between us and, for a decade, living in another country, I did not see Kim. In the interval, I wrote a novel based upon him. Pamela Moore had done the same ten years before in 'Chocolates for Breakfast', but kindlier. Mine was the raffish tale of an unprincipled adventurer; certainly,*

325

*the book was libellous. Before publication, I was*
*obliged to seek him out, with some misgivings. We*
*dined. I explained what I had done and how*
*inconvenient it would be should he injunct.*

Apparently, Kim's reaction was to laugh, saying:

*"If I worried about what people wrote, I should*
*have spent a quarter of my life in litigation."*

Kim was always quietly niggled that his ex-wife,
Penny Brahms, had married Jeremy Scott but he kept the
relationship on an even keel for the sake of their daughter,
Campbell. He 'supposedly' agreed that he wouldn't issue
libel proceedings against Jeremy Scott or his publishers.
Whatever happened between them, something changed
Kim's mind and once the book had been printed, he issued
proceedings in the High Courts of Justice as a self-litigant.
Amazingly, he won, without representation, and an out of
court settlement was made as well as costing poor Jeremy
Scott's publishers over £50,000 in lost sales and reprinting
costs.

Needless to say, Penny Brahms took her second
husband's side during this legal action and it caused a long-
term feud between them all that was only partially healed
before Kim's death.

Jeremy Scott later said:

*"I knew Kim three ways. Personally, from his*
*press cuttings and from his myth. It was not for*
*nothing that I had chosen him as main character in*
*my novel; as a personality, he fascinated me.*

*Michael George David Patrick Caborn-*
*Waterfield, 'Dandy Kim', Lord of the Manor of*
*Sedgehill, I thought, amateur jockey and gun-*
*runner... promotor of wild schemes. There were*
*planes and helicopters, race horses and polo ponies...*
*the Tangier night club and water ski school front for*
*his Mediterranean smuggling operation. Disaster and*
*triumph had alternated over the years with*
*bewildering rapidity, a rotation of penury with*

*fortune. He had walked a narrowed road and dabbled in criminality.*

*There was much that I knew about, more that I suspected, and much more that I would never know.*

*His story is at the same time the confession of an amoral, quick-witted chancer, and a chronicle of a louche social society of the past half-century. That social world which he has embraced is eclectic in the extreme, ranging from café society of New York, London and the Riviera, to the 'Chelsea Set' of the 1950's, in tandem with the shadowy international world of organised crime. From early youth Dandy Kim, has moved with equal ease and familiarity in these and other contrasting sets. Reportage of his follies are voluminously recorded in press cuttings ... of endless night club fracas, financial scandals and weeping heiresses. Mysteriously, his bizarre punch up in the celebrity restaurant Mimmo's with the road-rage and police killer Kenneth Noye has been unreported until now. There was the wanton extravagance of his life, the loves, the losses, the villainies and the sheer devil-may-care excess of it."*

Kim kept a note of this statement and later quoted it in his ridiculous blog which began in 2011.

Kim suddenly went quiet again. He didn't answer either his mobile or landline numbers until one day he called me and said that he had left Boo and that he was back in London. For the next two years, his whereabouts were supposed to be complete secret, except I knew he was living in a magnificent townhouse at Chelsea Harbour. The reason why it was such a secret was because he had been loaned the house free of charge, by an old girlfriend, who, he refused to name.

The ex-girlfriend was supposedly happily married to an American millionaire and living in New York. She had never lived her London home and allowed Kim to use the house, but she was terrified that her wealthy and powerful husband might find out and think the worst. He was therefore requested to keep it a secret and never invite anybody into the house.

It was quite ridiculous, I used to see Kim about fortnightly in those days, and he always insisted on being dropped outside the entrance to Chelsea Harbour rather than being taken to his front door, whatever the weather. It was during this period that he started giving me various folders and documents claiming that he had no storage space for them and that they were safer in my hands. I obliged at the time, merely thinking that he was becoming elder and perhaps, a little more eccentric. In fact, many of these files and dossiers have helped me immensely, to piece the timeline of this book together.

Kim had all but retired at this point. He constantly threatened to finish both his memoirs and the Ann Summers book. He had become a fitness fanatic and lived in the local gymnasium.

His claws began to show again when in 2004, Jacqueline Gold, the Ann Summers CEO, was voted one of Britain's 'Top 100' most influential women by the Daily Mail and 'Business Communicator' of the year. By now, the Ann Summers name was so accepted, that even H.R.H. Princess Anne's daughter Zara Phillips held an Ann Summers party at Gatcombe Park, her mother's country estate.

In 2005, I saw Kim frequently and unfortunately, he had been discovered living in Chelsea Harbour by his ex-girlfriend's husband. He had to find a new home, and quickly. He stayed with me for a while in Kent and then found an apartment in a great location, just off his beloved Kings Road. Coincidently, the property was almost next door to where his old colleague, Bobby Mckew was living, they had finally ended up becoming neighbours. The sight of the pair of them together could only be likened to Kirk Douglas and Burt Lancaster in the movie 'The Tough Guys'!

The usual problem transpired - he had very little money left.

I usually met Kim at Antipasto restaurant in Battersea, it was much cheaper than Mimmo d'Ischia, and it was near Campbell's home, so she invariably joined us for lunch. Over one of these many luncheons Kim informed me that he had been working on two new schemes that he felt would be both profitable and alleviate him from his currently diabolical financial position. He explained that he just needed someone to finance him. His words were definitely aimed at myself.

Kim was becoming fascinated by the rapid growth of the internet and he wanted to create an online website marketing erotic bronzes and artefacts. He also wanted to annually tour the World's 'hot spots', holding exhibitions in top hotels and organising auctions. I had never heard such nonsense in my life, but politely listened, knowing that the project was not one that I wished to be involved with.

The second scheme was even more bizarre. Kim had always been interested in sport and he recognised the iconic popularity of the footballer David Beckham. Beckham was the UK's number one celebrity at this time and was being featured in every newspaper and gossip magazine. Kim's idea was to create a poster based on the Leonardo da Vinci's 'Vitruvian Man'.

The 'Vitruvian Man' depicts a man in two superimposed positions with his arms and legs apart and inscribed in a circle and square. The drawing and text are sometimes called the 'Canon of Proportions' or, less often, the 'Proportions of Man'. Kim wanted to replace de Vinci's face with that of David Beckam's. He then wanted to dramatically enlarge da Vinci's testicles and apply genuine, thick gold leaf to his bollocks. The proposed poster was to be titled 'Goldenballs' and subsequently marketed on line for just under £100. I didn't know whether to laugh or cry. I thought the scheme was absurd.

Amazingly, the project was kick started with financial help from Angela Sieff and the first 500 copies were printed.

Not caring to consider copyright issues, Kim was looking for as much publicity as possible to market the new poster and after a disappointingly small launch party at a Kings Road wine bar, the poster appeared on the internet with its own website. Quite incredibly, via the internet, Kim received an enquiry from a Japanese departmental store who were interested in buying a large quantity of the posters. There was one stipulation, they wanted Kim to travel to Tokyo and make a presentation to their sales and management team.

To my utter astonishment, Angela Sieff agreed to sponsor Kim to travel to Tokyo. I just couldn't imagine a seventy-five-year-old man wandering around the streets of Tokyo with 'Goldenballs' posters under his arms... but he did! I was confounded when he returned with 100 copies sold. The sales in Japan were not successful and no more orders were ever taken but luckily, all the costs were recovered and Angela Sieff received all her investment monies back prior to her sad death in 2008 which left Kim heartbroken. She left a daughter, Rebecca, Chatelaine of Castle Howard, York, wife of the Hon Simon Howard.

What happened to the remaining 400 posters is still a complete mystery.

During 2007, Kim was mentioned in 'Ruth Ellis, My Sister's Secret Life' by Muriel Jakubait and 'Wigs and Wherefores' which was a biography of Michael Sherrard Q.C. by Linda Goldman.

Worse was to follow. He was yet again upset and furious to read that Jacqueline Gold had been included in 'Debrett's People of Today' for her contribution to British society, as well as being named as the second most powerful woman in the retail trade by 'Retail Week'. She was also voted the 'Most Inspirational Businesswoman' in a survey by Barclays Bank and 'Britain's Most Powerful Woman' by many publications including Cosmopolitan,

Good Housekeeping and Woman magazines. Kim really believed that he was responsible for all her distinguished achievements and awards.

The situation with Jacqueline Gold literally exploded when Kim discovered she had written her autobiography. In the book, she suggested that:

*"Kim had enjoyed an 'adulterous relationship' with the H.M. Queen Elizabeth's sister, H.R.H. Princess Margaret. Kim lived up to his name 'Dandy Kim' and was in the habit of illegally landing his helicopter in Hyde Park and walking over to his Ann Summers shop in the Edgeware Road, picking up the takings and then flying off to the races. He was spending money at a quicker rate than he was earning it."*

Kim was livid! The Gold family had by now written no less than five autobiographies between them and most of them had contained detrimental paragraphs about Kim in different contexts.

Kim saw these remarks as a great excuse to have yet another shot at the Golds, and hopefully receive monetary damages. He started preparing his case against them.

The next few years were very quiet, apart from an approach from Channel 4, who were genuinely interested in making a mini-series or documentary of Kim's life. I was present at a couple of meetings with their production team but the discussions rapidly diminished as Kim became more and more adamant that the project was going to be undertaken his way or no way. Needless to say, it ended up no way!

Kim was becoming elderly and obsessed with the British legal system. He had made 'the fall of the Golds' his mission. The more successful the Ann Summers brand became; the angrier Kim became. He was still driving and bought a second-hand BMW estate car and apart from watching the rugby on television, his days were taken up with reading legal case history, learning the intricate laws of libel and creating a ridiculous blog in which he would promote himself on the internet.

On January 1st 2010, Kim celebrated his eightieth birthday quietly with Campbell and his grandchildren in London and he featured in a new book called 'Life After Debt' by Peter Phillips.

It took a further three years for Kim's case to reach the High Court of Justice. Articles on the internet stated:

*'Mr Michael Caborn-Waterfield has lodged a writ at London's High Court settling the value of his claim in excess of £500,000. Mr Caborn-Waterfield is suing Mr David Gold for defamation in his autobiography 'Pure Gold' and Ms Jacqueline Gold, the current boss of the adult store over claims made about the alleged relationship with the Queen's sister in Ms Gold's autobiography 'Please Let It Stop'. The businessman, of Fulham, is also suing the publishers of the book, Random House Group Ltd and author Wendy Holden, who ghost-wrote another book about Ms Gold's life entitled 'Good Vibrations'.'*

Yet again and unbelievably, Kim self-litigated. In Court, Kim (the Claimant) pleaded the meanings he attributed to the words complained as follows:

*"In their natural and ordinary and/or inferential meaning and/or innuendo, the said words meant and were understood to mean that the Claimant was:*

*1.      A Blackmailer.*

*2.      Was no better than named convicted East London criminals.*

*3.      Was himself a criminal.*

*4.      Was having an adulterous relationship with H.R.H. Princess Margaret.*

*5.      Was prepared to 'kiss and tell' about his relationship with members of the Royal Family, and in particular Princess Margaret.*

*6.      Was prepared to bring the Royal Family into contempt and disrepute.*

*7.	Illegally landed his helicopter in Hyde Park.*

*8.	Was in the habit of emptying the till in the Edgeware Road shop and using the money for his own purposes.*

*9.	Was habitually irresponsible in the conduct of his affairs.*

*10.	Did not honour his personal or business debts.*

*11.	Was deceitful and unscrupulous concerning the ownership of intellectual property.*

*12.	Was a liar.*

*13.	Was a dissolute and profligate dilettante.*

*14.	Was a drunkard.*

*15.	Was an object of ridicule following a series of physical assaults.*

The Gold's defence narrated the histories of both Kim and the Ann Summers business. It went on to describe the dismissal of their ex-managing director, Ronald Coleman, not only for embezzling company funds but also the Golds claimed, that they were previously being blackmailed by Ron Coleman.

Apparently, over the years, Coleman had collected company computer readouts of confidential information which would have been valuable to the Ann Summers competitors. He promised to return all the documents in return for £50,000 and added that if they failed to meet his demands, he would take up employment with one of the Ann Summers' competitors and use the sensitive information against the Golds which would be extremely damaging to their own business. The Golds decided to pay Coleman, upon condition that he moved abroad and return all the documents, but he had died in 2000. The Golds didn't know that Kim had been holding a copy of certain documents for the previous twenty-six years. The Golds also alleged that some fourteen years earlier Kim had asked for £150,000 to not publish his book on Ann Summers.

The Court case became a farce. All parties concerned were really using the Royal Courts of Justice to air their 'dirty washing'. It was costing everybody an absolute fortune, except Kim.

The Golds, quite sensibly, came to the conclusion that it would be cheaper and more efficient in the long-term to offer Kim an out of court settlement to drop his case. The Golds' time was too valuable to be sitting in the High Court arguing with an eighty-two year-old gentleman, they had major businesses to operate. A 'without prejudice' offer was made to Kim subject to a non-disclosure statement being signed and an 'Oath of Silence' sworn in order that the final amount of monetary damages would never become public knowledge. Kim accepted.

After numerous lunches with Kim, the amount he received in settlement, always varied between £5000 and £80,000 depending how many bottles of wine had been enjoyed. I shall never know.

**Two of the offending autobiographies, 'Pure Gold' by David Gold (2006) & 'Good Vibrations' by Jacqueline Gold (1997)**

Kim at the launch of 'Goldenballs', Jacqueline Gold's
book 'Please Let It Stop', Kim's blog, Jacqueline Gold
& the High Court writ

# CHAPTER THIRTY-FIVE

## A FINAL F*CK & A FINAL FAREWELL
## (2014 – 2016)

During 2013, Peter Watson-Wood published his memoir 'Serendipity... a Life' and recalled the following about Kim:

*'A succession of women fell under Kim's spell. After seducing one such unfortunate, the daughter of an American millionaire, Waterfield had swept her off to Gretna Green for a quick marriage: The American tycoon had to part with very considerable money in order to rescue his beloved daughter from this unsuitable union. Kim did the decent thing and, with the bank seriously topped up, he told the girl it wouldn't work out after all and she should go back to daddy. Kim resisted the charms of the ex-wife of Randolph Churchill (née Pamela Digby, later Pamela Harriman, the US ambassador to Paris), whom he described as a true redhead... aflame, mop, collar and muffs.'*

I was surprised that I had never heard this story before. Kim was beginning to be mentioned in many books including 'Stoned' by Andrew Loog Oldham and 'Getting It Straight in Notting Hill Gate' by Tom Vague. In the final chapter of this book, I thought that it was only appropriate to make a last reference to Kim's favourite hobby, sex!

In Spring of 2014, Kim was a different person. He felt that he had been victorious in Court. He saw himself as a legal expert and believed that he had taught the Golds a well-deserved lesson. It was as if a cloud had been lifted. His sparkle and sense of humour had returned. He had purchased many new clothes and a large flat screen television in order to watch the rugby, but he still needed a purpose or more importantly a new project. I often suggested to him that he should write his autobiography, but his reply to my suggestion was always the same:

*"Nigel, if I blow the lid off that damned lot, I could open up a bloody can of worms that will come back and haunt me for what's left of my life. You have been privy to my most sensitive of papers, so best you write it after I have departed from this world."*

The truth was quite simply that he had never enjoyed writing. He still hadn't finished either the Ann Summers story or his memoirs, which he had started nearly twenty years before.

One summer Sunday morning, I received a telephone call from the estranged wife of an old colleague of mine. This particular lady, who shall remain nameless, had quite a reputation for being somewhat 'available' and outrageous as well as enjoying a drink. She invited me for Sunday lunch at her apartment in Mayfair. I politely refused the offer and told her that I was meeting Kim Waterfield in Battersea for lunch. She asked if she could join us, explaining that she had met Kim in Murray's club over thirty-five years before and that she would love to see him again.

The three of us met at our usual haunt, Antipasto, and duly ordered our lunch. The wine was flowing and the conversation between Kim and the 'nameless lady' was becoming more and more flirtatious. Just as we finished eating Kim ordered a fresh bottle of white wine and the 'nameless lady' quietly whispered in my ear:

*"He's amazing for his age. He certainly lives up to his reputation, do you think he still f\*cks?"*

Although Kim was eighty-four years old, he had the hearing of a much younger man and suddenly retorted:

*"Madam, I heard that. Of course, I still fuck, better to end with a bang than a farewell!"*

Laughter followed, and the 'nameless lady' discreetly

asked me:

*"Nigel, would it be alright if I took him home with me?*

I sensed that the joke had become a reality. I discreetly paid the bill and left the restaurant. I drove back to Kent, leaving the two lovebirds deep in conversation about the variations of sex whilst knocking back their third bottle of wine.

At about eleven o clock that evening, my telephone rang, it was Kim:

*"My God, she f\*cked me for two and a half hours. What a joyous enchanting lady, an absolute honey. She moves like a snake. I don't remember ever meeting her before, but she is a crazy randy nymphomaniac. Anyway, I'm back at home now. I'm going to take my pills and get some well-earned rest."*

I hung up, and the telephone rang again, this time it was the 'nameless lady':

*"Nigel, thank you for a great lunch. You will be pleased to hear that I now have an honorary membership to the 'Dandy Kim' club and in case you want to know, yes, he can still f\*ck!"* I was speechless, but highly amused.

Unfortunately, despite the fact that Kim could still f\*ck, he could no longer responsibly drive and he had sell his BMW estate car. Without a vehicle, Kim had lost his freedom, now his only journeys were to walk across the Kings Road to his second home, Franco's wine bar.

Kim was becoming tired. Although he still talked about moving to Thailand at eighty-five years of age, thinking that there would be a gorgeous young Thai girl waiting there for him, the irony is that there probably would have been!

Anthony Summers' and Stephen Dorril's new book 'The Secret Worlds of Stephen Ward- Sex, Scandal and Deadly Secrets' highlighted Kim's old friendship with

Stephen Ward.

At one of our last lunches at Antipasto in 2015, I couldn't help but notice Kim had lost his distinguished silver hair. I naturally asked him if there was a problem, suspecting that he had been receiving chemotherapy at the Chelsea and Westminster Hospital. Kim unequivocally denied that there was anything wrong with him. I knew it was time to change the subject.

I had a final lunch with Kim just before his eighty-sixth birthday at Christmas time in 2015. He was very melancholy, and reflectively said:

*"I always expected someone to come and put a knife in my back one day and paradoxically, that would get me off the hook. So much tittle tattle has been written about me over the years. I've always been just one glass of wine ahead of the gossip columns. I've met so many people who've tried to cover up things, not which I'd understand to protect their lives, but to preserve some petty vanity. I have many faults, more than most, but I've always sought to tell the truth. One needs an awfully good memory to be an accomplished liar. In the past, I was always anxious just to move on to the next thing… my life was all about wild schemes, race horses, polo ponies, helicopters, fast boats and even faster women. I've been extraordinarily lucky; my life has been full of adventure and fascinating people. I've got away with so much. I feel it's not so much of a story but that of a time that never can exist again, an unrepeatable chapter in history. Although I never really believed my attitude and lifestyle could be repeated in the 21st Century, there was always the vague thought that it might have. Today, I feel like a dinosaur, albeit a frisky one. I'm a naughty museum piece for the top shelf, or a Hollywood 'B' movie'; I couldn't be real in today's world. I should celebrate my birthday more. I was born at the right time in history."*

Unfortunately, it was to be his last birthday and sadly, Kim passed away on May 4th 2016 after a short battle with oesophageal cancer. He was eighty-six years old.

Some rather distasteful obituaries were written in most major newspapers including The Times, The Telegraph and The Mirror. The Old Cranleighan, his old-school magazine, acknowledged his passing and the socialite Chelsea designer, Nicky Haslam, somewhat cruelly wrote in The Oldie magazine:

*"In July, at the Church of the Holy Spirit in Clapham, Michael George Patrick Caborn-Waterfield, known to a near-forgotten generation as 'Dandy Kim' – adventurer, charmer, trickster, self-created myth and myth-creator – was commemorated in a memorial service attended by friends, enemies, creditors, flashy former crooks and Kray fag-ends, old lags and loving young family members. Kim made his spiritual exit in the same flamboyant manner he played out his whole life: publicly – except when constrained from doing so by several stretches in jail."*

The comedian Ronnie Corbett referred fondly to Kim in his autobiography 'High Hopes'. It was published just before his own death in 2016.

Jacqueline Gold was appointed Commander of the Order of the British Empire (C.B.E.) in the 2016 New Years for services to entrepreneurship, women in business, and social enterprise. Ann Summers continues to go from strength to strength.

Bobby McKew is alive, well and still living in Chelsea.

Jeremy Scott, Penny Brahms' husband, was later interviewed about Kim's life on Radio 4 by Matthew Bannister and said:

*"Kim was a restless spirit. He had a somewhat cavalier attitude to banks and when he was short of funds had a habit of evaporating into thin air."*

Even Richard James, the exclusive Savile Row tailors, have dedicated an entire Spring and Summer clothing collection on their website to Kim.

The publicity reads:

*"For Spring/Summer 2017, Richard James has taken inspiration from the exquisitely attired British gentleman, adventurer and contra bander Michael 'Dandy Kim' Caborn-Waterfield. So-called, for his copious collection of stunningly cut Savile Row suits. 'Dandy Kim' left Chelsea for a palatial hotel suite in Havana during 1958. This is a softly sun-bleached collection that captures all the energy and intrigue of Cuba's capital as the 'pleasure seekers' playground. Delicate pink, blue and mint pastels are punctuated by bright neon accents of the same hue."*

The tailoring company further quotes one of Kim's old sayings on its website:

*"Image is everything, substance is irrelevant, perception is reality, and image trumps all."*

But my favourite quote from Kim remains:

*"It's been a life of little merit, but God, how I'd love to live it all over again!"*

Even in his final years, Kim kept people guessing. There are still a number of questions that remain such as the secrecy surrounding his parents. He never liked to talk about his family or what happened to his mother, Yvonne. I know that she went on to marry a further two husbands and have another child, a daughter named Caroline who I believe is now a retired photographer. I also have learned that Kim moved his mother during her final years to a nursing home in Kent. I never found out if he had pursued the unanswered question of his father's untimely demise any further.

I think Kim's life was of great merit, a gentleman dandy to the end.

I will always miss him and his colourful stories. I duly dedicate this book to his memory.

MEMORIAL SERVICE of THANKSGIVING for the
LIFE of

## KIM WATERFIELD

1st January 1930 – 4th May 2016

Tuesday 12th July 2016 at 3.00pm

Church of the Holy Spirit, Clapham

London SW4

**Kim's final farewell**

Printed in Great Britain
by Amazon